The Wicked Sisters

THE
WICKED
SISTERS

Women Poets, Literary History,
and Discord

BETSY ERKKILA

New York   Oxford
OXFORD UNIVERSITY PRESS
1992

Oxford University Press

Oxford   New York   Toronto
Delhi   Bombay   Calcutta   Madras   Karachi
Kuala Lumpur   Singapore   Hong Kong   Tokyo
Nairobi   Dar es Salaam   Cape Town
Melbourne   Auckland   Madrid

and associated companies in
Berlin   Ibadan

Copyright © 1992 by Oxford University Press, Inc.

Published by Oxford University Press, Inc.,
200 Madison Avenue, New York, New York 10016
Oxford is a registered trademark of Oxford University Press

Library of Congress Cataloging-in-Publication Data
Erkkila, Betsy, 1944–
The wicked sisters: women poets, literary history, and discord
Betsy Erkkila
p. cm.   Includes bibliographical references and index.
ISBN 0-19-507211-1 (cl :).   —   ISBN 0-19-507212-X (pbk.)
1. American poetry—Women authors—History and criticism—Theory, etc.
2. English poetry—Women authors—History and criticism—Theory, etc.
3. Feminism and literature.   4. Women and literature.
I. Title.   PS310.F45E75   1992   811.009'9287—dc20   91-40918

The following page is regarded as an extension of the copyright page

2 4 6 8 9 7 5 3 1

Printed in the United States of America
on acid-free paper

I gratefully acknowledge permission to reprint material from the following sources:

Passages from *The Poems of Emily Dickinson*. Reprinted by permission of the publishers and the Trustees of Amherst College from *The Poems of Emily Dickinson*, Thomas H. Johnson, ed., Cambridge, Mass.: The Belknap Press of Harvard University Press, Copyright 1951, © 1955, 1979, 1983 by the President and Fellows of Harvard College.

Passages from *The Letters of Emily Dickinson*. Reprinted by permission of the publishers from *The Letters of Emily Dickinson*, edited by Thomas H. Johnson, Cambridge, Mass.: The Belknap Press of Harvard University Press, Copyright © 1958, 1986 by the President and Fellows of Harvard College.

Passages from *The Complete Poems of Marianne Moore*. Reprinted by permission of Viking Penguin Inc. and Macmillan Publishing Co., Inc., and Faber and Faber, Ltd. from *The Complete Poems of Marianne Moore*.

Passages from *The Complete Prose of Marianne Moore*. Reprinted by permission of Viking Penguin Inc.

Passages from Marianne Moore's letters to Elizabeth Bishop. Reprinted by permission of the Elizabeth Bishop Papers at Vassar College Library, Poughkeepsie, New York, and the Rosenbach Museum and Library, Philadelphia. Permission for the quotations from Marianne Moore's unpublished letters granted by Marianne Craig Moore, Literary Executor for the Estate of Marianne Moore.

Passages from H.D.'s letters to Marianne Moore. Reprinted by permission of the Rosenbach Museum and Library, Philadelphia; and Perdita Schaffner, Copyright © 1982 by The Estate of Hilda Doolittle.

Passage from a letter of Marianne Moore to Bryher. Reprinted by permission of the Rosenbach Museum and Library, Philadelphia.

Excerpts from *The Collected Prose* by Elizabeth Bishop. Copyright © 1984 by Alice Methfessel. Reprinted by permission of Farrar, Straus and Giroux, Inc.

Excerpts from *The Complete Poems, 1927–1979* by Elizabeth Bishop. Copyright © 1979, 1983 by Alice Helen Methfessel. Reprinted by permission of Farrar, Straus and Giroux, Inc.

Excerpts from the unpublished letters and notebooks of Elizabeth Bishop are used here with permission of her Estate, copyright © 1992 by Alice Helen Methfessel; the Elizabeth Bishop Papers at Vassar College Library, Poughkeepsie, New York; by permission of the Houghton Library, Harvard University; the Rosenbach Museum and Library, Philadelphia; and Washington University Libraries, St. Louis, Mo.

Passages from Adrienne Rich's *A Change of World*, 1951; *Necessities of Life: Poems 1962–1965*, 1966; *Snapshots of a Daughter-in-Law: Poems 1954–1962*, 1967; *Leaflets: Poems 1965–1968*, 1969; *The Will to Change: Poems 1968–1970*, 1971; *Diving into the Wreck: Poems 1971–1972*, 1973; *Adrienne Rich's Poetry*, 1975; *Of Woman Born: Motherhood as Experience and Institution*, 1976; *The Dream of a Common Language: Poems 1974–1977*, 1978; *On Lies, Secrets, and Silence: Selected Prose 1966–1978*, 1979; *A Wild Patience Has Taken Me This Far: Poems 1978–1981*, 1981; *Blood, Bread, and Poetry: Selected Prose 1979–1985*, 1986; and *Your Native Land, Your Life: Poems*, 1986. Reprinted by permission of W. W. Norton and Company, Inc., and Adrienne Rich.

Passages from Gwendolyn Brooks's *A Street in Bronzeville*, 1945; *Annie Allen*, 1949; *Maud Martha*, 1953; *The Bean Eaters*, 1960; *Selected Poems*, 1963; *In the Mecca*, 1968; *Report from Part One*, 1972; *Beckonings*, 1975; *A Capsule Course in Black Poetry Writing*, 1975; *Primer for Blacks*, 1980; *To Disembark*, 1981. Reprinted by the kind permission of Gwendolyn Brooks.

For Suli

Acknowledgments

I would like to thank the University of Pennsylvania for providing a University Research Grant that enabled me to travel to various library collections and to cover other costs of completing this manuscript. Pat Willis, formerly Curator of Literature at the Rosenbach Museum and Library, Philadelphia, Pennsylvania, and Lisa Browar, formerly Curator of Rare Books and Manuscripts at Vassar College Library, Poughkeepsie, New York, were especially helpful in guiding me through the Marianne Moore and Elizabeth Bishop materials in these collections. I would also like to thank Nancy S. Mackechnie, Curator of Rare Books and Manuscripts at Vassar College Library; Natania Rosenfeld, Assistant Curator of Books and Manuscripts at the Rosenbach Museum and Library; and Debra Thomas, Director of the Office of Public Information, and Caroline Rittenhouse, College Archivist, at Bryn Mawr College, for leading me to the cover photograph of Marianne Moore and H.D. at Bryn Mawr College. Several colleagues at the University of Pennsylvania and elsewhere have provided advice, commentary, and inspiration over many years. I would like especially to thank Stuart Curran, Deirdre David, Al Filreis, Lynda Hart, Thais Morgan, Vivian Pollak, Maureen Quilligan, and Martha Nell Smith. I would also like to thank my many talented graduate students at the University of Pennsylvania, especially Teresa Goddu (now at Vanderbilt University), Jay Grossman, Katherine Kinney (now at the University of California, Riverside), and Ashley Moss. Finally, I would like to thank Elizabeth Maguire and Ruth Sandweiss of Oxford University Press for their much-appreciated editorial advice.

As always, my husband, Larry, has given the love, laughter, and encouragement that make everything possible. For companionship, precociousness, and delight, I would also like to thank my daughter, Suli, who was born just in time for me to dedicate this book to her.

Contents

Illustrations

The Wicked Sisters

But I who am bound by my mirror
as well as my bed
see causes in color
as well as sex

and sit here wondering
which me will survive
all these liberations.

Audre Lorde
"Who Said It Was Simple"

1

Rethinking Women's Literary History

those who feel destined, under god's eye
need never ponder difference

and if they kill others for being who they are
or where they are

is this a law of history
or simply, *what must change?*
                    —Adrienne Rich, "Sources"

Through a study of the lives and works of Emily Dickinson, Marianne Moore, Elizabeth Bishop, Adrienne Rich, and Gwendolyn Brooks and their complex and troubled relations with both masculine and feminine literary culture, this book seeks simultaneously to engage and to explore feminist theory and practice as a field of cultural struggle. Broadly stated, this study attempts to "historicize" our understanding of particular women poets and particular (re)constructions of the "female poetic tradition" by focusing on the historical struggles and differences not only among and within women writers but also among feminists themselves. In particular, I argue that the emphasis among many white feminists on both patriarchy as the primal oppression and psychoanalysis as the primary mode of conceptualizing women's "experience" has tended to reduce all women writers to an economy of the same, transhistoricizing and universalizing the lives and works of women writers across race, class, sexual, and historically specific bounds. Moreover, I argue that under the influence of such French feminist theorists as Hélène Cixous, Luce Irigaray, and Julia Kristeva, recent feminist representations of women's literary history have tended to romanticize, maternalize, essentialize, and eternalize women writers and the relationships among them in ways that have worked to reconstitute the very gender stereotypes and polarities that have been historically the ground of women's oppression. By focusing on the historical struggles and differences among, between, and within writing women, this study seeks to reclaim women's literature and women's literary history as a site of dissension, contingency, and ongoing struggle rather than a separate space of some untroubled and essentially cooperative accord among women.

Without discounting the historical power of sisterhood and its strategic efficacy in particular political, cultural, or rhetorical contexts, *The Wicked Sisters* seeks to remain fully cognizant of the more negative and exclusionary practices of women writers, women's literary history, and feminist literary criticism. Against the tendency of earlier feminist critics to celebrate women writers and the female literary tradition, and to heroize strong literary foremothers and communities of women, this book considers the historical struggles and conflicts among women poets, as well as the problems of difference and otherness among and within women poets themselves. Finally, this book considers the ways some women poets—and, indeed, some feminist critics—have constructed their identities, traditions, and female worlds on the backs of sexual, racial, and class "others."

My title—*The Wicked Sisters*—is meant to suggest the discord that marks both the history of women poets and the history of feminist criticism. It is meant to problematize the familial metaphors that have been prevalent in feminist theory and practice by suggesting the impossible relation of women to Woman, the ways women are always at odds with and wickedly in excess of their identity as Woman—and sisters.[1] Whereas earlier feminists tended to treat women's literary history as something that was *there* to be recuperated and reclaimed by literary critics, the model that this study proposes is historically contingent: it treats the woman writer, women's writing, and women's literary history as cultural constructs, formulated by particular persons, in particular contexts, to serve particular political, social, and aesthetic ends. And thus this study proposes a model of women's literary history that engages the central paradox of feminism: it does its work even as it recognizes the instability and potential impossibility of its subject.

Encompassing the various historical significations of *wickedness* as evil, destructive, powerful, playful, witty, mischievous, and "not righteous," the term "the wicked sisters" has multiple permutations in this study. "*Muses . . .* are no better than *Harlots*," wrote Cotton Mather in *Manaductio ad Ministerium* in 1726; they have a "Tendency to excite and foment Impure *Flames,* and cast *Coals* into your *Bosom*" (42). *The Wicked Sisters* seeks to engage this historical conjunction between women, writing, and potentially destructive sociosexual power. It is meant to suggest the ways women poets in their multiple identifications as witches, warrior women, "bad" women, blueswomen, lovers of other women, and singers of songs have taken up the power and danger of the word in an effort to resist and disrupt the various systems of masculine power and dominance in their time. It is also meant to suggest the ways women poets have been enabled in their defiance by the sisterly bonds of assistance and resistance they have formed with other women, particularly other writing women.

In "Sorties," Hélène Cixous reflects on the importance of writing and reading for the oppressed, not merely as a means of escaping to a world elsewhere—"to leave the real, colonial space"—but as a means of discovering others, what she calls her "true ancestors," "my true allies, my true 'race.' " In this formulation, the act of reading itself becomes a political quest rather than an escape into an imaginary paradise: "I am searching: somewhere there must be people who are like me in their rebellion and their hope" (Cixous and Clément, *The Newly Born Woman* 72). Like Hélène Cixous questing for her "true ancestors," women poets have historically frequently turned to each other as a means of authorizing and validating themselves. They have also often had as their primary muse a mother, a grandmother, a woman friend, a woman artist, a woman performer, or an invented goddess.

Historically, too, women have at times written together. Instances of this include Sappho's colloquies with women in Lesbos; Emily Dickinson's "magic circle" of women correspondents and her lifelong literary and erotic bond with her sister-in-law, Susan Gilbert; the networks of mostly unpublished black women poets who were in constant contact during the Harlem Renaissance; Natalie Barney's Sapphic colony in Paris; Marianne Moore's "collaboration" over many years with her mother; Amy Lowell's description of her relationship with Ada Dwyer Russell as "Lowell & Russell, Makers of Fine Poems"; *Conspirito,* a magazine founded by Elizabeth Bishop, Muriel Rukeyser, Mary McCarthy, and Eleanor Clark at Vassar in the thirties; and Adrienne Rich's evocation of

> two women eye to eye
> measuring each other's spirit, each other's
> limitless desire,
>> a whole new poetry beginning here.
>>> (*The Dream of a Common Language* 76) ,

These instances of women writing together suggest modes of collective authorship that challenge traditional romantic individualist notions of author and text.

Struck by this evidence of bonding among literary women and drawing on the work of social historian Carroll Smith-Rosenberg, the object relations theory of psychologist Nancy Chodorow, Hélène Cixous's concept of *écriture feminine,* and such works of cultural feminism as Adrienne Rich's *Of Woman*

Born and *The Dream of a Common Language* and Mary Daly's *Gyn/Ecology*, several feminist critics constructed models of women's literary history and a distinctively female tradition that seemed to contest the more agonistic model of masculine literary history theorized by Harold Bloom in *The Anxiety of Influence*.[2] Whereas earlier radical feminists had urged women "to dare to be bad," to resist traditional constructions of male and female, and, in the words of Adrienne Rich, "to know the writing of the past . . . not to pass on a tradition but to break its hold over us" (*Adrienne Rich's Poetry* 91), this new feminist emphasis on the specificity and difference of women's culture, which corresponded with the rise of cultural feminism as a political movement in the mid-seventies, focused on the positive, nurturant, and essentially maternal and sisterly dimensions of women's literary history.[3]

" 'Thinking back through our mothers,' a necessary act for all women writers, would afford one maternal protection for one's own raids on the patriarchy and simultaneously raise female consciousness," wrote Jane Marcus in an article on Virginia's Woolf's relationship with literary and other women. "Woolf knew by experience how women influence each other," Marcus argues. "Far from Harold Bloom's concept of the 'anxiety of influence', it is rather the opposite, affording the woman the relief from anxiety, acting as a hideout in history where she can lick her wounds between attacks on the patriarchy" (7–8). Arguing that identification and communality are the primary characteristics of women's friendships in contemporary fiction, Elizabeth Abel similarly notes: "As the dynamics of female friendship differ from those of male, the dynamics of female literary influence also diverge and deserve a theory of influence attuned to female psychology and to women's dual position in literary history" (434).[4]

In "These Self-Invented Women: A Theoretical Framework for a Literary History of Black Women," Mary Helen Washington asks, "Whose history is literary history?," noting that Afro-American literary history represents a history of choices by black and white men that privileges the generic myth of Frederick Douglass's *Narrative*. Against this masculine paradigm, she argues that "the black woman's struggle for a literary voice is . . . often achieved under the influence of a nurturing female community or because of a female precursor who conveys to the writer the power and authority to speak" (5). This "woman-centeredness that is evidenced in the novels of nearly every American black woman writer," she says, "is the sign of a very special tradition. . . . The power of the mother/daughter bond that is articulated in the works of Alice Walker, Paule Marshall, Gayle Jones, Dorothy West, and Zora Hurston is one aspect of that unique tradition" (5–6). In fact, this "special tradition" sets black women writers against both black and white male and white female paradigms of literary history: "In contrast to white women, the black woman writer does not find 'infection or debilitation' in her quest for female precursors" (6), Washington concludes, citing Sandra Gilbert and Susan Gubar's influential version of white women's literary history as a Bloomian struggle between "mad" literary women and commanding patriarchs, in *The Madwoman in the Attic: The Woman Writer and the Nineteenth-Century Literary Imagination*.[5]

But while this "gynocritical" emphasis on what Elaine Showalter called "women as a distinct literary group" and "*the difference* of women's writing" ("Feminist Criticism in the Wilderness" 185) challenged and destabilized traditionally white masculine conceptualizations of literary history and aesthetic value, the emphasis on mutuality, nurturance, and familial bonding among literary sisters and/or mothers and daughters as the essential form of women's literary history tended to naturalize and indeed heroize the separate sexual space of women's historical colonization and to mask, silence, or write over women's culture as a site of historical struggle and difference among women themselves. The almost exclusive focus on sexual difference—the difference of woman from man—as the primary historical and cultural divide, along with the corresponding emphasis on women's culture, women's writing, and women's language, virtually erased the multiple and various race, class, ethnic, cultural, and other locations of women within a particular social field. "Woman" was equated with white middle-class women, and "woman's sexuality" was equated with heterosexuality and motherhood. Moreover, the critical emphasis on women's literature as a record of women's personal experience tended to privilege certain kinds of women writers. Among poets, Emily Dickinson, H.D., Sylvia Plath, and Nikki Giovanni were in; Marianne Moore, Elizabeth Bishop, Louise Bogan, and Gwendolyn Brooks were—and still are—out.

Critical of this American feminist preoccupation with the personal and sexual signature of literature, Alice Jardine argues that "it is not something called the 'Self' which speaks, but language, the unconscious, the textuality of the text" ("Gynesis" 56–57). To Showalter's gynocritics, Jardine opposes the French inflected theory of gynesis, "the putting into discourse of 'woman' as the process beyond the Cartesian Subject, the Dialectics of Representation, or Man's Truth" ("Gynesis" 58). In this model, woman becomes "neither a person or a thing" but "a reading effect, a woman-in-effect that is never stable and has no identity" (*Gynesis* 25).[6] The problem with this poststructuralist rejection of the category "woman," however, is that it (re)consigns women to invisibility within the grand master narratives and theories of the West, at the very moment when women—particularly women of color—are beginning to constitute themselves as subjects in history.[7] Rather than give up "women poets" or "women's writing" as categories of analysis, this study seeks to remain cognizant of the instability and provisionality of its subject; it seeks to maintain the concept of difference, without allowing that concept to solidify into an essential or totalizing subject; and it seeks to study the category "woman poet" as itself the subject of historical struggle.

Although some women poets, including Amy Lowell in "The Sisters," May Sarton in "My Sisters, O My Sisters," and Adrienne Rich in her seminal essay "Vesuvius at Home: The Power of Emily Dickinson," sought to locate themselves within a specifically female literary genealogy, others, like Elizabeth Bishop, resisted the category "woman poet" as a masculine category of exclusion and marginalization. For some, like Muriel Rukeyser, the tradition of female lyricism represented by Sappho was itself a reinscription of the bourgeois division between private and public, personal and political, female and male spheres. "Not Sappho, Sacco. / Rebellion pioneered among our lives," she declared at the outset of her first volume of poems, *Theory of Flight* (1935), to signify her break with traditionally female poetic modes and her commitment to a politically engaged and contemporaneous poetry that focused on the racial, class, and labor strife of what she later called "the first century of world wars" (*The Collected Poems* 3, 450).

For some women poets, the female poetic tradition was itself a site not of empowerment but disempowerment. In "Pro Femina," Carolyn Kizer represents women poets of the past as "a sickly effluvium," a "crew of self-pitiers, not-very-distant," who were all either "Old maids to a woman"; "Or the sad sonneteers, toast-and-teasdales we loved at thirteen" (*Knock upon Silence* 47). Similarly, Sylvia Plath set herself against a female poetic tradition she associated with "quailing or whining like Teasdale or simple lyrics like Millay" (*Letters Home* 24). As Sandra Gilbert and Susan Gubar note in rethinking their earlier assertion that contemporary women can "now attempt the pen with energy and authority" because they have been empowered by the struggles of their "eighteenth- and nineteenth-century foremothers" (*The Madwoman in the Attic* 51): "Confronting the lives and deaths of sometimes problematic foremothers," modernist and contemporary women writers "have had to ask, 'How usable, how energizing is a tradition of our own?' " (" 'Forward into the Past' " 240).

The difficulty and complexity of sisterhood as an affirming model of women's literary history is suggested by Amy Lowell's "The Sisters." Against the emphatically masculine genealogies of male modernist poets, "The Sisters" is a revisionary attempt to establish a distinctively female literary genealogy that runs from Sappho, to Elizabeth Barrett Browning, to Amy Lowell herself. Representing women poets as an exclusive, rare, and even "queer" group, the poet begins with an act of historical (mis)interpretation that immediately consigns to invisibility the large numbers of women poets who had been writing since at least the end of the eighteenth century, and who were particularly visible in the literary landscape of 1922, the year the poem was published:

> Taking us by and large, we're a queer lot
> We women who write poetry. And when you think
> How few of us there've been, it's queerer still.
> I wonder what it is that makes us do it,
> Singles us out to scribble down, man-wise,
> The fragments of ourselves. Why are we
> Already mother-creatures, double-bearing,
> With matrices in body and in brain?
>
> (*Complete Poetical Works* 459)

The category woman poet and the possibility of literary sisterhood are, from the outset, uncertain and fraught with contradiction. Are women poets "man-wise," and thus like men? Or are they different, with a "double-bearing" power as "already mother-creatures" to produce both poems and children? Or do they represent some other possibility, neither "man-wise" nor "mother-creature," but lesbian, for example? What is at stake in the poem is not only the category "woman poet" as a potential contradiction but the definition of womanhood itself—who does, and who does not, belong. Split between Victorian and modern discourse about the nature of woman, the poem locates itself within early twentieth-century debates about modernity, women's sexuality, the New Woman, and the mannish lesbian.[8]

Given the anti-Victorian thematics of the poem, Sappho is—or at least should be—its heroine:

> There's Sapho, now I wonder what was Sapho.
> I know a single slender thing about her:
> That, loving, she was like a burning birch-tree
> All tall and glittering fire, and that she wrote
> Like the same fire caught up to Heaven and held there,
> A frozen blaze before it broke and fell.
>
> (459)

Sappho is at the origins of a specifically female lyric tradition and a female desire uninhibited by the traditions of the Church Fathers and the prohibitions of Queen Victoria. Even more importantly, though more covertly in the poem, Sappho represents the beginnings of a tradition of women writing love poems for and about each other; thus she validates Amy Lowell's own lifelong love relationship with Ada Dwyer Russell as subject, audience, and context of many of her poems. The poet's fantasy encounter with Sappho is erotically charged, as the speaker appropriates the traditionally masculine position, and gazes lovingly at her:

> just to watch
> The crisp sea sunshine playing on her hair,
> And listen, thinking all the while 'twas she
> Who spoke and that we two were sisters
> Of a strange, isolated little family.
> And she is Sapho—Sapho—not Miss or Mrs.,
> A leaping fire we call so for convenience.
>
> (459)

Lowell's sexually nuanced bond with Sappho represents a different kind of sisterhood from the more general sisterhood of women poets with which the poem began. As a "strange, isolated little family" of self-identified and woman-loving lesbian poets, this sisterhood underwrites the poet's sense of identity and legitimacy as a lesbian poet even as it becomes the grounds for the exclusion of other women.

This process of exclusion is enacted in the poet's evocation of Elizabeth Barrett Browning, which begins by drawing "the perfect line" between Sappho and Mrs. Browning, "between sea-cliffs / And a close-shuttered room in Wimpole Street":

> Sapho could fly her impulses like bright
> Balloons tip-tilting to a morning air
> And write about it. Mrs. Browning's heart
> Was squeezed in stiff conventions. So she lay
> Stretched out upon a sofa, reading Greek
> And speculating, as I must suppose,
> In just this way on Sapho . . .
>
> (459)

In this formulation, Sappho represents the freedom, mobility, and sexual desire associated with the New Woman in early twentieth-century discourse; Browning represents the entrapment, stasis, and bodily repression of the Victorian era. As "an older sister / And not herself so curious a technician / As to admit newfangled modes of writing—," Browning is represented as the very figure of the quaint, old-fashioned, and tradition-bound Victorian poetess from whom Lowell seeks to escape and against whom she seeks to authorize and validate her own identity as an adventurous, experimental, modern woman poet.

Compared with Lowell's loving evocation of Sappho, her representation of Mrs. Browning seems rivalrous, hostile, and at odds with the sisterly context of the poem. This may be because Lowell, as the daughter of a prominent and genteel Boston family, also suffered bouts of nervous prostration and thus knew firsthand the repressiveness of Victorian convention:

For we are such a little family
Of singing sisters, and as if I didn't know
What those years felt like tied down to the sofa.
Confounded Victoria, and the slimy inhibitions
She loosed on all us Anglo-Saxon creatures!

(460)

But something more than common oppression is at stake in Lowell's apparent hostility to Browning, for why blame the victim? Or even Victoria for that matter? Browning, in fact, had something that Lowell did not. She is the very model of that "double-bearing" creature—a mother and a poet—that Lowell cannot finally be:

It seems miraculous, but she escaped
To freedom and another motherhood
Than that of poems. She was a very woman
And needed both.

(459)

For all Lowell's attempt to escape the inscriptions of Victorian womanhood, the poem still seems embedded in a Victorian sexual ideology that locates womanhood—and indeed woman's sexuality—in reproduction and maternity. If Browning's other "motherhood / Than that of poems" makes her "a very woman"—a phrase Lowell repeats twice in the poem—then by implication Lowell may not be a "woman"; she may indeed be the very image of the sterile, brainy, unwomanly poet—the mannish lesbian—who haunts the subtext of the poem.

In her attempt to find a positive lesbian identification as a poet, Lowell seems particularly hostile to Browning's heterosexuality. "I do not like the turn this dream is taking," Lowell quips, when "Robert" intrudes upon the "doubtful" scene of her encounter with Browning. Moreover, Lowell suggests that Browning's heterosexual love poems to Robert have been "fertilized" and legitimized in ways that, again by implication, her own love poems to Ada are not:

Suppose there hadn't been a Robert Browning,
No "Sonnets from the Portuguese" would have been written.
They are the first of all her poems to be,
One might say, fertilized. For, after all,
A poet is flesh and blood as well as brain
And Mrs. Browning, as I said before,
Was very, very woman. Well, there are two
Of us, and vastly unlike that's for certain.

(460)

The speaker not only asserts her difference. She also suggests that even for Mrs. Browning the lesbian position would have been the most effective means of reconciling the potential contradiction of being woman and poet:

> But Sapho was dead
> And I, and others, not yet peeped above
> The edge of possibility. So that's an end
> To speculating over tea-time talks
> Beyond the movement of pentameters
> With Mrs. Browning.
>
> (460)

But while Lowell seeks to legitimize a line of lesbian poetry that runs from Sappho to herself, she, too, resists giving up being "very woman," a concept which, in the context of the poem at least, cannot finally be loosened from its Victorian inscription as reproduction and maternity.

And thus the poem comes to turn on problems of sterility, unwomanliness, and doubt that cloud even Sappho's radiant image. Although Sappho is associated with the "glittering fire" of passion, it is a "frozen blaze" that "broke and fell"—lines that suggest a sterile passion that expends itself upon itself. More to the point, the lines suggest the legend, first articulated by Ovid, that Sappho abandoned women and writing for the love of Phaon—a love that ended tragically when he rejected her, and she leaped in despair from the Leucadian cliffs.[9] Whatever its precise reference, this "frozen" image appears to make any fully empowering bond with Sappho impossible.

Lowell's imaginary encounter with Emily Dickinson is similarly troubled by images of sterility and unwomanliness. Their meeting seems at first promising—in fact "even better than Sapho"—as the poet encounters Dickinson in the garden "Engrossed in the doing of a humming-bird / Among nasturtiums." Lowell appears to admire Dickinson's intellectual difficulty and her hide-and-seek gaminess:

> Sapho would speak, I think, quite openly,
> And Mrs. Browning guard a careful silence,
> But Emily would set doors ajar and slam them
> And love you for your speed of observation.
>
> (461)

But as a model of how to resolve the apparent split between woman and poet, Dickinson, too, proves inadequate. If Sappho erred in the direction of too much body and too much passion, and Browning in the direction of heterosexual love, marriage, maternity, and "very" womanhood, Dickinson erred in the direction of too much brain. Having begun in the sentimental mode of nineteenth-century romantic friendship among women, Lowell's evocation ends in the gothic mode, with Dickinson figured as a sterile and fragile Victorian anorexic who gave up "womanhood" for poetry and metaphysics:

> But Emily hoarded—hoarded—only giving
> Herself to cold, white paper. Starved and tortured,
> She cheated her despair with games of patience
> And fooled herself by winning. Frail little elf,
> The lonely brain-child of a gaunt maturity,
> She hung her womanhood upon a bough
> And played ball with the stars—too long—too long—
> The garment of herself hung on a tree
> Until at last she lost even the desire
> To take it down.
>
> (461)

As a New England sister, Dickinson is in some sense meant to figure a fate that Lowell herself all too narrowly escaped. But for all Lowell's desire to present herself as a "modern" sister in relation to her Victorian predecessors, Lowell's representation of Dickinson is once again embedded in a nineteenth-century sexual discourse that emphasized the natural balance of an essentially maternal female body against the neurasthenia, hysteria, and even insanity caused by overuse of the brain. And within this discourse, Lowell's own "womanhood" is also in question.

Although Lowell continues to insist on the metaphor of sisterhood, by the end of the poem what is most striking is the problem of difference:

> Strange trio of my sisters, most diverse,
> And how extraordinarily unlike
> Each is to me, and which way shall I go?
>
> (461)

As it turns out, none of the poet's literary sisters provides an adequate model or direction:

> Good-bye, my sisters, all of you are great,
> And all of you are marvellously strange,
> And none of you has any word for me.
> I cannot write like you.
>
> (461)

Still preoccupied by the problems of womanliness, maternity, and reproduction, the poet dreams hopefully forward, imagining herself as the progenitor if not of children then of some writing woman who will look back on her as she has looked back on her own literary precursors:

> I only hope that possibly some day
> Some other woman with an itch for writing
> May turn to me as I have turned to you
> And chat with me a brief few minutes.
>
> (461)

But given Lowell's contradictory and troubled impulses toward her own literary ancestors, even this dream of literary progeny seems inadequate to lift the pall of sadness, fear, and self-doubt that hangs over the final passages of the poem.

Rather than empowering Lowell, her literary sisters leave her feeling "sad and self-distrustful / For older sisters are very sobering things." For all their seeming strangeness, they are also paradoxically "near / Frightfully near, and rather terrifying" (461). The poet's initial desire to retrieve a distinctively female literary genealogy ends as a drive to exorcise her sisters as a frightening and terrifying presence. And thus what begins as an affirmation of literary sisterhood ends as a cautionary tale about sisterhood as an impossible and ultimately terrifying relation. What the poem suggests finally is that women poets and the concept "woman" itself are so written over and overwritten by the misogynist inscriptions of classical authorities, a "long line of Church Fathers," and the sexual ideologies of the Victorian and early modern periods in England and the United States, that any complete sisterly identification is impossible and, indeed, "rather terrifying."

"Lesbians are not women," Monique Wittig famously and provocatively wrote in her article "The Straight Mind" (110). Her words mark the distance and difference between the Sapphic communities of the early modern period and the theory and politics of lesbianism in the eighties and nineties in the United States, Britain, and France. Whereas in the later period several lesbian theorists would seek to escape the category "woman" and to use their position "outside" as a lever to criticize the heterosexual binary man/woman as a social construct rather than as an ontological given, Amy Lowell appears to have been struggling to stay *in* the category "woman" at a time when early modern discourse on the mannish lesbian was telling her that lesbians were indeed "not women."[10] She appears to have been looking for a way to be woman, man-wise, mother-creature, sexual, lesbian, and poet at a time when the only choices available to her were man, woman, or pervert.

"There is a pretense to a homogeneity of experience covered by the word *sisterhood* that does not in fact exist," writes Audre Lorde in *Sister Outsider* (116). Like the act of exclusion upon which Amy Lowell's "The Sisters" is founded, and like the exclusionary dynamics that operate throughout the poem, the bonds of assistance and resistance that women poets have formed with other women have also been bonds formed by the exclusion, silencing, or demonization of other women—particularly women of another race, class, ethnicity, or sexual orientation. With the exception of Susan Gilbert, the magic circle of women friends among whom Emily Dickinson honed and validated her poetic skills was formed exclusively with women of her own race and class from the surrounding community. Elizabeth Bishop's lifelong relationship with Marianne Moore was formed against a tradition of female lyricism represented by such "personal" poets as Sara Teasdale and Edna St. Vincent Millay; and it was also formed against her own sexual identification as a lesbian. The revisionary feminist politics and poetics that Adrienne Rich so powerfully invoked in "When We Dead Awaken: Writing as Re-Vision" (1971) was white and Eurocentric. And the empowering tradition of black literary mothers that Alice Walker reclaims in *In Search of Our Mothers' Gardens* was founded on the exclusion of more racially and less "womanist"-identified black women writers such as Gwendolyn Brooks.

Thus there is another and more troubling way that the term "wickedness" figures in this study to suggest the acts of violence and violation that women have practiced among and against each other. "The Radical Feminist must extend her own 'identity' politics to include her 'identity' as oppressor as well," writes Cherríe Moraga in *Loving in the War Years* (128).[11] As Teresa De Lauretis notes, the new feminist historical consciousness is considerably "less pure" than the earlier more patriarchally based phase of feminist consciousness:

> The subject of this feminist consciousness is unlike the one that was initially defined by the opposition of woman to man on the axis of gender and purely constituted by the oppression, repression, or negation of its sexual difference. For one thing, *it is much less pure*. Indeed, it is most likely ideologically complicit with "the oppressor" whose position it may occupy in certain sociosexual relations (if not in others).
>
> ("Eccentric Subjects" 137; emphasis added)

"The wicked sisters" is meant to suggest this new historical consciousness of women as "less pure," complicit, oppressive, and powerful—and thus it suggests the positiveness of their danger to and charge against not only patriarchy but also each other.

For all the earlier emphasis on feminine and feminist sisterhood, what is in fact most striking about the 1989 dialogue between Jane Gallop, Marianne Hirsch, and Nancy K. Miller in their chapter in *Conflicts in Feminism* is the extent to which they now fear the attacks not of men but of other women—particularly women of color. "The way [Deborah] McDowell has come to occupy the place of Lacan in my psyche," observes Gallop, "does seem to correspond to the way that emphasis on race has replaced for me something like French vs. American feminism" (364). Whereas for Annette Kolodny, in

"Dancing Through the Minefield" in 1980, the minefield was male, in the nineties the minefield appears to be located among women and on the very ground of feminism itself.

In "White Women, Listen! Black Women and the Boundaries of Sisterhood," Hazel Carby argues that "most contemporary feminist theory does not begin to adequately account for the experience of black women" (213). This gap between feminist theory and the experience of black women is particularly evident in the case of Gwendolyn Brooks, whose life and work have remained outside and elsewhere to traditional constructions of both white and black women's literary history. As I shall argue in the concluding chapter in this book ("Race, Black Women Writing, and Gwendolyn Brooks"), black women writers, and the life and work of Gwendolyn Brooks in particular, challenge and unsettle many of the fundamental assumptions about the woman writer, women's writing, and women's literary history still prevalent in feminist literary criticism and in the academy. Rather than posing Gwendolyn Brooks and the "black woman writer" as some fixed locus or romanticized "other" to unfix the ethnocentrism of white feminist constructions of the female literary tradition, however, this study poses unfixity, struggle, and ongoing transformation among and within women writers—black, white, lesbian, or otherwise—as the underlying dynamics of women's literary history.

Finally, in recognition of the struggle among, between, within, and *for* women which is the very ground of feminism as both social movement and critical and theoretical practice, "the wicked sisters" is meant to suggest the oppositional nature of feminist literary discourse, a discourse that has challenged the hegemony of the white masculine subject in literature and elsewhere and undermined traditional assumptions about the study of literature, the canon, the curriculum, aesthetic value, and the traditional divisions between elite and popular, private and public work. In this putatively "postfeminist" moment, I use the title *The Wicked Sisters* as a means of reclaiming the potentially radical and transforming energies of feminism as social movement and critical practice. Feminism is not merely about changing the family and the home, as the phrase "the personal is political" might lead us to believe. It is about changing the traditional binary male/female at the base of Western metaphysics, transforming traditional social orders of power and dominance, and radically altering our very ways of knowing, seeing, and being in the world. In this last permutation, then, "the wicked sisters" is meant to suggest that, at its most radical, feminism is not finally about reinstating the angel in the house.

2

Emily Dickinson and the Wicked Sisters

> Somehow or other I incline to other things—and Satan
> covers them up with flowers, and I reach out to pick
> them. The path of duty looks very ugly indeed—and
> the place where *I* want to go more amiable—a great
> deal—it is so much easier to do wrong than right—so
> much pleasanter to be evil than good, I dont wonder
> that good angels weep—and bad ones sing songs.
> —Emily Dickinson to Jane Humphrey, *The Letters of Emily Dickinson*

"What if the 'goods' refused to go to market?" asks Luce Irigaray in "Des marchandises entre elles" ("Female Commodities Among Themselves"). Reflecting on the use of women as objects of mediation, exchange, and transference between men in a patriarchal and ultimately homosexual economy, Irigaray wonders: "What if they maintained among themselves 'another' kind of trade?" (Marks and de Courtivron 110). Emily Dickinson's interaction with a select circle of women friends was her means of refusing to go to market. Getting the goods together in a separate community of female language and desire, Dickinson sought to maintain among women another kind of trade. Dickinson's community of women included her sister, Lavinia, and her sister-in-law, Susan Gilbert; her childhood friends Abiah Root, Abby Wood, Emily Fowler Ford, and Jane Humphrey; and later her friend Elizabeth Holland and her cousins Louise and Frances Norcross. Complementing the written "correspondence" that she carried on with her women friends, Dickinson also located herself within a tradition of literary women that included the Brontë sisters, Elizabeth Barrett Browning, and George Eliot.

Remembering the group of girls who attended Amherst Academy in the forties, Emily Fowler Ford said: "There was a fine circle of young people in Amherst, and we influenced each other strongly." The group included Emily Fowler, Emily Dickinson, Helen Fiske (Hunt Jackson), and perhaps Louisa

Bridgman—all of whom would become, albeit in different ways, poets and writing women. "We were in the adoring mood," Ford recalled, "and I am glad to say that many of those idols of our girlhood have proved themselves golden. The eight girls who composed this group had talent enough for twice their number, and in their respective spheres of mothers, authors or women, have been notable and admirable" (Mabel Loomis Todd 126).

Emily Dickinson remembered a group of five rather than eight—a group that included, along with herself, Sarah Tracy, Harriet Merrill, Abby Wood, and Abiah Root. At a time when Emerson was announcing a national mythos of self-definition through self-reliance, Dickinson was seeking identity and self-validation *within* and *through* an exclusive community of girlfriends. "How gay to love one's friends! . . . I would not exchange it for all the funds of the Father" (*The Letters of Emily Dickinson* 2: 351, hereafter referred to as *Letters*), she wrote Elizabeth Holland, in words that set an economy of affectional exchange among women in opposition to a religious and marketplace economy regulated by the "funds of the Father," both earthly and spiritual. For Dickinson heaven was a site not of personal salvation but of restoration to a lost community of friends. "How happy if we may be one unbroken company in heaven," she wrote to Abiah Root when she was only sixteen (*Letters* 1: 28). If friends never died, she later wrote Holland, there would be "no need of other Heaven than the one below" (*Letters* 2: 329).

The irony, of course, is that in her letters and poetry, Dickinson—the "Queen Recluse" of popular legend—is most potent when she defines herself not *apart from* but *in relation* to others. "I should be stronger if I could see you oftener—I am very puny alone," she wrote to Emily Fowler in 1850 (*Letters* 1: 90). At about the same time she wrote to Jane Humphrey: "Oh I have needed my trusty Jane—my friend encourager, and sincere conciller, my rock, and strong assister!" (*Letters* 1: 95). In a similar vein, she addressed Abiah Root as a sturdy oak around which she would entwine her tendrils "so full of faith and confidence and the most holy trust" (*Letters* 1: 166). Later, in her poems, it is within a select community, and not in solitude, that Dickinson's "Soul" shuts her door on the world:

> The Soul selects her own Society—
> Then—shuts the Door—
> To her divine Majority—
> Present no more—
> (*The Poems of Emily Dickinson* #303, hereafter referred to as *Poems*)

Dickinson's " 'withdrawal from general society,' for which she never cared," said her sister, Lavinia, "was only a happen." She found a more stimulating life among nature, books, and "her chosen friends" (qtd. in Sewall 153).

There was nothing particularly neurotic or abnormal about Dickinson's intense relationships with her women friends. Within the sexually polarized world of nineteenth-century America, intensely passionate, and sometimes even physical, relationships between women were common. In *Maternal Counsels to a Daughter* (1855), Matilda Pullan comments on the importance of female friendship in a girl's life: "Perhaps not even the acceptance of a love is a more important era in the life of a young girl than her first serious choice of a friend" (qtd. in Gorham 113). But as the loving bond between Cecilia and Alice in Henry Wadsworth Longfellow's *Kavanagh* (1849) suggests, female friendship was a privilege of adolescence and a preparation for adult womanhood: it was "a rehearsal in girlhood of the great drama of woman's life." As Carroll Smith-Rosenberg points out in "The Female World of Love and Ritual," in nineteenth-century America girls routinely slept together, kissed, and hugged in relationships that were emotionally and sometimes erotically intense: "Bounded by home, church, and the institution of visiting," this female world became an apprenticeship into the culture of true womanhood, and thus an initiation into the laws of the fathers (10).[1]

What made Dickinson's female world unique was that it became, for her at least, not an initiation into but a form of *resistance to* the structures of male power as they were embodied in home and school, church and state, workplace and marketplace. However unwillingly, Dickinson's friends became players in her own drama of self-creation, her attempt to interrupt, to rupture, the patriarchal script in order to write a revisionary script of her own. Like the hills she addressed as her "Strong Madonnas" in "Sweet Mountains—Ye tell Me no lie—" (*Poems* #722), Dickinson sought to construct her women friends as empowering figures who would enable her to look witch-like and "Oppositely" for the kingdom of heaven.

The Magic Circle

At a time when women were subject to the authority of the father in the home, legally "covered" in marriage, and deprived of citizenship and political being under the Constitution of the United States, Dickinson's exchanges with women appear to have served the same function as gift-giving in earlier societies, creating a noninstitutionalized form of social commerce that affirmed the social being and solidarity of women even as it became the site of competition, rivalry, and contest.[2] With her women friends Dickinson shared a culture of affection and dissidence, of writing and exchanging "papers," of gardening, secrets, and a joyous irreverence toward male law. "How many knights are slain and wounded, and how many now remain," she asks Jane Humphrey.

"Keep a list of the conquests, Jennie, this is an *enemy's* Land!" (*Letters* 2: 321). It is in her correspondence with women that we first hear the transgressive witch-voice—the heh! heh! heh!—that would become the high tone of her poems. "I have lately come to the conclusion that I am Eve, alias Mrs. Adam," she wrote to Abiah Root in 1846. "You know there is no account of her death in the Bible, and why am not I Eve?" (*Letters* 1: 24).

Identifying with Eve as the mother of sin, she launched her own satanic revolt against the kingdom of God. While Amherst underwent a series of religious revivals during the forties and fifties, Dickinson cast herself over and over in the figure of the "tempter," the "*wicked* friend," "one of the lingering *bad* ones," who refused to "give up and become a Christian" (*Letters* 1: 83, 89, 98, 67). When in the winter of 1846 her friend Abiah Root began moving toward a life in Christ, Dickinson was rocked with desire and fear. "Evil voices lisp in my ear," she says of her refusal to give herself up to Christ during the revival in Amherst the previous winter; she is "in a state of enmity to him & his cause" (*Letters* 1: 27, 28).

For a short time Dickinson, too, communed "alone with the great God." But, she confesses in a letter to Root in 1846, "the world allured me & in an unguarded moment I listened to *her syren voice*. From that moment I seemed to lose my interest in heavenly things by degrees" (*Letters* 1: 30–31; emphasis added). As Dickinson's comment suggests, periods of religious revival became for her periods of intense struggle between (male) heaven and (female) earth. "We do not know that he is God—and *will* try to be still—tho' we really had rather complain," she wrote to Jane Humphrey in 1850 (*Letters* 1: 84). Insofar as the religious revivals that marked the forties and fifties in the United States might be understood as a response to a rapidly changing social order in which, after the Compromise of 1850, even the stability of the political union was at stake, Dickinson's refusal to "yeild [*sic*] to the claims of He who is greater than I" (*Letters* 1: 28) committed her to negotiating her own way through the shifting and uncertain terms of a social and linguistic field that could bring both power and dissolution. Seeking to articulate and affirm a female "I" who is greater than "He," Dickinson clung to her women friends with an even greater sense of urgency. While she experienced some uneasiness about the state of her own soul, she experienced her greatest anxiety at the loss of her sacred band of girlfriends to the male God. "I love you better than ever notwithstanding the link which bound us in that golden chain is sadly dimmed," she wrote Abiah Root as they began growing apart after Abiah joined the Church. "I feel more reluctant to lose you from that bright circle, whom I've called *my friends*" (*Letters* 1: 71).

At the same time that Dickinson's golden circle of friends was being shattered by the pressures of adulthood, religion, and marriage, she found in *Jane Eyre* a fictive heroine who refused to give herself up to the demands of man or

Figure 1. Daguerreotype of Emily Dickinson taken at Mt. Holyoke in December 1847 or early 1848. "I dont wonder that good angels weep—and bad ones sing songs," Dickinson wrote to her friend Jane Humphrey in 1850. (Courtesy of Amherst College Library)

God. The book, which she appears to have read in 1849, had an "electric" effect.[3] Not only was Jane Eyre "poor, obscure, plain, and little" (Brontë 222) in contrast with more classic heroines like Austen's Emma, who was "handsome, clever, and rich, with a comfortable home and happy disposition" (Austen 1). In the eyes of the contemporary reviewer Elizabeth Rigby,

Jane Eyre was also a "heathen mind" in an "anti-Christian composition" that threatened the overthrow of "authority and violated every code human and divine" (Brontë 451, 452). Here, indeed, was a female heroine to match Dickinson's own satanic identification and longings.

In Jane Eyre she found a cohort in discontent, whose yearning to escape the dull round of "making puddings and knitting stockings," "playing on the piano and embroidering bags," was linked with the nightly howlings of the madwoman, Bertha Mason. Besides the female quest myth, what probably most electrified Dickinson about *Jane Eyre* was the figure of a woman who resisted her confinement by opening her "inward ear to a tale that was never ended—a tale my imagination created, and narrated continuously; quickened with all of incident, life, fire, feeling, that I desired and had not in my actual existence" (Brontë 95–96). What Jane Eyre suggested was not only a heroic model of the female life but the ways the imagination might be used as a source of creative resistance, a means of narrating her own open-ended story in opposition to the closed love and marriage plots of the fathers.

Written during her years of puberty and late adolescence, at a time when women were expected to put their bodies into circulation and production for the use of men and the service of the race, Dickinson's early letters to her "golden chain" of women friends became not only a means of creating a form of unmediated correspondence among women within *"enemy's* Land." Like Jane Eyre's "never ended" tale of female desire, Dickinson's letters to women became a means of writing and narrating an existence against and beyond patriarchal design.[4] She came to experience the demands of domesticity and dutiful daughterhood as an almost physical intrusion into the sacred text of her female correspondence.

In a letter to Jane Humphrey, written in January 1850 when she was 19, Dickinson described in explicit and humorous detail the split between her writer self and the pious, pure, domestic, and ultimately self-effacing role required of true womanhood in nineteenth-century America:[5]

> So *many* wants—and me so *very* handy—and my time of so *little* account—and my writing so *very* needless—and really I came to the conclusion that I should be a villain unparralleled if I took but an inch of time for so unholy a purpose as writing a friendly letter . . . mind the house—and the food—*sweep* if the spirits were low. . . . The halt—the lame—and the blind—the old—the in-firm—the bed-ridden—and superannuated—the ugly, and disagreeable—the perfectly hateful to me—all *these* to see—and be seen by—an opportunity rare for cultivating meekness—and patience—and submission—and for turning my back to this very sinful, and wicked world.
>
> (*Letters* 1: 82)

At a time when women reformers like Catharine Beecher and Lydia Maria Child were using the language of Christian benevolence to justify women's advance into the public sphere, Dickinson was using her letters to women to articulate a kind of creative work and a kind of writing that would enable her to exist simultaneously inside and on the margins of the system, as "Vesuvius at Home."

Unable to be the Victorian angel in the house, Dickinson identifies herself and her work with the subversions of Satan:

> Somehow or other I incline to other things—and Satan covers them up with flowers, and I reach out to pick them. The path of duty looks very ugly indeed—and the place where *I* want to go more amiable—a great deal—it is so much easier to do wrong than right—so much pleasanter to be evil than good, I dont wonder that good angels weep—and bad ones sing songs.

> > (*Letters* 1: 82)

Dickinson's association of her writing with the songs of bad angels is a sign of the Puritan culture in which she lived. Within Puritan New England, as Nathaniel Hawthorne reminds us in *The Scarlet Letter,* art and the imagination had always been associated with the seductions of Satan. And from the time of Plato's *Republic,* art and the imagination had also been associated with the seductions of the female. In reclaiming the power of the imagination in her letters and in her poems, Dickinson was in some sense recuperating a demonic power that was already her own. In her night writings she sought to use the power of the "word made flesh" to become herself a god, creating an imaginary universe that exploded the bounds of women's sphere, and mocked, questioned, reversed, and reinvented the laws of the fathers. She knew, if others did not, that in the eyes of her culture she was one of the bad angels and that, had she been born at an earlier time, she, like Anne Hutchinson, would have been banished as a heretic.

In her letters to women Dickinson transformed the nineteenth-century fashion of letter writing as a form of mutual improvement into a site of female protest that quickened her fictive-making powers. It was within the secret, shared, and private culture of her correspondence with women that she first began to enact her assault on the symbolic orders of language itself. After a wildly hyperbolic account of the visitation of a cold in an 1850 letter to Abiah Root, Dickinson apologized for her "wicked story": "Now my dear friend, let me tell you that these last thoughts are fictions—vain imaginations to lead astray foolish young women. They are flowers of speech, they both *make,* and *tell* deliberate falsehoods, avoid them as the snake, and turn aside as from the *Bottle* snake, and I dont *think* you will be harmed" (*Letters* 1: 88). Dickinson's "flowers of speech" became a means of planting her own garden within the kingdom of God and the fathers. Courting the devil as muse, she tells "deliberate falsehoods" as a means of making her own truth. Her densely metaphoric language, her fictions, become a means of recuperating the art of lying, of fiction making, that were part of her heritage as Eve, "alias Mrs. Adam."

Dickinson resists the Emersonian figure of the poet as Adamic namer in a linguistic economy in which words equal things. " *'Speech'*—is a prank of *Parliament,"* she wrote (*Poems* #688). Recognizing at once the power of language and its essential fictiveness, she realizes first in her letters to women and later in her poems that it is on the level of language that she can resist subjection to the systems of masculine power—religious, social, and linguistic—by questioning and destabilizing its terms. Her letters to women have some of the linguistic wildness of her poems. As in her poems, her refusal to give herself up to the law of the fathers is enacted as an assault on the grammar, logic, syntax, and univocal meanings that have constituted the traditional authority of language.[6] At age 15, in her first known letter to Abiah Root, Dickinson speaks the language of "nonsense" that would quicken into the "divinest sense" of her poems: "leave everything and sit down prepared for a long siege in the shape of a bundle of nonsense from friend E" (*Letters* 1: 9). At times she appears to speak an encoded female language of gaps and ellipses, silences and blanks. In a letter written to Emily Fowler in early 1850, she leaves a blank space at the top of the page: "That is'nt an *empty* blank where I began—," she explains; "it is so full of affection that you cant see any—that's all" (*Letters* 1: 90).

At about the same time she begins to share a similar form of invisible writing—what she called "sky" writing—with Jane Humphrey. "I have written you a great many letters since you left me—not the kind of letters that go in post-offices—and ride in mail-bags—but queer—little silent ones—very full of affection—and full of confidence—" (*Letters* 1: 81). These silent letters are more "precious" than the "ocular" ones, for there is "No need of shutting the door—nor of whispering timidly—nor of fearing the ear of listeners—." Through this silent writing Dickinson seeks to engage in an imaginary exchange—a spiritual correspondence among women—that avoids mediation, circulation, and containment by "mail-bags" and males. "Sometimes I did'nt know but you were awake—and I hoped you wrote with that spirit pen—and on sheets from out the sky. *Did* you ever—and were we together in any of those nights? I *do* love—and remember you Jane—" (*Letters* 1: 81–82). Dickinson's spirit pen gestures toward what Luce Irigaray describes as "a feminine syntax" of "what resists or subsists 'beyond' " (*This Sex Which Is Not One* 134). Her silent correspondence "on sheets out of the sky" might be read as an attempt to articulate a different kind of speaking among women that cannot be heard and thus cannot be interrupted by the potentially dangerous "ear" of a listening (male) world.

It is to her women friends that Dickinson first whispers in privately coded metaphors the secret of her poetic art. "I have dared to do strange things— bold things, and have asked no advice from any," she wrote to Jane Humphrey in the spring of 1850. "I have heeded beautiful tempters, yet do not think I am wrong." Dickinson's "curious" and "strange" things probably refer to her courtship of the muse, who is once again projected as a demonic visitant. She appeals to her friend as a source of sustenance in her growing sense of artistic vocation. "Oh I have needed my trusty Jane—my friend encourager, and sincere counciller, my rock, and strong assister! . . . Oh, Jennie, it would relieve me to tell you all, to sit down at your feet, and look in your eyes, and confess what *you only* shall know, an experience bitter, and sweet, but the sweet did so beguile me—and life has had an aim, and the world has been too precious for your poor—and striving sister!" (*Letters* 1: 95).

As this initial circle of girlfriends married and left the Amherst community, Dickinson carried on her effort to establish an exclusive bond among women in her relationships with Susan Gilbert, Elizabeth Holland, and her cousins Frances and Louise Norcross. For the remainder of Dickinson's life, Sue Gilbert, who became her sister-in-law, Elizabeth Holland, whom Dickinson consistently addressed as "Little Sister" and "Loved Little Sister," and the Norcross sisters, whom she called her "children" or "little children," became a kind of extended family and private female public through whom and among whom Dickinson sought to create, nourish, and sustain herself as a writing woman.

Dickinson's bond with Elizabeth Holland, whom she met in the early fifties, was particularly strong in the last two decades of her life. Although she began by writing to both Elizabeth Holland and her husband Josiah, who joined Samuel Bowles as editor of the *Springfield Republican* in 1849, after 1865 her letters were addressed almost exclusively to Mrs. Holland. "Smaller than David you clothe me with extreme Goliath," she wrote her in 1866, fascinated by the power that emanated from Holland's tiny figure (*Letters* 2: 452). In her role as "Spirit Sister" and "extreme Goliath," Holland energized Dickinson's drama of self-creation and called forth some of her most witty assaults on masculine authority and pretension.

Dickinson's letters to Holland are full of antic posturings, as she plays the role of the rebellious daughter, laughing Medusa-like at the absurdities of the male order and challenging their sacred myths. "If God had been here this summer, and seen the things that *I* have seen—I guess that He would think His Paradise superfluous," she wrote in one of her earliest exchanges with Holland (*Letters* 2: 329). In another letter, Dickinson comments on the fact that as a child she used to spell Phoebe "Fee Bee." "[I] have seen no need to improve!," she exclaims. "Should I spell all the things as they sounded to me, and say all the facts as I saw them, it would send consternation among more than the '*Fee Bees!*' " (*Letters* 3: 774). Flaunting her defiance, Dickinson suggests that her irregular orthography and slant vision are—like her fracture of poetic line, image, and syntax—part of her self-conscious refusal to straighten and improve under the laws of the fathers.[7]

Compared with her fervent exchanges with Sue Gilbert and Elizabeth Holland, Dickinson's correspondence with the Norcross sisters seems more conventional in both sentiment and style, but this may be because the sisters carefully excised the more transgressive voice of their aunt before they made an edited and transcribed version of the letters available to Mabel Loomis Todd for publication.[8] With the Norcross sisters Dickinson played the role of a kind of culture mother, packing her letters full of exchanges about books, women writers, and literary culture, and occasionally enlisting them to procure exotic books for her from Burnham Antique Book Shop in Boston. " 'Burnham' must think Fanny a scholastic female," she wrote in 1860. "I wouldn't be in her place! If she feels delicate about it, she can tell him the books are for a friend in the East Indies" (*Letters* 2: 368).

Although the voice of conventional sentiment and the gospel of love is more emphatic in Dickinson's correspondence with the Norcross sisters, even here her letters treat reading and writing as realms of subversive activity shared by women against men. In one letter Dickinson describes her father's irritation when he catches her reading a book she obscurely refers to as "the South Sea rose": "Father detecting me, advised wiser employment, and read at devotions the chapter of the gentleman with one talent. I think he thought my conscience would adjust the gender" (*Letters* 2: 427). In her consciousness of the ways women are excluded from male-defined systems of language, literature, and law, Dickinson wittily suggests that insofar as the Bible is written for, by, and about a generic male figure, she is exempt from its laws.

"The Leaves like Women, interchange," Dickinson wrote, in a poem that simultaneously naturalizes female creation and the "Exclusive Confidence" and "Inviolable compact" among women as part of nature's law (*Poems* #987). But this "interchange" among women was not only or always a female world of love and ritual: it was also a site of ambivalence, contest, and pain. By conducting her friendships with women largely through the medium of writing, Dickinson avoided the risks and dangers of social contact. She wanted her friends to mirror and affirm her own needs and desires. As her childhood friends began to move toward adult womanhood and a life in Christ, she experienced an increasing sense of anxiety, separation, and difference: "We are growing away from each other, and talk even now like strangers," she wrote to Abiah Root in 1850 (*Letters* 1: 104). After Abby Wood's conversion into a "sweet, girl christian," their relationship breaks off:

"Our lots fall in different places; mayhap we might disagree," she wrote to Root. "We take different views of life, our thoughts would not dwell together as they used to when we were young—how long ago that seems! She is more of a woman than I am, for I love so to be a child" (*Letters* 1: 98, 104).

In her attempt to establish an intimate bond with her women friends, Dickinson could be possessive in the extreme, at times even excluding her sister, Lavinia, from her sacred circle of correspondence. When Elizabeth Holland sent a joint letter to both of them, Dickinson responded curtly: "Sister, A mutual plum is not a plum. I was too respectful to take the pulp and do not like a stone. Send no union letters" (*Letters* 2: 455). Defining herself against the conventionally Christian, benevolent, and true womanly lives chosen by her friends, at times Dickinson could be openly mocking, even hostile: "I presume you are loving your mother, and loving the stranger, and wanderer, visiting the poor, and afflicted, and reaping whole fields of blessings," she wrote to Abiah Root in one of their last exchanges (*Letters* 1: 99). Even in her relatively untroubled relationship with Elizabeth Holland, Dickinson made it clear that Holland's choices—husband, marriage, motherhood, and what she called her "sunshiny" God—were not her own. When she read that Josiah Holland was about to return from a lecture tour, Dickinson wrote: "I gather from 'Republican' that you are about to doff your weeds for a Bride's Attire. Vive le fireside! Am told that fasting gives to food marvellous Aroma, but by birth a Bachelor, disavow Cuisine" (*Letters* 2: 350).

Although we know what role Dickinson's friends played for her, we do not finally know what role she played for them. What did her girlfriends think of her satanic confessions? Were they secret sharers or appalled witnesses of her resistance and defiance? To what extent might the riddled style and wicked pose of her letters be read as a form of hostility to the more conventional lives of her women friends? In part because Lavinia destroyed the other half of the correspondence, there is a curiously monologic quality about Dickinson's relations with her women friends. Her friends never speak, they never respond, and thus they remain problematically "other." Nowhere is this problem of otherness more evident than in Dickinson's intense love relationship over many years with her friend and later sister-in-law, Susan Gilbert.

"Satan, or Sue"

Among Dickinson's "bright circle" of women friends, it was Sue Gilbert more than any other who was the presiding presence in the birth chambers of her poetic art. Having said this, one is immediately struck by the extent to which the "Master" plot and narratives of heterosexual love still dominate critical interpretations of Dickinson's life and work, and, correspondingly, by the ways in which Dickinson's central and troubled love relationship with Sue has been by turns erased, mutilated, demonized, and sentimentalized in the history of Dickinson scholarship. Dickinson's brother Austin quite literally erased and scissored out references to Sue in the correspondence he presented to his lover, Mabel Loomis Todd, who with Thomas Higginson undertook to "edit" Dickinson's poetry and correspondence after her death.[9] According to Todd's daughter, Millicent Todd Bingham, "Mr. Dickinson stipulated that if Emily's letters to him were to be used, the name of one of her girlhood friends must be left out—that of Susan Gilbert—his wife. But omitting her name was not enough. Before turning over the letters he went through them, eliminating Susan Gilbert's name and in some instances making alterations to disguise a reference to her"(Bingham, *Emily Dickinson's Home* 54).

While Austin sought to cut out or cover over his sister's passionate references to his wife, after Susan's death in 1913, she was demonized by local Amherst society as a dark lady and a villain. Lavinia's friend Mary Lee Hall says she told her that "Sue had been cruel to Emily and herself, and they each had suffered keenly from her insincerities, her insane jealousies, as well as her intentional deceit" (Sewall 256). According to Mabel Loomis Todd, Susan was "quite generally disliked and thoroughly distrusted" (Sewall 278). Elaborating upon her mother's version of Sue as a lower-class woman who married above her station, Bingham calls her "a relentless alien," "a low being, the daughter of a stable keeper whom the Squire had married by mistake" (Sewall 260, 300).[10] Referring to her as "Satan, or Sue," Mary Lee Hall wrote: "You cannot imagine such a fiend, for Sue could appear like 'an angel of light', when it served her purpose to do so" (Sewall 261). To Sarah Tuckerman, whose husband taught at Amherst College, Susan and her daughter Martha Dickinson [Bianchi] were "the two black devils" (Sewall 258).

In *The Life and Letters of Emily Dickinson,* Bianchi seeks to counter these negative versions of her mother with a story of her own, a carefully "edited" and sentimentalized version of the relationship between Dickinson and Sue as an idyllic friendship between sisters. In the last decade, following Rebecca Patterson's lead and Adrienne Rich's call for a revisionary look at "intense woman-to-woman-relationships" as "a central element in Dickinson's life and art" (*On Lies, Secrets, and Silence* 157), feminist critics have begun to break the historical and literary silence surrounding Dickinson's relationship with Sue Gilbert. But in their attempt to enact and enforce a feminist and politically correct model of loving sisterhood, these critics have also tended to romanticize the relationship between Dickinson and Sue, covering over the difference, the pain, and the "bladed" words that were also part of their love.[11]

Although the stories about Sue's cruelty and duplicity may not be true, they do suggest something of the role she played not only for the townspeople but for Dickinson herself, as the "torrid Spirit," "Siren," and "Stranger" through whom and against whom she defined herself. It is Sue's story, finally, that never gets told. What we do know is that the "War Between the Houses" was a war between women, a war that had as its site and center the volcanic and transgressive love relationship between Dickinson and Sue.

Susan Gilbert arrived back in Amherst in 1848, after completing her formal schooling, and there is evidence that at some time in their late teens or early twenties she and Dickinson began writing poetry together (Fig. 2). We "please ourselves with the fancy that we are the only poets, and everyone else is *prose*," Dickinson wrote to Sue in October 1851 (*Letters* 1: 144). Sometime around March 1853, she sent Sue one of her first poems—"On this wondrous sea"—preceded with the injunction "*Write! Comrade, write!*" (*Letters* 1: 226). The same month, in a letter to her brother, Austin, she made her first overt announcement of her own literary ambitions. Teasing her "Brother Pegasus" about the poem he enclosed in a letter to her, she says: "I'll tell you what it is—I've been in the habit *myself* of writing some few things, and it rather appears to me that you're getting away my patent, so you'd better be somewhat careful, or I'll call the police!" (*Letters* 1: 235).

By the early fifties Dickinson came to equate what she called "*real life*" with the world of the fathers. "We do not have much poetry," Dickinson wrote to Austin in 1851, "father having made up his mind that its pretty much all *real life*. Fathers real life and *mine* sometimes come into collision, but as yet, escape unhurt!" (*Letters* 1: 161). Dickinson was aided in the process of resisting her father's "*real*" and discovering the sources of her own creative power by her passionate and erotically intense love relationship with Sue Gilbert. "Susie, will you indeed come home next Saturday, and be my own again, and kiss me as you used to?" she wrote in June 1852, when Sue was teaching in Baltimore. "I hope for you so much, and feel so eager for you, feel that I *cannot* wait, feel that *now* I must have you—that the expectation once more to see your face again, makes me feel hot and feverish, and my heart beats so fast—" (*Letters* 1: 215).

When Dickinson speaks her desire in her correspondence with Sue, language breaks down. She speaks silence—not in words but with her body:

> Susie, forgive me Darling, for every word I say—my heart is full of you, none other than you in my thoughts, yet when I seek to say to you something not for the world, words fail me. If you were here—and Oh that you were, my Susie, we need not talk at all, our eyes would whisper for us, and your hand fast in mine, we would not ask for language.

> (*Letters* 1: 211–12)

Figure 2. Susan Gilbert, about 1851. "Where my Hands are cut, Her fingers will be found inside," Dickinson wrote of her lifelong love relationship with her sister-in-law, Susan Gilbert Dickinson. (By permission of the Houghton Library)

In her attempt to express what had been unnamed and unrepresented by her culture, Dickinson's letters to Sue, like her letters to her other women friends, begin to speak the elliptical, hyperbolic, densely figural language of her verse. In fact, as their relationship grew, Dickinson's letters to Sue became shorter and shorter, until, finally, in the last few decades of her life, the letters, and indeed the poems to Sue, have all the quality of cryptic code messages delivered across enemy lines.

Whether or not Dickinson's relationship with Sue was lesbian in the modern sense of the term is open to question.[12] Catharine Stimpson has argued that "lesbianism partakes of the body, partakes of the flesh. That carnality distinguishes it from gestures of political sympathy with homosexuals and from affectionate friendships in which women enjoy each other, support each other, and commingle a sense of identity and well-being. Lesbianism represents a commitment of skin, blood, breast, and bone" ("Zero Degree Deviancy" 364). In its early phases, at least, Dickinson's relationship with Sue had a physical dimension, but by the mid-sixties their relationship was carried on largely through writing and most often through poems. What is apparent is that the lifelong bond between them exists within what Adrienne Rich calls the "lesbian continuum" of woman-identified existence. Dickinson's relationship with Sue Gilbert is part of the history of women who "as witches, *femmes seules,* marriage resisters, spinsters, autonomous widows, and/or lesbians— have managed on varying levels *not* to collaborate" (Rich, "Compulsory Heterosexuality" 635). Dickinson's love for Sue was a form of saying *No* to the masculine and heterosexual orders of Church and State in order to say *Yes* to herself.

After Sue, along with Dickinson's father, joined the Church in August 1850, Dickinson sought to seduce her back into her own personal religion of female love. "The bells are ringing, Susie, north, and east, and south, and *your own* village bell, and the people who love God, are expecting to go to meeting; don't *you* go Susie, not to *their* meeting, but come with me this morning to the church within our hearts, where the bells are always ringing, and the preacher whose name is Love—shall intercede there for us!" Having refused to go to "the usual meetinghouse, to hear the usual sermon," Dickinson has "the old *king feeling*" as, in the "sweet Sabbath" of their communion, she seeks to "poeticize" the world for Sue (*Letters* 1: 181). As Sue's "Idolater" Dickinson makes her the central "Shrine" of a mother-goddess religion that eclipses the religion of the New England patriarchs and releases her into song.

In an 1852 letter to Sue, Dickinson makes her own profession of faith. Passionate thoughts of "Thee," she says:

> filled my mind so full, I could not find a *chink* to put the worthy pastor; when he said "Our Heavenly Father," I said "Oh Darling Sue"; when he read the 100th Psalm, I kept saying your precious letter all over to myself, and Susie, when they sang—it would have made you laugh to hear one little voice, piping to the departed. I made up words and kept singing how I loved you, and you had gone, while all the rest of the choir were singing Hallelujahs. I presume nobody heard

me, because I sang *so small,* but it was a kind of a comfort to think I might put
them out, singing of you.

(*Letters* 1: 201)

Over and over in her letters and poems, Dickinson rewrites scriptural passages
to express her idolatry at what she calls the "Shrine" of Sue (*Letters* 2: 458).
She counters the Calvinistic religion of the fathers with a religion of female
love, and empowered by her love for Sue, she imagines her *small* voice
growing so strong that she will "put out" the voice of Calvinist patriarchy in song.

But Sue Gilbert was not only a source of love. Cultured, worldly, demonic,
and magnetically attractive, she was also a source of knowledge and power.
As Richard Sewall points out, hyperbole is the ruling figure in Dickinson's
letters to Sue: "Images of uniqueness, size, power, totality abound" (202).
Under Sue's influence, Dickinson discovered an elastic power that enabled
her to dance "like a Bomb, abroad" and dream terrorist dreams of annihilat-
ing the Puritan fathers, New England culture, and ultimately the entire edifice
of America itself. Writing to Sue of how her " 'life' was made a 'victim',," at
Church meeting, Dickinson longs for the assistance of her women friends in
destroying the "Phantom" that pursues her. "How I did wish for you—how,
for my own dear Vinnie—how for Goliah, or Samson—to pull the whole
church down" (*Letters* 1: 283–84).

When her father is sent as a delegate to the Whig Convention in Baltimore
in 1852, she wonders why she cannot be a delegate. The knowledge of her
exclusion from the constituted orders of masculine political power leads her
into a fantasy of destruction. "I don't like this country at all, and I shant stay
here any longer! 'Delenda est' America, Massachusetts and all!" (*Letters* 1:
212). While Sue probably did not share Dickinson's terrorist dreams of violence against the system, it was Dickinson's explosive and transgressive desire for Sue that called forth and validated the volcanic persona who would
emerge in the poems as a "Loaded Gun" and "Vesuvius at Home."

In her multiple incarnations as "absent Lover" and a "real beautiful hero,"
"Imagination" and an "Avalanche of Sun," an "emblem of Heaven" and the
"garden *unseen,*" Susan Gilbert served finally as a bewitching Muse-like
presence who poeticized Dickinson's world and called forth her own art of
song. "You sketch my pictures for me," Dickinson wrote Sue in 1853; "and
'tis at their sweet colorings, rather than this dim real that I am used, so you see
when you go away, the world looks staringly, and I find I need more vail"
(*Letters* 1: 229). At times, Sue seemed the essence of creation itself. "Dear
Susie, when you come, how many boundless blossoms among those silent
beds!" (*Letters* 1: 208). Sue's presence brings the "warm and green, and
birds" of spring. When she is absent it is waste and stone (*Letters* 1: 304).

In the poem "Dying! Dying in the night!" it is Sue as Dollie, and not Jesus Christ, who brings salvation and light:

> And "*Jesus*"! Where is *Jesus* gone?
> They said that Jesus—always came—
> Perhaps he does'nt know the House—
> This way, Jesus, Let him pass!
>
> Sombody run to the great gate
> And see if Dollie's coming! Wait!
> I hear her feet upon the stair!
> Death won't hurt—now Dollie's here!
>
> (*Poems* #158)

Experiencing herself as hungry and insufficiently nurtured by either God the Father or her biological mother, in the early stages of their relationship Dickinson turned to Sue as a compensatory source of mother-religion and mother love: "Oh Susie, I would nestle close to your warm heart, and never hear the wind blow, or the storm beat, again," she wrote her in the winter of 1852. "Is there any room there for me, or shall I wander away all homeless and alone?" (*Letters* 1: 177).

From the first, however, it was Sue's role as sister rather than maternal protectress that shaped the relationship between them. This sisterly relation might, as some feminist critics have argued, appear to foreground the familial, horizontal, and essentially egalitarian nature of their bond in contrast to the more hierarchical relationship of dominance and submission that characterized Dickinson's relationship with the male figures in her life and poems.[13] But as "precious Sister," Sue was also and always not the same. If their sisterhood was marked by passionate love, it was also a scene of contest and struggle for possession, power, and dominion.

In "One Sister have I in our house," Dickinson represents Sue as a bird whose "different tune" becomes a source of sustenance in the journey from childhood to adulthood:

> She did not sing as we did—
> It was a different tune—
> Herself to her a music
> A Bumble bee of June.
>
> Today is far from Childhood—
> But up and down the hills
> I held her hand the tighter—
> Which shortened all the miles—
>
> (*Poems* #14)

Even in this sisterly poem of praise, however, there are ambiguous references to a "hum" that "Deceives" and eyes that "lie," references that suggest that Sue's "different tune" was also a source of tension between them.

Sue's difference was, I would argue, at least in part a difference of class and privilege. As the orphaned daughter of a tavern owner, Sue was from a lower social class than Dickinson, and thus she could not, like Dickinson, exercise the privilege of choosing not to circulate. Smart and ambitious for status and power, Sue had designs in and on the social world that placed her at odds with Dickinson's dream of an exclusive female bond. "Sue always made a point of associating principally with daughters of the better class," wrote Mabel Loomis Todd. "She was a bright girl, who knew how to put herself on confidential terms with daughters of the upper class in Amherst, and for some years she and Lavinia and Emily were trusting friends" (Sewall 282).

Having made her own profession of faith and aspiring to rise socially, Sue may have been uneasy with the urgency, intensity, and seeming irreverence of Dickinson's love. It was probably what Dickinson called her "*idolatry*" that provoked a disagreement between them sometime in the mid-fifties: "Sue— you can go or stay—," Dickinson wrote abruptly. "We differ often lately, and this must be the last." She links the causes of their disagreement with her own private worship at the shrine of Sue: "Sue—I have lived by this. It is the lingering emblem of the Heaven I once dreamed, and though if this is taken, I shall remain alone, and though in that last day, the Jesus Christ you love, remark he does not know me—there is a darker spirit will not disown it's child" (*Letters* 1: 306).

If Dickinson was angered by the loss of Sue to Jesus Christ, there is also evidence that Sue's marriage to Austin Dickinson in 1856 may be responsible for the mysterious silence—the total absence of letters—between 1856 and 1858. During the courtship of Sue and Austin, Dickinson expressed her own ambivalence about the potentially repressive rituals of love and marriage: "You and I have been strangely silent upon this subject, Susie," she wrote in June 1852:

> How dull our lives must seem to the bride, and the plighted maiden, whose days are fed with gold, and who gathers pearls every evening; but to the *wife*, Susie, sometimes the *wife forgotten*, our lives perhaps seem dearer than all others in the world; you have seen flowers at morning, *satisfied* with the dew, and those same sweet flowers at noon with their heads bowed in anguish before the mighty sun. . . . they know that the man of noon, is *mightier* than the morning and their life is henceforth to him. Oh, Susie, it is dangerous. . . . It does so rend me, Susie, the thought of it when it comes, that I tremble lest at sometime I, too, am yielded up.
>
> (*Letters* 1: 209–210)

The imagery of female flowers being dried up by the "man of noon" suggests the threat that marriage represented to Dickinson during the period of her creative growth. But the letter is more than a confession of her fear of being "yielded up" to male power. Dickinson's hyperbolically charged language may be an attempt to seduce Sue away from the heterosexual orders of courtship and marriage and back into the garden of their own female love.

In "Ourselves were wed one summer—dear—," Dickinson represents the tale of her loss of Sue to the masculine orders of religion and marriage:

> Ourselves were wed one summer—dear—
> Your Vision—was in June—
> And when Your little Lifetime failed,
> I wearied—too—of mine—
>
> (*Poems* #631)

The syntactical oddness of "Ourselves" suggests the "difference" of their female marriage—the autoerotic awakening to an enriched consciousness of self that a woman can experience in loving someone who is like rather than different from herself. Dickinson's syntactical construction might be paraphrased to read: we married our selves when we married each other.

Sue's "Vision" in June appears to telescope two events: her profession of faith in August 1850 and her marriage to Austin in July 1856. Associating their relationship with the creative bloom of summer, Dickinson experiences her loss of Sue to both religion and marriage as a kind of death in which Sue's life is "yielded up" to the masculine and heterosexual orders of man and God. She overcomes her own experience of death and waste by yielding herself—not to man or God—but to the "light" and call of her poetic muse:

> And overtaken in the Dark—
> Where You had put me down—
> By Some one carrying a Light—
> I—too—received the Sign.
>
> (#631)

Having received the "Sign" of her poetic vocation as another kind of religious and marital vow, Dickinson inscribes the difference of her own life in lines that suggest both the heroism of her quest and her experience of loss:

> 'Tis true—Our Futures different lay—
> Your Cottage—faced the sun—
> While Oceans—and the North must be—
> On every side of mine
>
> 'Tis true, Your Garden led the Bloom,
> For mine—in Frosts—was sown—

> And yet, one Summer, we were Queens—
> But You—were crowned in June—
>
> (#631)

Whereas Sue's life is contained within the daily social round of cottage and sun, Dickinson lives sterile and witch-like on the margins, facing the open space of oceans and the north. Once again, Sue is associated with the creativity and bloom of a garden, but it is a garden circumscribed by the round of the male order signified by sun/son. The line "Your Garden led the Bloom" may in fact refer to the birth of Sue's son, Edward, on June 19, 1861. Dickinson sows her own garden—her poems—in "Frosts" that suggest the cold and waste of her separation from Sue, her existence on the margins of the social world, and a barrenness that gives birth to poems rather than children. In their separation from each other, Dickinson suggests, both have lost some of the potency of their primal bond together when they were "Queens" under another law. And thus, the "crown" of power that Sue receives as the Bride of Christ and man is also a crown of limits, blows, and thorns.

This loss of the female to the law of the fathers is a central and almost obsessively recurrent motif in Dickinson's letters and later in her poems. In her very first letter to Abiah Root, written when she was fourteen, Dickinson presents herself as part of a female universe of blooming gardens and singing birds, continually embattled by a tyrannical and all-powerful masculine force: "I have heard some sweet little birds sing, but I fear we shall have more cold weather and their little bills will be frozen up before their songs are finished. My plants look beautifully. Old King Frost has not had the pleasure of snatching any of them in his cold embrace as yet, and I hope will not" (*Letters* 1: 9).

Dickinson's myth of paradise was not the Biblical story of Adam and Eve in Genesis, but the anterior matriarchal myth of female community inscribed by the myth of Demeter and Köre. Over and over in her poems Dickinson returns to the story of a primal female bond ruptured by the intrusion of a Plutonian figure in the shape of man, God, or death itself. The essence of this myth of origins is contained in the following poem:

> We talked as Girls do—
> Fond, and late—
> We speculated fair, on every subject, but the Grave—
> Of our's, none affair—
>
> We handled Destinies, as cool—
> As we—Disposers—be—
> And God, a Quiet Party
> To our Authority—

> But fondest, dwelt upon Ourself
> As we eventual—be—
> When Girls to Women, softly raised
> We—occupy—Degree—
>
> We parted with a contract
> To cherish, and to write
> But Heaven made both, impossible
> Before another night.
>
> (*Poems* #586)

The poem represents a fantasy of female power in which, as in Dickinson's "Oh Darling Sue" letter, "Girl" talk silences the "Authority" of the male voice. This female contract of two as one—figured in the grammatical fracture of "Ourself"—is at once affectional and creative: "To cherish, and to write." But this primal bond is interrupted by the masculine "Authority" of "Heaven," perhaps in the form of religion, marriage, adulthood, or death.

From a psychoanalytic point of view the poem might be read as an inscription of the daughter's desire to return to what French feminists have called the body and the language of the mother. But this underlying psychic drama of Dickinson's poems also had a particular historic formation, enacting dimensions of her early relationships with her sacred band of girlfriends. As a woman poet seeking to "occupy" a subject position and "Degree" in a cultural economy in which the only socially valorized route from girlhood to womanhood was through the masculine orders of religion, marriage, and motherhood, Dickinson imagines the loss of paradise not as a fall away from man or God, but as the loss of a specifically female bond that enabled her to achieve a sense of agency, "Authority," and voice. The female contract "To cherish, and to write" calls up even as it breaks the woman's traditional marital vow "to love, cherish, and obey" her husband and her God.

When Sue Gilbert married Austin in 1856, Dickinson lost the possibility of an exclusive female relation under another law. Insofar as the social order is, as Claude Lévi-Strauss argues, rooted in the incest taboo and the exchange of women among men, Dickinson's own refusal to marry and her attempt to create an alternative exchange among women might be read as a gesture of political resistance, an attempt to block the cultural and social order at its very foundations. In fact, if Sue's marriage to Austin separated her from Dickinson, Sue's new status as sister-in-law also served paradoxically to reinforce Dickinson's refusal to circulate by transforming their erotic bond into an actual kinship "in law" and thus a form of incest. By ultimately strengthening the kinship between Dickinson and Sue, Sue's marriage became a rather inventive means for Dickinson to love her and to make a family with her within the conventional domestic arrangements of nineteenth-century genteel New England society. Within this familial arrangement, Dickinson undertook her own form of production, articulating one possible answer to what Luce Irigaray calls "the question of what the social status of women might be—in particular through its differentiation from a simple reproductive-maternal function" (*This Sex Which Is Not One* 128).

After Sue's legal incorporation into the family and sometime during the mysterious break in correspondence between 1856 and 1858, Dickinson began arranging and sewing her poems into groupings that Mabel Loomis Todd called "fascicles."[14] Among Dickinson's manuscripts there are thirty-nine groupings that have been threaded and bound together and twenty-five other groupings that have not been sewn. Although Dickinson may have been preparing her poems for eventual publication, she also may have been engaged in a private form of publication. Folding, sewing, and binding four to five sheets of paper together in groupings of eighteen to twenty poems, Dickinson, in effect, converted traditional female thread-and-needle work into a different kind of housework and her own form of productive industry.

"*My* business is to *sing,*" she wrote to Elizabeth Holland during the period of her most intense poetic creation, at a time when she was seeking to articulate a valuable and productive kind of women's work that did not merely subtend the interests and orders of men. In the same letter she wrote; "Perhaps you laugh at me! Perhaps the whole United States are laughing at me too! *I* can't stop for that! *My* business is to love" (*Letters* 2: 413). Like such women reformers as Emma Willard and Julia Ward Howe, who sought to ground their arguments for women's education and women's suffrage in domestic ideology and traditional notions of woman's sphere, Dickinson seeks to justify her poetic "business" by linking it with the traditionally feminine business of affection and love.[15] But in her attempt to legitimize her creative work and to resist the traditionally commercial business of men with her own affectional economy, Dickinson paradoxically risks reinstating the very dichotomy of male and female work that underwrites the essential illegitimacy of her business as a writing woman. This dichotomy is a point of stress in Dickinson's poems as her speaker swings between the more conventional notion of women's art as loving and healing inscribed in the lines "If I can stop one Heart from breaking / I shall not live in vain" (*Poems* #119) and a more transgressive notion of women's art as the power to wound and to kill expressed in the poem "My Life had stood—a Loaded Gun—" (*Poems* #754).

Although Sue is often criticized for failing to cooperate in Mabel Loomis Todd's project to publish Dickinson's poems, the bowdlerized version in which her *Poems* first appeared in 1890 and 1891—with Dickinson's poems neatly titled and thematicized and her fracture of meter and rhyme, grammar and syntax carefully corrected and regularized—suggests that Sue may have had a better understanding of the kind of poetic business in which Dickinson was engaged. Although Dickinson appears to have flirted with the notion of publishing, with the exception of a few poems, she in fact never did. This refusal to publish might be read as a further gesture in her refusal to go to market. She appears to have been engaged in a kind of cottage industry, a pre-capitalist mode of manuscript production and circulation that avoided the commodity and use values of the commercial marketplace.

Along with the manuscripts that Dickinson produced, threaded, and bound herself, she also engaged in a further form of self-production and self-publica-tion by enclosing and circulating her poems in letters to her friends.[16] Within this private system of publication, it was Sue Dickinson who received more poems than anyone else. As the recipient of at least 276 of Dickinson's poems, Sue served over many years as the primary audience for Dickinson's work. She was the subject of several poems and the inspiration for many more, perhaps even some of the marriage poems that appear to be addressed to men.

Their exchange over "Safe in their Alabaster Chambers—" around 1861 indicates that she also served, perhaps frequently, as a knowledgeable critic of Dickinson's work. Commenting on the first stanza, Sue wrote: "You never made a peer for that verse, and I *guess* you[r] kingdom does'nt hold one—I always go to the fire and get warm after thinking of it, but I never *can* again." Sue's praise fed Dickinson's own ambitions as a poet: "Your praise is good—to me—because I *know* it *knows*—and *suppose*—it *means*. Could I make you and Austin—proud—sometime—a great way off—'twould give me taller feet—" (*Letters* 2: 380). When Thomas Higginson later asked her to define poetry, she borrowed Sue's "fire and ice" response to "Safe in their Alabaster Chambers—": "If I read a book [and] it makes my whole body so cold no fire ever can warm me, I know *that* is poetry" (*Letters* 2: 473–74).

As a subscriber to the *Atlantic*, Sue may have urged Dickinson to respond to Higginson's "Letter to a Young Contributor" in the spring of 1862; and it may have been Sue who prevailed on her friend Samuel Bowles to publish five of Dickinson's poems in the *Springfield Republican*. After "Safe in their Alabaster Chambers—" appeared in the *Springfield Republican* on March 1, 1862, Sue sent Dickinson an enthusiastic note: "*Has girl read Republican?* It takes as long to start our Fleet as the Burnside" (Leyda 2: 48). The note suggests that Dickinson's poetry writing was part of a cooperative enterprise between them and that Sue was, at least momentarily, urging Dickinson to "launch" her work and their "Fleet" in the world.

Although critics and biographers have suggested that the relationship be-

tween Sue and Dickinson broke off or changed radically in the mid-fifties, the
letters and poems that Dickinson sent her over many years suggest that their
relationship never really cooled—that Sue continued as sister-spirit, witch-
goddess, erotic center, and muse at the very sources of Dickinson's poetic
creation. But the relationship between them was not easy, and it was never
free from ambivalence, tension, and pain. This ambivalence is evident even in
their exchange over "Safe in their Alabaster Chambers—." Sue's words,
"You never made a peer for that verse," might also suggest that Dickinson
had written only one good poem. And Dickinson's response, "Your praise is
good—to me—because I *know* it *knows*—and *suppose*—it *means*—," might
also suggest that she is not really sure what and if Sue's advice *means*; it might
only be *mean*. When the poem was published in the *Springfield Republican* it
was in fact published in Dickinson's original version, the one Sue appears to
have objected to.

The complex nature of their relationship is suggested by a note that Dickin-
son wrote to Sue in 1864. "Sweet Sue—," she wrote from Cambridge where
she was being treated for eye trouble, "There is no first, or last, in Forever—
It is Centre, there, all the time. . . . [f]or the Woman whom I prefer, Here is
Festival—Where my Hands are cut, Her fingers will be found inside—"
(*Letters* 2: 430). As loved one, power, and muse Sue was the "Sister of
Ophir" and the "Festival" that enabled Dickinson to overcome her sense of
amputation and lack under the regime of the fathers in order to give birth to
herself and her poems. But if Dickinson's "hands-cut-fingers" image suggests
Sue's agency and power, the image also suggests the intensely erotic nature of
the bond between them and the potentially painful nature of that bond as a
wound that never heals, a love that is never finally consummated. Sue's
"fingers" inside Dickinson's "cut" hands may be a source of "Festival" and
power, but they also keep the wound always open.

The poems that Dickinson sent to Sue or that were inspired by her—and
there were probably many more of these than we think—were not only poems
of love, sisterhood, power, and *jouissance*. They were also and often poems
that registered a sense of separation, loss, rejection, and inexpressible pain.
"You love me—you are sure—," Dickinson wrote in one of her more anxious
poetic addresses to Sue as "Dollie":

> Be sure you're sure—you know—
> I'll bear it better now—
> If you'll just tell me so—
> Than when—a little dull Balm grown—
> Over this pain of mine—
> You sting—again!
>
> (*Poems* #156)

If Sue offered "Sunrise" and "Balm," she also had her "sting": she could be cool, aloof, and, if we are to believe local Amherst gossip, cunning, cruel, arrogant, and self-serving. "She dealt her pretty words like Blades—," Dickinson wrote, perhaps with Sue in mind (*Poems* #479). But Dickinson could also be a difficult, imperious, and demanding friend, sister, and lover, and the art of bladed words was one to which she was herself no stranger. In fact, "She dealt her pretty words like Blades—" could also refer to her own wounding and killing power as both poet and sister.

In her desire to secure an alternative affectional economy among women, Dickinson was not only in some sense possessed by Sue, she also wanted to possess her. "To own a Susan of my own," she wrote:

> Is of itself a Bliss—
> Whatever Realm I forfeit, Lord,
> Continue me in this!
> (*Poems* #1401)

Having in effect forfeited God for Sue, Dickinson never fully accepted the fact that she did not finally get Sue in exchange. "But Susan is a Stranger yet—," she said in a rewrite of the poem "What mystery pervades a well!" that she sent to her about 1877:

> To pity those who know her not
> Is helped by the regret
> That those who know her know her less
> The nearer her they get—
> (*Letters* 2: 598)

For all Dickinson's dream of female oneness and possession under another law, Sue remained finally "other," "A Different Peru," as Dickinson said in "Your Riches—taught me—Poverty," an earlier poem she addressed to her.

But while it is important that we recognize Sue's difference from Dickinson, and the very real differences that marked the relationship between them, it is also important to recognize the centrality of this relationship in the text of Dickinson's life and work. Despite the efforts of the Dickinson family and later critics to erase and write over the erotic traces of this relationship, it was Dickinson's intense, passionate, and sometimes troubled love relationship with Sue and not her love relationship with the Master—or any of the various men who have been proposed to play that role—that was the central and enduring relationship of her life. "With the exception of Shakespeare, you have told me of more knowledge than any one living—To say that sincerely is strange praise," Dickinson wrote Sue in 1882 (*Letters* 3: 733). If she could never really "own" a Susan of her "own," she could never finally separate herself from her either: "The tie between us is very fine, but a Hair never dissolves," she wrote to Sue shortly before her death in 1886 (*Letters* 3: 893). Sue was at once both "Stranger" and "Sister," a woman like herself who called forth, mirrored, and affirmed the power, the knowledge, the creation, and the transgressive desire that became finally their "Fleet" and part of what Dickinson called "my letter to the World / That never wrote to Me—" (*Poems* #441).

Sisterhood and Difference

The playful, cryptic, riddled, and wicked language that emerges first in Dickinson's letters to women and later in her poems might be read as a particularly compelling example of what French feminists have called "feminine writing" and a "feminine text." Dickinson's fracture of grammar, logic, and meaning, her attempt to "ride indefinite," to keep herself open, flexible, and multiple, might be read as an attempt to *voler,* an attempt to fly and steal that, like Hélène Cixous's bird and thief, takes pleasure in "scrambling spacial order, disorienting it, moving furniture, things, and values around, breaking in, emptying structures, turning the selfsame, the proper upside down" (Cixous and Clément, *The Newly Born Woman* 96). Insofar as Dickinson's disruptive and explosive language is a language that emerges among women, it might also be read as an instance of what Luce Irigaray calls "Speaking-among-women" as "the place where a speaking (as) woman may dare express itself" (*This Sex Which Is Not One* 135). Dickinson's shifting and shifty language of breaks, ellipses, and logical contradiction also gestures toward what Julia Kristeva calls *le sémiotique,* the language of the "maternal body" that traverses and ruptures the symbolic language of the fathers (*Revolution in Poetic Language*). But while Dickinson's work appears to intersect with and affirm the work of contemporary French feminists, it also questions and challenges some of the more problematic grounds of recent feminist theory and practice.

It is one thing to argue that, within a particular social formation, women might speak an elliptical and coded language that sounds different from traditional masculine discourse. It is quite another to argue that this language is a reflex of a biologically different female body—a language that inscribes the particular female sexuality of what Irigaray calls two lips speaking together, of what Cixous calls the "white milk" of the mother, and of what Kristeva calls the "sublime repressed" of the maternal body. Although Dickinson's multiple, fluid, and mobile language contests masculine logic and masculine orders of power, it does not in any literal sense of the term write the female body. Her grammar of fracture and dislocation is grounded in her historical experience of exclusion, danger, and contradiction as a woman seeking to write within and resist a particular socioeconomic order.

"I do not care for the body," Dickinson wrote Abiah Root in 1850, "the bold obtrusive body—Pray, marm, did you call *me*?" (*Letters* 1: 103) Figuring the body as a servant of the lower class, Dickinson registers her experience of the body as the site of her oppression, the place where female nature—in particular, the female capacity for reproduction—can be made to serve the needs of man and the race. The fact that Dickinson's friendships even with women were carried on largely through writing suggests the ways that writing became for her a means of avoiding the risks and dangers of both bodily contact and being reduced to her body. Through her writing Dickinson sought to enter a mental space beyond the colonized space of the female body. "A Letter always feels to me like immortality," she said, "because it is the mind alone without corporeal friend" (*Letters* 2: 460). To interpret Dickinson's language as an inscription of female corporeality denies the terms of her own writing practice; it also reinscribes the notion of an essentially different male and female nature that has been historically the source of women's oppression.

In *This Sex Which Is Not One*, Irigaray speculates on how a separatist exchange among women might socialize "in a different way the relation to nature, matter, the body, language, and desire" (191). She imagines an idyllic female community in which "Nature's resources would be expended without depletion, exchanged without labor, freely given, exempt from masculine transactions: enjoyment without a fee, well-being without pain, pleasure without possession" (197). She calls on women to create an other, better world: "Let's never lay down the law to each other, or moralize, or make war. Let's not claim to be right, or claim the right to criticize one another. If one of us sits in judgment, our existence comes to an end" (217). For all their visionary and utopic power, Irigaray's words suggest the ease with which feminist notions of an essential "women's sexuality," "women's language," and "women's imaginary" slip into a kind of nineteenth-century rhetoric of female moral superiority.

It was precisely this rhetoric of female moral superiority, deployed by women reformers and popularized by the sentimental women writers of her time, that Dickinson sought to resist in representing herself as one of "the bad ones," who took pleasure in being "evil" rather than "good." In a letter to Jane Humphrey, Dickinson mocks the benevolent notion of women as the feeders, caretakers, and reformers of the world represented by the local Sewing Society to which she refuses to belong: "Sewing Society has commenced again—and held its first meeting last week—now all the poor will be helped—the cold warmed—the warm cooled—the hungry fed—the thirsty attended to—the ragged clothed—and this suffering—tumbled down world will be helped to it's feet again—which will be quite pleasant to all. *I dont attend*—notwithstanding my high approbation—which must puzzle the public exceedingly. *I am already set down as one of those brands almost con-sumed—and my hardheartedness gets me many prayers"* (*Letters* 1: 84; em-phasis added).

Dickinson's women friends became enabling figures in her attempt to create a subject position and a place to speak from as a woman writing in a culture that would either keep her "still" or lock her in the "prose" of the domestic and sentimental writers of her time. These friendships—particularly Dickin-son's relationship with Sue—reveal the way some women have historically turned to each other as a means of naming themselves and representing their desire. But these friendships also suggest that relationships among women can be just as troubled and complex as relations between men or between men and women. If Dickinson, too, dreamed of a separate female community of nur-turance, mutuality, and love, her actual relations with women suggest the impossibility of this dream, not because as Irigaray and others have argued "men have organized a *de facto* rivalry among women" (*This Sex Which Is Not One* 164), but because women have differences among and within them-selves, and sisters can also be wicked.

Placing Dickinson in History

In the attempt to theorize women's subjectivity and the difference of women's experience, French as well as Anglo-American feminist critics have tended to privilege psychoanalytic discourse and an essentially Freudian/Lacanian fam-ily paradigm that reads women's history and women's texts as an inscription of the daughter's desire to return to an initial mother/daughter bond that has been ruptured by the language and law of the Father.[17] Although Dickinson's quest for female community and a language of self-representation might be read as a desire to be mothered, I would argue against essentializing this desire as part of a univocal female psychology, the quest of every woman to return to the body of the mother and the *langue maternelle*. Through an almost exclusive focus on gender, psychosexuality, and patriarchy as the only oppres-sion, feminist critics have tended paradoxically to take Dickinson out of history, (re)privatizing her in the space of the home and the psyche, and subsuming the particularity and difference of Dickinson's life and work into a repeat across time of the same familial romance: the story of the daughter's revolt against a perpetually demonized and transhistorical patriarch and her desire to return to a preoedipal and prehistorical mother.

As Gayle Rubin argues in "The Traffic in Women," "Sex/gender systems are not ahistorical emanations of the human mind; they are products of histor-ical human activity. . . . There is an economics and politics of sex/gender systems" (204–205). Dickinson's desire for female community and the "remoter green" of a motherland occurred within a particular historical and class formation, a formation grounded in the separation of male and female spheres and in a particular social construction of the woman, the mother, the daughter, and the female body. "I never had a mother," Higginson remembers Dickinson saying in conversation with him. "I suppose a mother is one to whom you hurry when you are troubled" (*Letters* 2: 475). Dickinson's words have spurred psychoanalytic critics to attribute her seeming "neurosis" to a cold and unloving mother.[18] But there is no evidence that Dickinson was abused or mistreated by her mother. Echoing the words of her favorite literary heroine, Aurora Leigh—"I felt a mother-want about the world"—Dickinson's words have a larger socioeconomic resonance. What Dickinson's words do suggest is the ways a white upper-class girl child in nineteenth-century America might experience herself as hungry and unmothered within an increasingly bourgeois market economy rigidly segregated into male and female spheres.

Quiet, passive, sickly, and dependent, Dickinson's mother—Emily Norcross Dickinson—represented the very model of true womanhood against which Dickinson had to rebel in order to escape dutiful daughterhood. Perceiving her own mother as an advocate for the fathers, Dickinson sought guidance and nurturance from a number of countervailing female figures, who enabled her to claim a right in herself and a right to her own production and self-representation in a masculine system of exchange that only valorized woman's reproductive role as mother. But Dickinson's desire to enclose herself within a sacred band of girlfriends was not only a means of resisting the pressures of adulthood, marriage, and the reproductive plot. Her community of women friends also became a means of resisting the forces of democratic, commercial, technological, and nationalist transformation at a time when the privilege of Dickinson's own class position as the daughter of a conservative Whig squire was itself under siege.[19]

Dickinson's childhood and adolescence had been marked by the panic of 1837 and a depression in the economy from which the country did not fully recover until the mid-forties. During these years, the traditionally privileged socioeconomic status of the Dickinson family in the Amherst community was not at all secure. In 1830, the year of Emily Dickinson's birth, her father, Edward Dickinson, had to buy half of the family "Mansion" on Main Street from her grandfather, Samuel Fowler Dickinson, who had lost the family fortune by overinvesting his time and money in public projects such as the founding of Amherst College.[20] In 1833, Samuel left town in financial ruin, and the remaining half of the "Mansion" was sold to an outsider, General David Mack, who came to Amherst to set up a factory for the manufacture and sale of straw hats.

Left with half a house, a failing law practice, and his father's debt, Edward experienced a sense of panic that he was losing status and ground to a new breed of entrepreneur. "I must make money in some way," he wrote to his wife on September 7, 1835: "To be shut up forever 'under a bushel' while hundreds of mere Jacanapes are getting their tens of thousands & hundreds of thousands, is rather too much for my spirit—I must spread myself over more ground—half a house, & a rod square for a garden, won't answer my turn" (Leyda 1: 30). During Edward Dickinson's tenure as a Representative in the Massachusetts state legislature from 1837 to 1839, his personal fortunes do not appear to have improved much. By 1840, David Mack's prosperous hat business enabled him to buy the entire Dickinson mansion. The Dickinson family moved to a house on North Pleasant Street where they lived until 1855, when they were able to repurchase the "Old Homestead" from Mack.[21]

As a student at Mount Holyoke in 1847, Emily Dickinson registered her own sense of anxiety that the Dickinson class position was under siege by the forces of Jacksonian democracy represented by the locofoco postmaster Seth Nims—the same postmaster whose gaze Dickinson sought to avoid in the sky writing she shared with Jane Humphrey. In October 1847, she wrote to Austin: "Well, I dreamed a dream & Lo!!! Father had failed & mother said that 'our rye field which she & I planted, was mortgaged to Seth Nims.' I hope it is not true but do write soon & tell me for you know 'I should expire with mortification' to have our rye field mortgaged, to say nothing of it's falling into the merciless hands of a loco!!!" (*Letters* 1: 48–49). In the same letter, Dickinson half-humorously protested the expansionist and nationalist Democratic policies of President Polk, policies that had led to the Mexican war and that seemed to endanger Dickinson's own privileged sense of identity, status, and place in rural New England. "Has the Mexican war terminated yet & how?," she asks her brother. "Do you know of any nation about to besiege South Hadley? If so, do inform me of it, for I would be glad of a chance to escape, if we are to be stormed" (*Letters* 1: 49).

During the fifties as the Whig Party dissolved under the pressure of the slavery controversy and Edward Dickinson held steadfastly to the conservative party faith of Daniel Webster, even as many of his friends joined the newly formed Republican Party, Emily Dickinson sought to enclose and secure herself within an ever tighter circle of family and friends. Not only did she set herself against the abolitionist, reformist, and democratizing energies of the times; she also set herself against the public and political engagement of her father. When Edward Dickinson was serving as a Representative in Congress between 1852 and 1854, Dickinson resented the fact that he, like her grandfather, Samuel Fowler Dickinson, neglected the family for the public interest. "Caesar [Father] is such 'an honorable man,' " she wrote Austin in

1853, "that we may all go to the Poor House, for all the American Congress will lift a finger to help us" (*Letters* 1: 275).

Moreover, while her father was instrumental in bringing the Belchertown Railroad to Amherst in 1853, Dickinson looked on the railroad as an intrusion from abroad that quickened the pace of life and thrust Amherst into the grip of outsiders and the "almighty dollar." "Our house is crowded daily with the members of the world," Dickinson wrote Austin; "the 'poor in this world's goods,' and the 'almighty dollar,' and 'what in the world are they after' continues to be unknown—But I hope they will pass away, as insects on vegetation, and let us reap together in golden harvest time—that is you and Susie and me and our dear sister Vinnie" (*Letters* 1: 257).

The train's arrival in Amherst was only one of a number of signs of the erosion of traditional New England communities and traditional rural values under the pressures of the new market economy. Like Catharine Sedgwick, Lydia Sigourney, and other domestic novelists of the time, Dickinson set a familial and essentially woman-centered culture of affection and mutual nurturance against the commercial ethos of self-interest and capital gains.[22] As in the poem she sent to Sue—"Your Riches—taught me—Poverty"—money and wealth were recurrent themes of Dickinson's verse. But, as if to secure herself against the periodic collapses in the new commercial economy and the reality of her own financial dependence in what she always called "my Father's house," the riches she celebrates are psychic rather than material, affectional rather than commercial, communal rather than capitalist.

"My friends are my 'estate,' " Dickinson wrote Samuel Bowles in 1858, at a time of economic depression when even the *Hampshire and Franklin Express* was urging its readers to seek mental culture as a bulwark against the "monotony of the hard times" in Amherst and the surrounding community (Leyda 2: 351). In response to each of the successive personal and political crises that marked her life, Dickinson reaffirmed her investment in an earthly, exclusive, and predominantly female "estate" of friends as a means of securing herself against the disruptive incursions of democratic and national transformation. "Sorrow seems more general than it did, and not the estate of a few persons, since the war began," Dickinson wrote the Norcross sisters during the Civil War (*Letters* 2: 436). After a moving account of the death of Frazar Stearns, a local Amherst boy who was killed at New Bern, North Carolina, in 1862, Dickinson reaffirms the bond of love she shares with the Norcross sisters as a kind of armor against the violation and general sorrow of the Civil War: "Let us love better, children, it's most that's left to do" (*Letters* 2: 398). Similarly, in a letter written to Elizabeth Holland after the stock market crash of 1873, Dickinson represents the affectional investment they share as a security against the financial ruin of the time: "Owning but little

Stock in the 'Gold of Ophir' I am not subject to large Reverses" (*Letters* 2: 511).

When Dickinson's father, Edward Dickinson, died on June 16, 1874, Dickinson became part of an exclusively female household. Within the female trinity formed by herself, her sister, Lavinia, and her mother, Emily, the traditional structures of the patriarchal family were transformed, as mother, sister, and daughter were reconstituted into a new kind of family. With age, Emily Norcross Dickinson became increasingly dependent on her daughters. Becoming mothers to their mother, Emily and Lavinia felt that the affectional bond between mother and daughter had been strengthened and renewed: "We were never intimate Mother and Children while she was our Mother," Dickinson wrote Elizabeth Holland after her mother's death in 1882, "but Mines in the same Ground meet by tunneling and when she became our Child, the Affection came—" (*Letters* 3: 754–55).

Dickinson's return to her mother has been read as part of an empowering female teleology, the final act in the daughter's process of self-creation: "Without union with other women and this reunion with Mother, Psyche— woman recreating herself and making herself over in her own image—cannot be reborn," writes Martha Nell Smith of this passage (21). Read in relation to the specific circumstances that made Dickinson's "reunion" with her mother possible, however, her new sense of intimacy does not appear to be part of any essential or essentially empowering return to the primal dyad between mother and daughter. Dickinson's affection for her mother came at about the same time as her own menopause, when motherhood no longer represented a threat to the poetic work she had already pursued on her own terms. Moreover, the words "when she became our Child, the Affection came—" suggest that even though Dickinson's father was dead, the hierarchies of the traditional patriarchal family had not completely collapsed. In fact, the image suggests that it is only when their mother became dependent on them and thus safely under their power, as "Child" to "Mother," that the "Affection came."

In a letter to Elizabeth Holland, written in the last year of her life, Dickinson called attention to the exclusion of the female under the law of the Father. "So Madonna and Daughter were incomplete, and Madonna and Son, must supersede!" she wrote Holland when a grandson was born to her daughter in 1885 (*Letters* 3: 869). "Say to the Son that the Little Boy in the Trinity had no Grandmama, only a Holy Ghost" (*Letters* 3: 871). Both comments reveal Dickinson's witty recognition of female absence from the Christian religion of the patriarchs. Not only does she suggest a prior Mother/Daughter bond beneath the patriarchal bond of Father and Son, but pointing out the absurd lack—the unnatural female absence in the figure of the Trinity—she also suggests the ways the creative power of women has been appropriated by the religion of the fathers. Against and beyond the male trinity she invoked as "Burglar! Banker—Father!" (*Poems* #49), Dickinson imagined and sought to create in her life an alternative female community—a trinity of "Summer—Sister—Seraph!"—through whom and with whom she continued to utter her witch-like "No" to the orders of the fathers (*Poems* #18). "Don't you know," she said in turning down the marriage proposal of Judge Otis P. Lord in the final decade of her life, "that 'No' is the wildest word we consign to Language" (*Letters* 2: 617).

But what, we might ask in conclusion, were the terms of Dickinson's "No"? If Dickinson challenged the masculine orders of authority in home and family, church and state, it was an assault launched from within the confines and class privilege of her "Father's house." If from the point of view of gender her refusal to marry, to publish, and to circulate might be read as a radical act, from the point of view of class that refusal was paradoxically grounded in the privilege of her status as the daughter of a conservative Whig squire. In fact, Dickinson's decision not to marry was underwritten by her father, whose reluctance to have his daughters leave his house may well have been related to his desire to keep family and class position intact against the potentially corrosive—and democratizing—influences of the time. It was because Dickinson had the economic privilege of being able to choose to stay at home that she could finally refuse to go to market. "Poverty—be justifying / For so foul a thing / Possibly," Dickinson wrote in "Publication—is the Auction" (*Poems* #709), apparently oblivious to the fact that other writers, including her friend Helen Hunt Jackson, really did have to write and to publish for money and survival.

At the same time that Dickinson was writing her satanic letters to her women friends, the Seneca Falls Convention of 1848 was calling upon women to organize for women's rights, women's suffrage, and real political power; Margaret Fuller, in *Woman in the Nineteenth Century,* was enjoining women to redeem the lost political ideals of America and pay for what she called "Isabella's jewels"; and other women writers, including most notably Harriet Beecher Stowe and Harriet Jacobs, were celebrating the networks among black and white women as a powerful means of subverting and contesting the slave system. Although Dickinson's recognition of the oppression she shared with other women had the effect of politicizing that experience, the bonds of assistance and resistance she formed with her women friends lacked any larger political reference. She never conceived of taking her struggle into the public sphere. Her object appears to have been separation among rather than political transformation through women.

"I am sorry I smiled at women," she wrote Samuel Bowles in 1860. "I fear I am your little friend no more, but Mrs Jim Crow," she said in words that suggest that she had derided women who were active in the antislavery movement (*Letters* 2: 366). As the genteel daughter of a Whig squire, Dickinson set herself apart from both the women reformers and the women's suffrage movement of her time. Dependent on her father's political and class status for her own privileged position, Dickinson resisted the forces of democratic transformation and manifested an almost Know-Nothing aversion to outsiders. In fact, with the exception of her relationship with Sue Gilbert, Dickinson's circle of women friends was limited exclusively to women of her own class from the surrounding community.

Although Dickinson challenged her own exclusion and privation under the laws of the fathers, she lived apart from the specific forms of material and economic oppression suffered by black, immigrant, and other working class women, and she manifested little concern about the problems of slavery, industrialism, the urban poor, and the dispossession of American Indians that sent other New England women, including Lydia Maria Child and her friend Helen Hunt Jackson, into the public sphere to struggle against social injustice. "She wore white, she shut herself away from her race as a mark of her separation from the mass of minds," wrote Dickinson's friend Emily Fowler Ford (Mabel Loomis Todd 132). It was this same separation from the "common daily strife" of the masses that Ford emphasized in a poem to Dickinson published in the *Springfield Republican* on January 11, 1891:

> Nor will you touch a hand, or greet a face,—
> For common daily strife to you is rude
> ("Eheu! Emily Dickinson!")

Within the political order of Dickinson's verse, the multitude and the democratic masses are consistently demonized. In "The Popular Heart is a Cannon first—" and "The Ditch is dear to the Drunken man," the masses are associated with intemperance, criminality, and an explosive violence without past or future. The poem "I'm Nobody! Who are you?" appears to parody the politics of title and place:

> How dreary—to be—Somebody!
> How public—like a Frog—
> To tell your name—the livelong June—
> To an admiring Bog!
>   (*Poems* #288)

From a gender point of view, the poet's lack of settled identity as "Nobody" represents a form of liberation from the structures of social authority that define and limit a woman's life. But this seemingly democratic "Nobody" masks an aristocrat who refuses to be defined in and through the demonized body of the democratic masses figured as "an admiring Bog."

Like Tocqueville in *Democracy in America* (1835), Dickinson was critical of the dull conformity of democratic and majority rule. If her poems bear traces of the antiauthoritarian political rhetoric of her times, it is a rhetoric that is translated not into a dream of democracy but into a royalist dream of rule by hereditary and divine right. Thus, in the poem "I'm ceded—I've stopped being Their's—," Dickinson deploys the politically charged language of secession, but the secession she imagines is not in favor of a sovereign republican self or state. Rather, "With Will to choose, or to reject," she secedes into an essentially monarchical order in which she will be "Queen."

Whereas Frederick Douglass, Henry David Thoreau, Walt Whitman, and Herman Melville, and many of the women writers of her age, including Harriet Beecher Stowe, Margaret Fuller, Lydia Maria Child, and Harriet Jacobs, embraced the democratic language of republican ideology even as they turned that language to a critique of the actual practice of the American government, Dickinson returned to a pre-Revolutionary and aristocratic language of rank, titles, and divine right to assert the sovereignty of her self as absolute monarch. Not only does she set herself against the possibilities of democracy as they were being invoked by other writers of her age. At a time when a woman, Victoria, was the Queen of England, Dickinson's royalist language also bears witness to the political irony that it is under an aristocratic order of hereditary and divine right rather than under a democratic order of contract and inalienable rights that a woman was entitled to political power and to rule.

"If women have a role to play," says Julia Kristeva in "Oscillation Between Power and Denial," "it is only in assuming a *negative* function: reject everything finite, definite, structured, loaded with meaning, in the existing state of society. Such an attitude places women on the side of the explosion of social codes: with revolutionary movements" (166). If Dickinson was on the side of revolution, for her, as for Kristeva, it was a revolution located not in the political and economic but in the linguistic sphere. Like Kristeva and other French feminists, including Cixous and Irigaray, Dickinson showed little concern with bringing about a political transformation in the material conditions of women's lives. Her revolution was enacted on the level of language by rupturing "everything finite, definite, structured, loaded with meaning" and thus challenging a metaphysical order and an entire way of knowing and signifying grounded in the transcendent power of the Word as Logos and Father.

Insofar as language is the symbolic structure that constitutes the social order, Dickinson's disruption of language and syntax might, as Kristeva suggests in *Revolution in Poetic Language,* register or anticipate a revolutionary transformation in the political sphere. But while Dickinson's poetic assault on the patriarchal orders of language parallels the more public agitation for a change in woman's social, economic, and legal status in the United States, it is unclear how her poetic revolution might become an agent of political change. As Catherine Clément notes in *The Newly Born Woman,* in a comment on the distinction between Hélène Cixous's notion that language can be a vehicle of historical transformation through the writing of female desire and a more traditional Marxist notion of language and history as seemingly different realms of struggle: "There is imagination, desire, creation, production of writing . . . and then somewhere else, on another level of reality, there is class struggle, and within it, women's struggle. There are missing links in all that, which we should try to think in order to succeed in joining our two languages" (159).

These "missing links" between desire and language, writing and history, textual politics and sexual politics have in some sense been forged by the poststructuralist emphasis on the discursive construction of reality. But although some interpretations (including Jacques Derrida's argument that "There is nothing outside of the text" [*il n'y a pas de hors-texte,* 158]; Jacques Lacan's theorization of a subject constituted in language; Louis Althusser's Marxist theorization of an individual interpellated as subject in ideology; and Julia Kristeva's representation of poetic language as the inscription of a subversive, and specifically maternal, libidinal economy) have freed literary critics to talk about textual struggles as a form of political struggle, the poststructuralist emphasis on the constitutive power of language has also had the curiously *ahistorical* effect of underwriting a kind of neoformalist discourse analysis that examines textual struggle as if it were the "thing" itself. The question still remains: What finally is the relation between textual struggle and political change? How does a revolutionary textual strategy connect with the *materiality* of women's oppression and the possibility of changing the conditions of women's lives? And, perhaps more significantly for our topic, is female desire an agent of political liberation and change, or is it, as it appears to be in Dickinson's work, the base for the reinscription of the imperial axioms of the ruling class on the backs of racial and class "others"?

The gap between Dickinson's revolutionary poetics and the revolutionary struggles of blacks, women, and workers that marked her time suggests a potential problem and contradiction in the current theoretical—and feminist—emphasis on language as the site of political transformation. Dickinson's revolutionary poetic practice appears to be unconnected with any real transformation in woman's historical status as "object" and "other" in a system of production and exchange controlled by men. As in the work of

James Joyce, Antonin Artaud, and other celebrated modern poetic "revolutionaries," her radical poetics was conjoined with an essentially conservative and in some sense reactionary and Know-Nothing politics. If on the level of language Dickinson might be celebrated as a kind of literary terrorist—a "Loaded Gun" and dancing "Bomb"—who blew up the social and symbolic orders of patriarchal language, it is also important that we recognize the fact that her poetic revolution was grounded in the privilege of her class position in a conservative Whig household whose elitist, antidemocratic values were still at the very center of her work. In fact, given the ways literary modernism often intersects with conservative and reactionary politics, it is no coincidence that it was among the modernists, and Allen Tate and the Southern Agrarians in particular, that Dickinson was first raised to canonical status.[23]

Moreover, for all the nay-saying power of Dickinson's poetic revolution, her attempt to challenge the logocentric order of the Word as God the Father was not finally successful. Despite her satanic and pagan identification with the bloom of female creation, that bloom was always under arrest by the absolute power of Death, which Dickinson consistently represented as a male figure whose tyrannical power is associated with the "marauding Hand" of a punishing and at times sadistic God. Like the figure of "Old King Frost" whom Dickinson imagines freezing her plants and the beaks of the singing birds in her early letter to Abiah Root, in the poem "Apparently with no surprise," the "Frost beheads" the "happy Flower" of female creation "In accidental power":

> The blonde Assassin passes on—
> The Sun proceeds unmoved
> To measure off another Day
> For an Approving God.
>
> (*Poems* #1624)

Dated only a few years before her death in 1886, the poem suggests the fear and awe that Dickinson continued to experience in the face of the "blonde Assassin" and the seemingly cruel and arbitrary power of the Calvinist God.

In *Madness and Civilization*, Michel Foucault comments on the relation between religion and madness. The constant talk of despair, revenge, and punishment, he argues, can lead to melancholia and fill the mind with anxiety. In fact, if "religion loosens its hold but maintains the ideal forms of remorse of conscience, of spiritual mortification, it leads directly to madness" (216). Although Dickinson never finally yielded herself up to the Calvinist God, she never fully freed herself from subjection to His terms either—terms that included what she called "the subject of perdition" (*Letters* 1: 309). "Oh Future! thou secreted peace / Or subterranean wo—," she wrote in one of her late poems (*Poems* #1631). If Dickinson celebrated and indeed flaunted her satanic identification in her exchanges with women, and if at times she might dance "like a Bomb, abroad," in her soul's "Bandaged moments" she also realized not with a sense of *jouissance* but with "ghastly Fright" and a "Horror" "not brayed of Tongue" that if the God of the fathers was true then she might indeed be "one of the lingering *bad* ones" and one of the damned (*Poems* #512).

3

Dickinson, Women Writers, and the Marketplace

> I too have my vocation,—work to do,
> The heavens and earth have set me since I changed
> My father's face for theirs, and, though your world
> Were twice as wretched as you represent,
> Most serious work, most necessary work
> As any of the economists' . . .
> —Elizabeth Barrett Browning, *Aurora Leigh*

In 1843, a reviewer for the prestigious and Whig-oriented *North American Review* expressed anxiety about the increasing commercialization and democratization of literature as the production of the written word and authorship became subject to the laws of a marketplace economy: "Literature begins to assume the aspect and undergo the mutations of trade," he noted. "The author's profession is becoming as mechanical as that of the printer and the bookseller, being created by the same causes and subject to the same laws. The nature of the supply seems likely to be as strictly proportioned to the demand, as in any other commercial operation" ("The Works of Alexander Dumas" 110).

In "Myself was formed—a Carpenter—," Dickinson registers a similar anxiety about the literary marketplace. At a time when the traditional artisan economy of craft and handwork was being reduced to wage labor, Dickinson imagines herself as an artisan whose craft is under siege by the marketplace values of speed, cost, and efficiency:

> Myself was formed—a Carpenter—
> An unpretending time
> My Plane—and I, together wrought
> Before a Builder came—
>
> To measure our attainments—
> Had we the Art of Boards

                    Sufficiently developed—He'd hire us
                    At Halves—
                                        (*Poems* #488)

Representing herself as a Christ-like figure, Dickinson responds "Against the
Man" that she is engaged in another, more immortal kind of work: "We—
Temples build—I said—."

Dickinson offered a similar response "Against the Man" in refusing to let
her "Mind" be published and put to "use" by the male publishing world. In
1862, she wrote to Thomas Higginson: "Two Editors of Journals came to my
Father's House, this winter—and asked me for my Mind—and when I asked
them 'Why,' they said I was penurious—and they, would *use it for the
World*—" (*Letters* 2: 404–405; emphasis added).[1] The terms of Dickinson's
refusal to publish are inscribed in poem #709:

                    Publication—is the Auction
                    Of the Mind of Man—
                    Poverty—be justifying
                    For so foul a thing

                    Possibly—but We—would rather
                    From Our Garret go
                    White—Unto the White Creator—
                    Than invest—Our Snow—
                                        (*Poems* #709)

Deploying a highly charged political language in which the rhetoric of antislavery protest intersects with the rhetoric of protest against wage labor as a
new form of human enslavement, Dickinson pleads against the "Auction"
block of commercial publication: "reduce no Human Spirit / To Disgrace of
Price—."

And yet, for all Dickinson's aristocratic refusal to yield herself up to the
commercialization and democratization of the literary marketplace, she continued to be simultaneously fascinated and repelled by the idea of publication.
Throughout her life she cultivated relationships with male writers, editors,
and publishers, including Samuel Bowles, Josiah Holland, Thomas Higginson, and Thomas Niles, who might help her "to print." And she was particularly drawn to the lives and works of a select group of women writers who had
entered the literary marketplace with apparent success.

At the time Dickinson began writing, the American literary marketplace
had in fact become a markedly female literary marketplace, dominated by a
sentimental domestic literature written by, for, and about women. By mid-
century, a number of women writers, including Catharine Sedgwick, Susan
Warner, and Harriet Beecher Stowe, had been able to enter the public sphere,

become best-selling authors, and for the first time assume a primary role in
the production of American culture. By mid-century, too, Lydia Sigourney
had earned enough money writing poetry to become the first professional
American poet. Between 1848 and 1849, no less than three anthologies of
verse by women poets were published: *The American Female Poets,* edited by
Caroline May; *The Female Poets of America,* edited by Thomas Buchan
Read; and *The Female Poets of America,* edited by Rufus Griswold. Hundreds
of women poets were also being published by popular journals of the time,
including *Godey's Lady's Book,* the *Saturday Evening Post,* and *Harper's.*[2]

If Dickinson experienced an "anxiety of authorship," as Sandra Gilbert,
Susan Gubar, and others argue, it was not for lack of women poets. As Emily
Stipes Watts observes: "It was actually easier and more 'respectable' for
women to publish poetry at this time than it was for men" (67). In fact, the
marketplace was so full of women writers that male writers began to suffer
their own form of gender and authorship anxiety in response to what Ann
Douglas has called "the feminization of American culture." With so many
women publishing poetry, Henry Wadsworth Longfellow worried that the
public might come to see poetry as "effeminate nonsense" (Watts 68). And in
1855, in a now famous exchange with his publisher, William D. Ticknor,
Nathaniel Hawthorne complained: "America is now wholly given over to a
d—d mob of scribbling women, and I should have no chance of success while
the public taste is occupied with their trash" (*The Letters, 1853–1856* 304).

Rather than experiencing a sense of solidarity with her American literary
sisters, Dickinson appears to have shared Hawthorne's anxiety about the mob
of "scribbling women." Her ambivalence about publication was not so much
a response to the lack of women writers—there were hundreds—as it was a
response to domestic ideology and the kind of "feminine" writing she would
be forced to produce if she entered the literary marketplace. In an essay on the
"Genius" of the popular British poet, Felicia Hemans, Lydia Sigourney defined this "essentially feminine" writing as the expression of the "whole
sweet circle of the domestic affections—the hallowed ministries of woman, at
the cradle, the hearth-stone, and the death-bed" (Hemans, *The Works of Mrs.
Hemans* xv). It was this same kind of religious, moral, domestic, and "essentially feminine" verse that Sigourney herself produced in formally conventional poems that glorified rather than challenged the cult of true womanhood.
In one of her more popular poems, "Connecticut River," Sigourney describes
the domestic economy of the female:

> Her pastime when the daily task is o'er,
> With apron clean, to seek her neighbour's door,
> Partake the friendly feast, with social glow,
> Exchange the news, and make the stocking grow;

Then hale and cheerful to her home repair,
When Sol's slant ray renews her evening care,
Press the full udder for her children's meal,
Rock the tir'd babe—or wake the tuneful wheel.
                                    (*Select Poems* 17–18)

Although Dickinson's writing bears traces of the sentimental gospel of love, as Barton St. Armand argues in *Emily Dickinson and Her Culture,* she never consciously identified with American sentimental writers—male or female. In fact, in her own writing she worried about producing conventional literary sentiment in stock form. In an 1853 letter to Josiah and Elizabeth Holland she confessed: "I wrote to you last week, but thought you would laugh at me, and call me sentimental, so I kept my lofty letter for 'Adolphus Hawkins, Esq.' [the sentimental poet of Longfellow's *Kavanagh*]" (*Letters* 1: 264).

Dickinson was equally resistant to domestic ideology. "*My* kitchen," she wrote Abiah Root in 1850, "God forbid that it was, or shall be my own—God keep me from what they call *households*" (*Letters* 1: 99). To Dickinson, "home" was the space of creative freedom rather than the site of what Catharine Beecher called female "domestic economy." She was interested in woman not as homemaker or childmaker but as *maker.* She hated housework and was only interested in those kinds of traditional female work like baking and gardening that involved not cleaning up or ministering to the messes of the world but some kind of creative and making power.

In her poems she consistently mocked the "Dimity Convictions" of the angel in the house:

What Soft—Cherubic Creatures—
These Gentlewomen are—
One would as soon assault a Plush—
Or violate a Star—

Such Dimity Convictions—
A Horror so refined
Of freckled Human Nature—
Of Deity—ashamed—
                                    (*Poems* #401)

It was precisely these "Dimity Convictions"—virtue, piety, purity, and refinement—that women sentimental writers bore with them as they advanced into the traditionally masculine and public space of the marketplace between 1820 and the end of the Civil War. During these years the writing of white middle-class American women became an extension of domesticity, a form of what Mary Kelley calls "literary domesticity" that "represented a new, public telling of old, private tales" (222).

It was this same kind of "literary domesticity" that Dickinson's male circle of literary friends fostered and admired among women writers. With the possible exception of "Sic transit gloria mundi" (*Poems* #3), which was published as "A Valentine" in the *Springfield Republican* on February 20, 1852, the few poems that Dickinson published in her lifetime were all diligently "edited" to conform with the formal and sentimental conventions of contemporary feminine verse. From the publication of "I taste a liquor never brewed—," which appeared as "The May-Wine" in *The Springfield Republican* on May 4, 1861, to the publication of "Success is counted sweetest," which appeared in *A Masque of Poets* in 1878, to the publication of the first edition of Dickinson's *Poems* in 1890, well-meaning editors and friends consistently titled and thematicized Dickinson's poems, regularized her rhyme and meter, eliminated her dashes and other oddities of punctuation, and altered her language, syntax, and meaning in acts of literary intervention that mutilated all that was most innovative in her work.

When in 1872 Dickinson was approached by a "Miss P" (perhaps Elizabeth Stuart Phelps, the editor of *The Woman's Journal* and author of *The Gates Ajar* (1868), a popular novel that materialized heaven as a middle-class, female-centered household complete with pianos), she responded with an irony that verged on hostility. "Of Miss P——I know but this, dear," she wrote Louise Norcross late in 1872: "She wrote me in October, requesting me to aid the world by my chirrup more. Perhaps she stated it as my duty, I don't distinctly remember, and always burn such letters, so I cannot obtain it now. I replied declining. She did not write to me again—she might have been offended, or perhaps is extricating humanity from some hopeless ditch." (*Letters* 2: 500).

Having already undergone the "surgery" of Samuel Bowles and Thomas Higginson, Dickinson is clearly unwilling to submit her work to the literary domestic gaze of Miss P, who may in fact have written to her at the suggestion of Higginson. Dickinson explicitly mocks and in effect "burns up" the concept of women's writing as an extension of women's domestic role—the missionary idea that it is her "duty" to "aid the world by my chirrup more." Her choice of the term "chirrup" underlines the trivialization of women's songs and puns on the literary domestic notion that it is the woman writer's role to "cheer-up" the world rather than, in Dickinson's terms, to make it "see" complexly, oppositely, and at times somberly. She also takes a parting shot at women reformers, aimed perhaps at Miss P[helps]'s involvement in temperance reform and the work of "extricating humanity from some hopeless ditch." The ellipses that close the letter are themselves tantalizing. What further shots at socially engaged and reforming women like Elizabeth Phelps did the Norcross sisters see fit to excise from Dickinson's letter against the sentimental women writers of her time?

In her own writing Dickinson was more interested in being immortal than in being merely useful, helpful, dutiful, or moral. Adhering to an essentially aristocratic and high cultural notion of literature as the production of mind and genius for eternity, she set herself against not only the new commercialization and democratization of literature but also the sentimental women writers who had gained money and fame in the American literary marketplace. While her reading included Harriet Beecher Stowe's *Uncle Tom's Cabin* (1852), *The Last Leaf from Sunnyside* (1855) by Elizabeth Stuart Phelps (the mother of the Phelps who may have written to her in 1872), Rebecca Harding Davis's *Life in the Iron Mills* (1861), and Helen Hunt Jackson's *Verses* (1870), *Bits of Travel at Home* (1878), and *Ramona* (1884), she was more drawn to British women writers like the Brontë sisters, Elizabeth Barrett Browning, and George Eliot, whose work appeared to challenge rather than merely to rationalize and confirm domestic ideology and traditional notions of women's sphere. Whereas white middle-class American women writers tended to enter the marketplace as traditional women, spreading women's influence and domestic ideology to the public sphere, the British women writers that Dickinson admired often adopted male pseudonyms as they sought to enter literature and the profession of authorship as individuals and competitors on equal terms with men.[3] "Happily, we are not dependent on argument to prove that Fiction is a department of literature in which women can, after their kind, fully equal men," wrote George Eliot in "Silly Novels by Lady Novelists" (324).

It tells us a good deal about Dickinson's implicit critique of American domestic, democratic, and national ideology that the women writers she found most admirable were all foreigners. At a time when both Whigs and Democrats, from Ralph Waldo Emerson to Walt Whitman and the Young America writers at the *Democratic Review,* were calling on American writers to turn away from the courtly muses of Europe in order to write a distinctively American literature, Dickinson transgressed national bounds in order to draw inspiration and self-validation from the lives and works of women writers in England and France. She read Elizabeth Barrett Browning's "Vision of Poets," *Aurora Leigh,* "Catarina to Camoens," and *Last Poems.* In addition to *Jane Eyre,* she read Charlotte Brontë's *Villette,* Emily Brontë's *Wuthering Heights,* Anne Brontë's *The Tenant of Wildfell Hall,* and the volume of *Poems by Culler, Ellis, and Acton Bell* published in 1846. An 1860 edition of George Eliot's *Adam Bede* is inscribed to Emily Dickinson from Sue [Dickinson]; she also read Eliot's *Mill on the Floss, Middlemarch, Daniel Deronda, The Legend of Jubal and Other Poems,* and *The Spanish Gypsy: A Poem.* And there is also evidence that she read George Sand's *Mauprat.*[4]

Dickinson's dog Carlo was named after the dog of St. John Rivers in *Jane Eyre,* and, as Sandra Gilbert and Susan Gubar have shown, Dickinson sought to create her own life in the image of the lives of the fictive heroines of Browning, the Brontë sisters, and Eliot. Portraits of Elizabeth Barrett Brown-

Figure 3. Portrait of Elizabeth Barrett Browning, the "Foreign Lady" whose "Tomes of solid Witchcraft" "enchanted" Emily Dickinson. Drawn by Field Talfourd in 1859. (Courtesy of the National Portrait Gallery)

ing (Fig. 3) and George Eliot (Fig. 4) hung in her room, and she turned to their works as a source of transport and power. " 'What do I think of *Middlemarch?*' " she wrote to the Norcross sisters in 1873, "What do I think of glory—except that in a few instances this 'mortal has already put on immortality.' George Eliot is one. The mysteries of human nature surpass the 'mys-

Figure 4. Portrait of George Eliot in 1864 drawn by Frederick Burton. "God chooses repellant settings, dont he, for his best Gems?," Dickinson wrote of "the Face of George Eliot," whose portrait hung in her room.

teries of redemption,' for the infinite we only suppose, while we see the finite" (*Letters* 2: 506). To Dickinson, Eliot was a Christ-like figure whose works bore the lesson of art's redemptive and immortalizing power. As an explorer of the complexities and mysteries of human nature, Eliot was in Dickinson's view a heroic figure who had opened new imaginative terrain: "She is the Lane to the Indes, Columbus was looking for," Dickinson wrote after Sue "smuggled" her a copy of *Daniel Deronda* in 1876 (*Letters* 2: 551).

But the lesson she learned from her Victorian sisters was not one of power only. She also recognized the long sufferance of women writers split between their sense of possibility, of creative and queen-like power, and the actual limits of their lives as women entrapped in the conventions of the Victorian Age. "That Mrs. Browning fainted," she wrote the Norcross sisters, "we need not read *Aurora Leigh* to know, when she lived with her English aunt;

and George Sand 'must make no noise in her grandmother's bedroom.' Poor children! Women, now, queens, now! And one in the Eden of God" (*Letters* 2: 376). Perhaps alluding to Jane Eyre's ruminations on the limits imposed on women's lives, Dickinson remembered Charlotte Brontë saying: " 'Life is so constructed that the event does not, cannot, match the expectation' " (*Letters* 2: 543).

Literary Sisterhood: The Brontë Sisters

Dickinson felt a particular bond of affinity with the Brontë sisters, whose cloistered lives in Haworth Parsonage seemed so nearly to mirror her own secluded existence in rural Amherst. Like the little pieces of paper that the Brontë sisters stitched into the saga of Angria and Gondol, Dickinson's similarly stitched poems became a means of writing herself out of her father's "real" and into an imaginary "other" world where women could be queens. For Dickinson, as well as for the Brontës, the fantasy-dominated world of childhood became a kind of enchanted female ground that released her from the demands of the body and thus from the demands of a true womanly role under Victorian patriarchy. "I wish we were *always* children, how to grow up I don't know," Dickinson wrote Austin when she was twenty-three (*Letters* 1: 241).

Dickinson's poems bear traces of the imaginary worlds and demonic female energies of *Jane Eyre, Wuthering Heights,* and the *Poems of Acton, Currer, and Ellis Bell.*[5] The figure of a captive female longing to escape the entrapment of cage and cave, body and prison is at the center of the creative worlds of Dickinson and the Brontë sisters. Like Emily Brontë in "Riches I hold in light esteem," Dickinson longs to be a "chainless soul," liberated from her subjection to male power:

> I never hear the word "escape"
> Without a quicker blood,
> A sudden expectation,
> A flying attitude!
>
> I never hear of prisons broad
> By soldiers battered down,
> But I tug childish at my bars
> Only to fail again!
> (Dickinson, *Poems* #77)

The dungeon is for both poets paradoxically double: it is at once an emblem of female entrapment and a fortress that shields and frees them from the intrusions of the male world. Both Brontë and Dickinson figure the demands of a masculine order of power in the image of a male sun continually threatening to penetrate and scorch the flower of female creation. In "Ah! why, because the dazzling sun," Brontë's female speaker seeks to escape the penetration of the sun's rays in the "cool radiance" of darkness and dreams:

> Why did the morning rise to break
> So great, so pure a spell,
> And scorch with fire the tranquil cheek
> Where your cool radiance fell?
>
> Blood-red he rose, and arrow-straight
> His fierce beams struck my brow:
> The soul of Nature sprang elate,
> But mine sank sad and low!
>   . . .
> O Stars and Dreams and Gentle Night;
> O Night and Stars return!
> And hide me from the hostile light
> That does not warm, but burn—
> (*The Complete Poems of Emily Jane Brontë 226*,
> hereafter referred to as *Complete Poems*)

Similarly, in Dickinson's "The *Sun—just touched* the Morning—" the female dawn is left feeble and uncrowned by the blaze of the "wheeling King," and in "The Daisy follows soft the Sun—" Dickinson's female flower seeks to eclipse the power of the Sun/Son world in "Night's possibility!"

Entrapment is for both poets the site of imaginative visitation. In "To Imagination," it is within the darkness and enclosure of the dungeon world that Brontë experiences the radiance of her own internal sun:

> What matters it that all around
> Danger and grief and darkness lie,
> If but within our bosom's bound
> We hold a bright unsullied sky,
> Warm with ten thousand mingled rays
> Of suns that know no winter days?
> (*Complete Poems* 206)

For Brontë and Dickinson, as for other Romantic poets, the imagination represented a means of escaping the world of time, change, history, and mortality. But for women poets, the imagination also had special significance as a possible avenue of escape from what Brontë called "Nature elate"— the world of a maternally-defined adult sexuality that threatened to place the female body in the service of the race. Sealed off from the sun world, the dungeon becomes for both poets the locus and condition of female imaginative power. Entrapment opens paradoxically into "Night's possibility," a kind of creative free space in which the woman poet can, like Dickinson, "ride indefinite" in a world where "Summer—lasts a Solid Year—" (Dickinson, *Poems* #569).

Among Dickinson's favorite poems was Emily Brontë's "No coward soul is mine," which Thomas Wentworth Higginson read at Dickinson's funeral in 1886. In this poem on divine calling, Dickinson may have recognized her own translation of the Calvinist religion of the fathers into a form of personal artistic devotion to a potent and nongendered "Thee" who is the "Being and Breath" of creation itself:

> O God within my breast
> Almighty ever-present Deity
> Life, that in me hast rest
> As I Undying Life, have power in Thee
> (Brontë, *Complete Poems* 243)

Brontë's God was like Dickinson's a personal "God of Visions." This all-powerful "Thee" who figures at the very center of their poems is not a deity existing outside the self but, rather, a demonic, sometimes masculine but frequently nongendered muse who projects and indeed mirrors their own power of creation.

"Gigantic Emily Brontë," Dickinson wrote in a letter to Elizabeth Holland, remembering Charlotte's words on her sister in the biographical introduction to *Wuthering Heights*: "Full of ruth for others, on herself she had no mercy" (*Letters* 3: 721). As Dickinson's comment suggests, she was as interested in the lives of British women writers as she was in their works. Lacking female precursors with whom she could identify in the United States, Dickinson appears to have sought in the lives of the Brontë sisters, Elizabeth Barrett Browning, and George Eliot both validation for her own poetic ambitions and particular instances and models of the female artist life.

Having read Elizabeth Gaskell's controversial *Life of Charlotte Brontë*, Dickinson was no doubt struck by the peculiar parallels between her own life and that of Charlotte Brontë.[6] Despite Gaskell's effort at containment—her attempt to present Brontë in a moralistic and dutiful daughter role—Dickinson may have heard the witch-voice of a spirit sister. Like Dickinson, Brontë refused to give up her "fiery imagination" to the Calvinist law of the fathers. In letters to her friend and confidant, Ellen Nussey, she described her "clouded and repulsive view" of religion. Like Dickinson, she experienced "a dread lest, if I made the slightest profession, I should sink at once into Phariseeism, merge wholly into the ranks of the self-righteous. . . . If the Doctrine of Calvin be true I am already an outcast" (qtd. in Gerin 100, 101).

In her life and her fiction, Brontë not only set herself against what she called the "black pillar" and "carved mask" of the Calvinist religion, but also, like Dickinson, she pursued her art in secret against her father's will:

> I carefully avoid any appearance of pre-occupation and eccentricity which might lead those I live amongst to suspect the nature of my pursuits. Following my father's advice—who from my childhood has counselled me, just in the wise and friendly tone of your letter—I have endeavoured not only attentively to observe all the duties a woman ought to fulfil, but to feel deeply interested in them. I don't always succeed, for sometimes when I'm teaching or sewing I would rather be reading or writing; but I try to deny myself, and my father's approbation amply rewarded me for privation.
>
> (Gaskell 127)

Like Dickinson, too, Brontë composed a series of "Master" letters. Brontë's were sent to M. Heger, the head of a Pensionnat in Brussels where she attended and later taught school; Dickinson's letters may never have been sent and the recipient is unknown. Although Dickinson could have no way of knowing of Brontë's letters, the fact that both were the authors of letters in which they give themselves up to a potent "Master" is interesting in what it reveals about the subject position of a woman writer in a culture in which the terms male and female are rigidly split and hierarchized. As Simone de Beauvoir argues in *The Second Sex,* in an economy in which women experience themselves as "other," their passionately self-effacing love for the male subject might be read as an attempt to invest themselves with masculine subjectivity and power. But because masculine presence would threaten to overpower the woman, her romantic passion is often most intense when the male figure is either absent or unavailable. "By choosing someone who is not attainable," says de Beauvoir, "she may make of love an abstract subjective experience with no threat to her integrity; she feels the emotions of longing, hope, bitterness, but without real entanglement" (325–26). For similar reasons, de Beauvoir suggests, women artists frequently seek same-sex relationships as a means of strengthening their sense of identity and power.

Although little is known about the male subjects who called forth the erotic and seemingly all-consuming desire of Brontë and Dickinson, what both "Masters" had in common was distance and unavailability. As de Beauvoir says: "It is one thing to kneel before one's personally constructed god who remains afar off, and quite another to yield oneself to a male of flesh and blood" (326). The abstract, subjective, and ultimately autoerotic nature of the Master figure for Brontë and Dickinson is unmistakable: for both women writers, the Master becomes at once the subject and the mirror of their own creative power.

It is perhaps one of the ironies of Charlotte Brontë's biography that after years of saving her life for and through literature, she married in 1854 and died only nine months later, carrying her first child. The fact could not have been missed by Dickinson, who no doubt read in Brontë's early death a cautionary tale that strengthened her own posture as marriage resister and religious outcast.

Dickinson's sense of identification with Charlotte Brontë is evident in the two verse elegies she wrote on her death.[7] In the first, Dickinson appears to be troubled by the fact that Brontë as "Nightingale" has been covered over and silenced by her death:

> All overgrown by cunning moss,
> All interspersed with weed,
> The little cage of "Currer Bell"
> In quiet "Haworth" laid.
> *(Poems #148)*

In the second elegy, Dickinson performs a kind of rescue mission, seeking to retrieve the name "Brontë" from the "cunning moss" and "weed" of female anonymity and misperception. While Brontë has escaped from the "sharp frosts" to which she was subjected on earth, Dickinson imagines her carrying on her rebellion in heaven:

> Gathered from many wanderings—
> Gethsemane can tell
> Thro' what transporting anguish
> She reached the Asphodel!
>
> Soft fall the sounds of Eden
> Upon her puzzled ear—
> Oh what an afternoon for Heaven,
> When "Brontë" entered there!
> *(Poems #148)*

Since Brontë died in 1855 and these elegies were composed around 1859, Dickinson may have been responding to her recent reading of Gaskell's biography. Like Gaskell, Dickinson presents Brontë's life as a Christ-like pattern of suffering and triumph. But by figuring Brontë's triumph in the image of the "Asphodel," Dickinson links her "transporting anguish" and her immortality with the pagan—and female—flower of creation. Whereas Gaskell presents Brontë as a proper Christian lady who subordinated art to duty, the Brontë Dickinson names in her poem is a heroic artist figure whose creation appears to rival the creation of God himself.

But while Dickinson eulogizes Brontë's apparently timeless and godlike power, it is also important to note that in her elegies she focuses on the more negative dimensions of Brontë's life: her suffering, her public neglect, the anomymity of her death. Had Brontë lived a more happy life, Dickinson might in fact have been less interested in her. As in her relations with other women writers, Dickinson appears to *need* Brontë's "transporting anguish" to justify her own life choices. The "sharp frosts" that Brontë suffered at the hands of the public appear to confirm Dickinson's own retreat from society and public life; moreover, Brontë's ultimate triumph in "Heaven" appears to promise the triumph of Dickinson's own artistic creation against and beyond her time.

Dickinson's elegies on Brontë are the first of a number of commemorative lyrics that she wrote on women writers. These poems are matched by no similar tributes to male writers. As a woman poet seeking to authorize herself and her voice within a predominantly male literary tradition, Dickinson seeks in effect to locate herself and her creative practice in relation to the most articulate women writers of her age. Although she read and admired the work of Henry Wadsworth Longfellow, Ralph Waldo Emerson, Nathaniel Hawthorne, and Robert Browning, it was in relation to Charlotte Brontë, Elizabeth Barrett Browning, George Eliot, and Helen Hunt Jackson that Dickinson chose to position, measure, define, and at times exalt herself through her own art of song.

"Tomes of Solid Witchcraft": Elizabeth Barrett Browning

In her formative years, the writer of her age with whom Dickinson felt the most intense bond of kinship was Elizabeth Barrett Browning. The powerful effect that Barrett Browning had on Dickinson is evident in an 1854 letter to her friend Henry Emmons, who appears to have sent her a copy of Browning's *Poems of 1844:*

> I find it Friend—I read it—I stop to thank you for it, just as the world is still—I thank you for them all—the pearl, and then the onyx, and then the emerald stone.
> My crown, indeed! I do not fear the king, attired in this grandeur.
> Please send me gems again—I have a flower. It looks like them, and for it's bright resemblances, receive it.
> A pleasant journey to you, both in the pathway home, and in the longer way—*Then* "golden morning's open flowings, *shall* sway the trees to murmurous bowings, in metric chant of blessed poems"—.
>
> (*Letters* 1: 303)

In this first known response to Browning's poems, Dickinson represents them as "gems," a "crown," that empower her in her own poetic quest. At a time when Browning's work was being generally acclaimed by the critics, Dickinson, in effect, clothes herself in Browning's poetic attire as a means of securing her own advance on the male literary tradition: "My crown, indeed! I do not fear the king, attired in this grandeur." Rather than resist Browning's influence, Dickinson hungers for more poems and proudly points the "bright resemblances" between Browning's "gems" and the poetic "flower" she sends to Emmons.

The final lines of the letter allude to Browning's "A Vision of Poets," which appeared in her *Poems of 1844.*[8] The object of this philosophical, allegorical poem, said Browning, was to indicate "the necessary relations of genius to suffering and self-sacrifice" (*The Poetical Works of Elizabeth Barrett Browning* 128, hereafter referred to as *Poetical Works*). At a time when the literary marketplace was being flooded by men and women writing for money and the masses, Browning's vision of the "Poet-God" as a heroic figure of self-sacrifice in the quest for divine truth and knowledge provided an inspiring high cultural model of the vocation of the poet. Traces of Browning's "A Vision of Poets" are evident in Dickinson's life as well as in her poems—most notably in the poem "I died for Beauty":

> I died for Beauty—but was scarce
> Adjusted in the Tomb
> When One who died for Truth, was lain
> In an adjoining Room—
>
> He questioned softly "Why I failed"?
> "For Beauty", I replied—
> "And I—for Truth—Themself are One—
> We Brethren, are", He said—
>
> (*Poems* #449)

These lines are a clever reworking of Browning's own pairing of the martyrs of Truth and Beauty: "these were poets true," she says of a community of poets that includes Sappho, Shakespeare, Milton, Keats, and Shelley, "Who died for Beauty as martyrs do / For Truth—the ends being scarcely two" (*Poetical Works* 131).

After Browning's death in 1861, Dickinson remembered her in her poems and in her life. When her good friend Samuel Bowles went abroad in the spring of 1862, Dickinson wrote: "Should anybody where you go, talk of Mrs. Browning, you must hear for us—and if you touch her Grave, put one hand on the Head, for me—her unmentioned Mourner—" (*Letters* 2: 410). As Browning's "unmentioned Mourner," Dickinson wrote no less than three poems in commemoration of her poetic work: "I think I was enchanted," "Her—'last Poems'—," and "I went to thank Her—."

In "I think I was enchanted" Dickinson writes what amounts to a poetic manifesto invoking and inviting Browning as her first specifically literary muse:

> I think I was enchanted
> When first a sombre Girl—
> I read that Foreign Lady—
> The Dark—felt beautiful—
>
> And whether it was noon at night—
> Or only Heaven—at Noon—
> For very Lunacy of Light
> I had not power to tell—
>
> (*Poems* #593)

As in Elizabeth Bishop's later "Invitation to Miss Marianne Moore," Dickinson invokes Browning as a witch woman whose influence brings "enchantment," magical transformation, and a "very Lunacy of Light." In fact, Dickinson's poetic invocation suggests that Browning, and in particular *Aurora Leigh*, as a figure of dawn and light, may have been the "Some one carrying a Light" who gave Dickinson the "Sign" of her poetic vocation and thus guided her out of the "Dark" where Sue had "put her down" (*Poems* #631).

Under the spell of Barrett Browning's influence, Dickinson's "sombre Girl" is transformed into a visionary poet. She recreates herself and the world as she discovers the plastic and metamorphosing powers of art:

> The Bees—became as Butterflies—
> The Butterflies—as Swans—
> Approached—and spurned the narrow Grass—
> And just the meanest Tunes
>
> That Nature murmured to herself
> To keep herself in Cheer—
> I took for Giants—practising
> Titanic Opera—
>
> The Days—to Mighty Metres stept—
> The Homeliest—adorned
> As if unto a Jubilee
> 'Twere suddenly confirmed—
>
> (*Poems* #593)

Like the trees that sway "In metric chant of blessed poems" in Barrett Browning's "A Vision of Poets," the universe yields to the metamorphic gaze of Dickinson's poet: Nature's "meanest Tunes" are transformed into "Titanic Opera," and "The Days—to Mighty Metres stept—."

Appropriating and refiguring the terms of a Calvinist conversion experience, Dickinson compares Browning's influence to the reception of divine grace. She experiences the awakening of her poetic powers as a form of religious sanctification:

> I could not have defined the change—
> Conversion of the Mind
> Like Sanctifying in the Soul—
> Is witnessed—not explained—
>
> 'Twas a Divine Insanity—
> The Danger to be Sane
> Should I again experience—
> 'Tis Antidote to turn—
>
> To Tomes of solid Witchcraft—
> Magicians be asleep—
> But Magic—hath an Element
> Like Deity—to keep—
>
> (*Poems* #593)

Unlike the madwoman who giggles out of control in "The first Day's Night had come—," Dickinson's representation of her artistic "Conversion" as "a Divine Insanity" functions as a sign not of psychotic breakdown but of poetic self-preservation, a witch-like refusal to be "sane" under the law of the fathers. The "Antidote" to the "Danger" of sanity within a patriarchal economy is the "Divine Insanity" inscribed in and through women's writing and women's texts. As "Tomes of solid Witchcraft," Browning's writing preserves, "Like Deity," the "Magic" of a female art of transformation and trespass: her bewitching "Tomes" represent a kind of reading, a kind of writing, and a kind of death to patriarchal design.

The "Tomes of solid Witchcraft" that brought about Dickinson's "Conversion of the Mind" were probably the nine books of *Aurora Leigh* (1856), which Browning described as the "most mature" of her works and the one into which her "highest convictions upon Life and Art have entered."[9] Dickinson owned the 1859 edition of *Aurora Leigh,* and she probably read the book some time between 1857—the date of Sue Gilbert's edition—and 1861, when she first refers to the book in her letters.

In associating her own poetic creation with the work of Elizabeth Barrett Browning, Dickinson was not identifying herself with the sentimental love poet of *Sonnets from the Portuguese* (1850) who was popularized and marginalized by twentieth-century creators of the Victorian canon. On the contrary, Dickinson was identifying her work with the most powerful woman poet of her time—a woman who was regarded as a major poet and a serious contender for the title of poet laureate when Wordsworth died in 1850.[10] While the critics continually tried to place Barrett Browning in the tradition of the Anglo-American poetess represented by Felicia Hemans, she refused to stay put in this category. By her own admission, she aspired to be Homer rather than Hemans, an aim corroborated by the fact that as an epic of female development, *Aurora Leigh* advances into a traditionally male genre and breaks the silence surrounding such topics as women's sexual desire, wife and child abuse, prostitution, rape, illegitimacy, and women's poverty. When Browning's "novel-poem" was published, even sympathetic reviewers were disturbed by the violence, aggression, and masculinity of her work.[11]

Dickinson's association of *Aurora Leigh* with "Witchcraft" suggests that she, too, recognized the radicalism and potential danger of a poem that posed as its outsetting subject a woman poet who resists love, marriage, and men in order to pursue an independent career as a writing woman in London. "Witchcraft" is indeed the word that Romney, Aurora's rejected lover, uses to describe her poetic work:

> Read it? Not a word.
> I saw at once the thing had witchcraft in't,
> Whereof the reading calls up dangerous spirits:
> I rather bring it to the witch.
> *(Poetical Works* 271)

Openly addressing such specific women's issues as domestic entrapment, economic dependence, and a woman writer's conflict between career and marriage, art and love, and the poet and the poetess, Browning's verse epic on the growth of a young woman poet in Victorian England had particular relevance for Dickinson. In fact, *Aurora Leigh* tells Dickinson's own story of an inverted female fall away from the open experiential field of childhood into the innocent "cage-bird life" of gender and true womanhood. As Aurora's aunt seeks to educate her into a model of English womanliness, Aurora asserts her imaginative freedom:

> I had relations with the Unseen, and drew
> The elemental nutriment and heat
> From nature, as earth feels the sun at nights,
> Or as a babe sucks surely in the dark,
> I kept the life thrust on me, on the outside
> Of the inner life with all its ample room
> For heart and lungs, for will and intellect,
> Inviolable by conventions.
> *(Poetical Works* 261)

Within her green chamber, Aurora Leigh, like Dickinson in her room in Amherst, finds a source of resistance, sustenance, and freedom in nature, books, and writing. In the image of a woman poet, "inviolable by conventions," speaking "what lies beyond / Both speech and imagination," Dickinson may have found the courage and the inspiration to pursue her own relations with the "Unseen" *(Poetical Works* 277). At the time that she read *Aurora Leigh*—between 1857 and 1861—her poetic output increased from about fifty poems written in 1858 to over 300 written in 1862.

While Dickinson never imitates Browning, her witty assault on the conventions and values of traditional New England society sometimes echoes Aurora Leigh's aggressive and ironic confrontation with Victorian social morality. As several critics have shown, Dickinson's poems are also resonant with lines, images, and phrases that appear to be borrowed and recast from *Aurora Leigh*. [12] Her representation of herself as a self-crowned "Queen" in "I'm ceded—I've stopped being Their's—" may owe something to the wreath of ivy Aurora Leigh draws across her brow at the outset of her poetic career: "What, therefore, if I crown myself to-day / In sport, not pride, to learn the feel of it" (*Poetical Works* 271). Like Browning, Dickinson makes recurrent use of flowers, birds, dawn, jewels, royalty, and crowns to represent female creative power.

But the most notable resemblances between Dickinson and Browning are social and cultural rather than imagistic. It was not only Browning's gender that drew Dickinson to her work: it was also her privileged class position, her conservative politics, and her essentially aristocratic notion of the role of the poet. Raised like Barrett Browning in a conservative upper middle-class household in which her primary knowledge of the world came through books and reading, Dickinson shared Barrett Browning's distrust of the democratic masses, her resistance to utopian social reform, and her dedication to art as the privileged mode of social transformation.

As a Carlylean critique of the materialism of the industrial age, *Aurora Leigh* is centrally concerned with the use and value of work, particularly women's artistic work. Drawing on Romantic and Victorian notions of the poets as "truth-tellers" and speakers of soul and God whose words burn "you through with a special revelation," Aurora defends poetry as the most "noble" and "holy" vocation:

> Ay, and while your common men
> Lay telegraphs, gauge railroads, reign, reap, dine,
> And dust the flaunty carpets of the world
> For kings to walk on, or our president,
> The poet suddenly will catch them up
> With his voice like a thunder,— 'This is soul,
> This is life, the word is being said in heaven,
> Here's God down on us! what are you about?'
> (*Poetical Works* 266)

What made Aurora's notion "That carpet-dusting, though a pretty trade, / Is not the imperative labor after all" particularly compelling for Emily Dickinson was that as a woman poet, Aurora Leigh also defended poetry writing as the most valuable and "imperative labor" for women.

In her copy of *Aurora Leigh* Dickinson marked the following passage for special emphasis:

> By the way,
> The works of women are symbolical.
> We sew, sew, prick our fingers, dull our sight,
> Producing what? A pair of slippers, sir,
> To put on when you're weary—or a stool
> To stumble over and vex you . . . "curse that stool!"
> Or else at best, a cushion, where you lean
> And sleep, and dream of something we are not
> But would be for your sake. Alas, alas!
> This hurts most, this—that, after all, we are paid
> The worth of our work, perhaps.
>   (*Poetical Works* 260–61)

Wanting to do work that was more than symbolical, eager to produce more than a stool for men to trip over, ambitious to be something other than the dream woman of patriarchy, Aurora articulates Dickinson's own creative desire as a woman writing in Puritan New England. Whether responding to what Ann Douglas calls the "disestablishment" of middle-class New England women with the coming of the Industrial Revolution or to what Engels described as a more general devaluation and marginalization of the "works of women" under patriarchy, Dickinson's marking underlines her own struggle for significant vocation, her desire to produce a work of "worth" that would have more than merely symbolic, commodity, or use value.

At a time when Dickinson was beginning to pursue her own poetic "business," Aurora Leigh provided a compelling model of poetry as a serious vocation for women, a divine calling that was, in effect, more "holy" than the traditional vocation available to women as "doating mothers, and perfect wives, / Sublime Madonnas, and enduring saints" (*Poetical Works* 273). "Singing at a work apart / Behind the wall of sense," Aurora not only resists her Aunt's attempt to "flatten" and "bake" her into "a wholesome crust / For household uses and proprieties" (269). In a sequence that Dickinson would recast in parodic form in "She rose to His Requirement—dropt," Aurora also resists Romney's request that she join him in the "nobler work" of wife, "helpmate," and "sister of charity" in ministering to "the social spasm / And crisis of the ages" (274).

Declaring her self-dependence—"That every creature, female as the male, / Stands single in responsible act and thought," Aurora asserts the dignity and value of her own poetic calling:

> I too have my vocation,—work to do,
> The heavens and earth have set me since I changed
> My father's face for theirs, and, though your world
> Were twice as wretched as you represent,

> Most serious work, most necessary work
> As any of the economists' . . .
> *(Poetical Works* 276)

Representing poetry as a higher and more spiritual power than political action, Aurora's words on the "serious" and "necessary work" of the poet may have given Dickinson just the "Antidote" she needed in choosing not to marry and not to join her American sisters in the "noble work" of social reform. Affirming the spiritual, transcendent, and ultimately immortalizing power of art, Aurora sets the "holy" work of poetry against the material work of economists and reformers. In lines that Dickinson would echo in such artist poems as "I cannot dance upon my Toes—," "Myself was formed—a Carpenter—," "We play at Paste—," and "Publication—is the Auction," Aurora also sets "art's pure temple" against the commodity and use values of the commercial marketplace represented by the tradition of the poetess. She distinguishes between the "sublime art" of poetry and the frivolity of "mere women's work" practiced by the popular women poets of her time: "I would not condescend . . . to such a use / Of holy art and golden life." "I would rather dance / At fairs on tight-rope," she declares, "than shift the types / For tolerable verse, intolerable / To men who act and suffer" *(Poetical Works* 274).

Aurora is in fact so emphatic in her critique of the literary marketplace and what she calls art for "hire" that she may have played a more determining role than Higginson in persuading Dickinson not "to print." The best poet, Aurora argues, resists being defiled by popularity and the use values of the marketplace:

> And whosoever writes good poetry,
> Looks just to art. He does not write for you
> Or me,—for London or for Edinburgh;
> He will not suffer the best critic known
> To step into his sunshine of free thought
> And self-absorbed conception and exact
> An inch-long swerving of the holy lines.
> If virtue done for popularity
> Defiles like vice, can art, for praise or hire,
> Still keep its splendor and remain pure art?
> Eschew such serfdom. What the poet writes,
> He writes: mankind accepts it if it suits,
> And that's success: if not, the poem's passed
> From hand to hand, and yet from hand to hand
> Until the unborn snatch it crying out
> In pity on their fathers' being so dull,
> And that's success too.

> *(Poetical Works* 327)

Aurora's exalted vision of the integrity and purity of art is in some sense acted
out by Dickinson in her resistance to the marketplace values of "the Man" in
"Myself was formed—a Carpenter—"; her refusal to yield "an inch-long
swerving" to what she called the "surgery" of Higginson; and her later refusal
to publish when approached by Helen Hunt Jackson and the publisher Thomas
Niles. Passing her poems "From hand to hand, and yet from hand to hand" in
the handwritten manuscripts she enclosed in her letters to friends, Dickinson
did her own work for immortality and, in effect, prepared for her later "success" with what Aurora Leigh called "the unborn."

But while Aurora Leigh may have strengthened and encouraged Dickinson
in her refusal to give herself up to the uses of men, marriage, and the marketplace, she also offered a potentially problematic model. For all her resistance to the use values of the literary marketplace, "being but poor" Aurora
is finally

> constrained, for life,
> To work with one hand for the booksellers,
> While working with the other for myself
> And art.
>
> *(Poetical Works* 292)

For all her devotion to "Art's pure temple," Aurora is also, like her author,
finally tripped up by what she calls "This vile woman's way / Of trailing
garments" (*Poetical Works* 325). The recurrent imagery of breasts and other
parts of the female body that seemed so radical when the poem first appeared
finally embeds the text, its heroine, and its author in an essentialist notion of
female biological destiny that Dickinson resisted in her own life and work.

Despite the apparent radicalism of Elizabeth Barrett Browning's critique of
patriarchal ideology in *Aurora Leigh,* Aurora's story ultimately supports that
ideology by suggesting that a woman writer cannot resist the instinctual
demands of the female body and the essential desire of a woman for the love
of a man.[13] Whereas at the outset of Browning's epic, Aurora turns away from
writing "For others' uses" in order to write a story for her "better self," at the
close she declares, "Art is much, but Love is more" as she places herself in
the service of Romney and God (*Poetical Works* 254, 405). Begging Romney
to use her "roughly," "As men use common things . . . To any mean and
ordinary end," Aurora finally renounces the part of herself that "must ana-
lyse, / Confront, and question" rather than be "satisfied" with the love of
man and God (*Poetical Works* 405–406).

In her own life and work, Dickinson in effect rewrote the ending of *Aurora
Leigh.* Continuing to push toward what Aurora called "the intense significance / Of all things," she never finally stopped analyzing, confronting, and
questioning patriarchal dominance. Nor did she, like Aurora, move toward

heterosexual marriage and the subordination of art to love, self to God. Insofar as her relationship with Susan Gilbert was the major relationship of her life, Dickinson stopped short at the radical female possibility suggested by the fatherless trinity formed by Aurora Leigh, Marian Erle, and her child at the center of Browning's epic of the woman artist's life.

While others have noted Browning's unmistakable influence on Emily Dickinson, in their emphasis on the sisterly bond between them, these critics have tended to play down their differences and the extent to which Dickinson's life and work represented a swerve away from rather than a continuation of the female literary life represented by Barrett Browning.[14] Dickinson did not, as Browning did, "cross" her "Father's ground" to marry and flee to Italy with a dashing young poet. She did not write poems on such public subjects as slavery, child labor, and Italian nationalism. Nor did she, as Browning did, aspire to the role of social or religious prophet or seek to "represent her age" in epic form. Although she was by turns tempted and repelled by the fame of the literary marketplace, she could not and would not ever finally publish and succeed as a popular poet in the ways that Barrett Browning had.

Traces of Dickinson's ambivalence about her literary precursor are evident in her elegy on Elizabeth Barrett Browning's death, "Her—'last Poems'—." In this poem, Dickinson represents Browning as the very essence of the poet whose death after the publication of her *Last Poems* (1862) signifies the death of poetry itself:

> Her—"last Poems"—
> Poets—ended—
> Silver—perished—with her Tongue—
> Not on Record—bubbled other,
> Flute—or Woman—
> So divine—
>
> (*Poems* #312)

Confessing her own inadequacy to praise this "Head too High to Crown," Dickinson concludes with a comparison of her own suffocating woe with the pain of loss experienced by Barrett Browning's husband Robert Browning:

> Nought—that We—No Poet's Kinsman—
> Suffocate—with easy wo—
> What, and if, Ourself a Bridegroom—
> Put Her down—in Italy?
>
> (*Poems* #312)

Although the poem is obviously intended as an expression of grief at the loss of Barrett Browning's poetic power, Dickinson's hyperbolic language masks an undercurrent of irony and envy that tends to "Put Her down" in the very act of exalting her.[15] Perhaps remembering the more radical fatherless household formed by Aurora Leigh and Marian Erle in Italy in *Aurora Leigh*, Dickinson suggests that Barrett Browning was in some sense "put down" by her marriage and flight to Italy with her "Bridegroom," Robert Browning. Responding to Barrett Browning on her own high cultural aesthetic ground, Dickinson also suggests that, like the figure of the poetess she struggled against, Barrett Browning was perhaps too "divine" and "bubbled" and "Gushed too free for the Adoring—." Insofar as "Poets—ended—" with the publication of Barrett Browning's " 'last Poems,' " Dickinson's identity as poet appears to be eclipsed: she is "No Poet's Kinsman" and her utterance is "Nought." At the same time, however, the death of Barrett Browning and the publication of her last work, has left the place of the poet—now marked by the name "Woman" for the first time "on Record"—free for Dickinson herself to occupy.

Dickinson's second elegy on Barrett Browning is a more straightforward expression of grief and gratitude:

> I went to thank Her—
> But She Slept—
> Her Bed—a funneled Stone—
> With Nosegays at the Head and Foot—
> That Travellers—had thrown—
>
> Who went to thank Her—
> But She Slept—
> 'Twas Short—to cross the Sea—
> To look upon Her like—alive—
> But turning back—'twas slow—
>
> (*Poems* #363)

The suggestion that Dickinson was on her way to thank Browning when she died links this elegy with the curious poem "Going—to—Her!," which exists in two versions, one with a feminine and the other with a masculine pronoun. Dickinson's poem "I taste a liquor never brewed" appeared anonymously in *The Springfield Republican* on May 4, 1861. With the exception of the valentine "Sic transit gloria mundi" that appeared in the *Republican* in 1852, "I taste a liquor" was the first of Dickinson's poems to be published. She may have intended to send "Going—to—Her!" to Browning as a verse-letter of gratitude.[16] The poem begins:

> Going—to Her!
> Happy—Letter! Tell Her—
> Tell Her—the page I never wrote!
> Tell Her, I only said—the Syntax—

And left the Verb and the Pronoun—out!
Tell Her just how the fingers—hurried—
Then—how they—stammered—slow—slow—
And then—you wished you had eyes—in your pages—
So you could see—what moved—them—so—

(Poems #494)

Alluding to lines from book 8 of *Aurora Leigh* in which Romney refers to "The verb being absent, and the pronoun out," Dickinson once against suggests the cryptic, allusive, and sometimes invisible writing that characterized her exchanges with her women friends. The poem itself speaks a kind of coded language, suggesting the privacy of a shared and secret art as Dickinson pays tribute to Browning in the very act of representing the travail and dedication of their common craft.

Dickinson's elegies to Elizabeth Barrett Browning register a complex of attitudes: admiration, gratitude, competition, envy, difference, the fear of inadequacy, and the desire to excel. If Dickinson was "enchanted" by Barrett Browning's "Tomes of solid Witchcraft," her life and writing suggest that once the initial enchantment wore off, she moved against and away from her literary precursor. Although she continued to be drawn by Barrett Browning's exalted high cultural notion of the poet's life and work, she never finally placed herself or her art in the service of what Barrett Browning called "God's / Complete, consummate, undivided work" (*Poetical Works* 372). Rather than speaking *for* God, Dickinson sought to speak *as* God, competing with Him for the power of the Word and the power of creation. "A Word that breathes distinctly / Has not the power to die" (*Poems* #1651), Dickinson wrote, appropriating to herself the authority of language and the power of creation as she did her own "Work for Immortality" (*Poems* #406). Dressed in white and enacting her own revisionary revelations, Dickinson was in some sense truer to her "better self" and more of a witch than the "Foreign Lady" who first "enchanted" her.

Superior Women: George Eliot

During her years of literary maturity, Dickinson was particularly drawn to the life and work of George Eliot, whose portrait hung in her room along with those of Elizabeth Barrett Browning and Thomas Carlyle (Fig. 4). Beginning with *Adam Bede* (1859), which was given to her by Sue, Dickinson read virtually all of Eliot's major works, and her letters are full of fervent and sometimes cryptic exchanges about Eliot's life and work. *Middlemarch: A Study of Provincial Life* (1871–72) was in Dickinson's view a form of "glory" that had brought Eliot "immortality" in time; and *Daniel Deronda* (1874–76) was "the Lane to the Indes" that offered a kind of earthly and humane sustenance. "But have you read Daniel Deronda," she wrote Maria Whitney in 1885. "That wise and tender Book I hope you have seen—It is full of sad (high) nourishment—" (*Letters* 3: 865).

The terms Dickinson uses to characterize *Daniel Deronda*—"wise and tender," "sad (high) nourishment"—draw attention to the qualities of compassion and wisdom that mark Eliot's work at the same time that they set Eliot apart from a less "high" tradition of more conventional women writers who catered to popular taste in being merely pious, didactic, and cheerful. As in her relationship with Elizabeth Barrett Browning, in choosing George Eliot as an artistic model, Dickinson was positioning herself in relation to a powerful and intellectually ambitious woman writer—a woman writer who had assumed a male pseudonym and entered the literary marketplace cloaked not as a woman but as a man. After the popular success of *Adam Bede* in 1859, Eliot was ranked along with Charles Dickens and William Makepeace Thackeray as one of the major novelists of the Victorian Age. And by 1863, when she moved to the Priory with her lover, George Henry Lewes, Eliot had attained the status of a Victorian sage, who, in the words of her friend, the evolutionary philosopher Herbert Spencer, possessed "that breadth of culture, and universality of power, which have since made her known to all the world" (qtd. in Blind 103).

Like Dickinson at the outset of her own poetic career, Eliot set herself against the popular and sentimental women writers of her time in an article entitled "Silly Novels by Lady Novelists," which was written while she was working on her first story. Although there is no evidence that Dickinson read Eliot's article, which was published in the *Westminster Review* in 1856, the essay is a virtual checklist of Dickinson's own high cultural notion of the artist's work. Embarrassed by the fact that the popular "lady novelists" appear to confirm the male idea that women lack intelligence and should not be educated, Eliot dismisses their "silly novels" as a "composite order of feminine fatuity" characterized by "the frothy, the prosy, the pious, or the pedantic" (301).

Like Dickinson in "Publication—is the Auction," Eliot scoffs at the notion that acceding to the demands of the literary marketplace is necessitated by poverty: "We had imagined that destitute women turned novelists, as they turned governesses, because they had no other 'lady-like' means of getting their bread" ("Silly Novels" 303). But, Eliot realizes, these women novelists have no real knowledge of poverty; they often write in luxurious middle-class households, "inexperienced in every form of poverty except poverty of brains" (304). Countering the merely commercial notion of feminine literary production with "a sense of the responsibility involved in publication, and an appreciation of the sacredness of the writer's art," Eliot stresses the "equal" and "rigid requirements" of intelligence, discipline, and "the right elements—genuine observation, humour, and passion" that contribute to "literary excellence" among men as well as women writers (323, 324).

Although Eliot's privileged medium was prose and Dickinson's was poetry, the two women writers shared a similar intellectual and moral universe. As political conservatives, identified with the landed gentry and the values of the preindustrial past, both women distrusted the revolutionary and reform movements of their times, including the agitation for women's rights. The works of both women express a longing to return to an idyllic preindustrial rural community, often associated with women. Both give precedence to the inward psychic event, stressing the complexity and fundamental "mystery" of human nature and the suffering, waywardness, and pain that are inseparable from human life. Both writers also emphasize the discipline of pain and desire that must come not through outward changes in legislation or economics but through inward struggle and personal control.

In reading George Eliot, Dickinson was particularly drawn to the emphasis on renunciation of immediate pleasure in the interest of some higher ideal that marked the narratives of *Adam Bede, Middlemarch, The Mill on the Floss,* and *Daniel Deronda*. For the poet who had herself written "Renunciation—is a piercing Virtue— / The letting go / A Presence—for an Expectation—," the self-renouncing lives of Eliot's characters, particularly such female characters as Dorothea Brooke and Maggie Tulliver, served to affirm the domestic limits within which Dickinson sought to realize the "Expectation" and "larger function" of her own creative desire (*Poems* #745). As a woman who had achieved a kind of heroism within the limited space of provincial Middlemarch and the home, Dorothea Brooke confirmed the pattern of Dickinson's own "simple and stern" life in rural Amherst. While Dorothea lacked the "medium" of St. Theresa and Antigone, her "finely-touched spirit" and "unhistoric acts" had in the end contributed their part to the "growing good of the world" (*Middlemarch* 613).

But whereas Eliot denied her female characters the success she herself had achieved, teaching the moral values of patience, renunciation, and self-sacrifice in the interest of the higher social good of the family, the community, and the law of the father, Dickinson translated the "piercing Virtue" of "Renunciation" into her own personal discipline of art, emphasizing the value of self-expression as a social and ultimately immortalizing act. She suggests the perimeters of this discipline of art in poem #544:

> The Martyr Poets—did not tell—
> But wrought their Pang in syllable—
> That when their mortal name be numb—
> Their mortal fate—encourage Some—
>   (*Poems*)

In Dickinson's poetics of renunciation, the martyrdom of pain and suffering becomes bound up with the practice of artistic creation, providing at once a means of personal release and what Dickinson called "Some—Work for Immortality—" (*Poems* #406). Unlike Eliot, who veiled herself in a masculine persona, advanced into the public sphere, and punished, contained, and controlled female aspiration and desire in her artistic work, Dickinson masked herself in an ultrafeminine-seeming persona, retreated from the world, and transgressed and challenged patriarchal law and traditional female bounds in the imaginative space of her poems.

Having reached her own literary maturity during the same years that Eliot rose to fame as the most celebrated woman writer and intellectual of her age, Dickinson was as interested in Eliot's professional and private life as she was in the renunciation, suffering, and passion of her literary heroines. In Dickinson's later years, as her struggle with the problem of religious belief intensified, she was particularly fascinated and troubled by the apparent faithlessness of Eliot's life. When Eliot died in 1880, Dickinson mourned her death and expressed anxiety about her afterlife. "Perhaps she who Experienced Eternity in Time, may receive Time's omitted Gift as part of the Bounty of Eternity," she wrote to Sue, alluding at once to the immortality of Eliot's artistic creation and her lack of traditional Christian faith (*Letters* 3: 689). Herself a spiritual orphan, who loved her brother's wife and may have had one or more love affairs with married men, Dickinson was intensely curious about the life of this woman writer whose troubled childhood, turn away from Christianity, life with another woman's husband, and exile from general society had been widely publicized in the American press. "Watching like a vulture for Walter Cross's life of his wife," Dickinson wrote the Norcross sisters in 1885 (*Letters* 3: 856), referring to the recently published biography of Eliot written by her husband in the final year of her life. As soon as she received a copy of the biography, she sent it to Thomas Higginson, as if the risky and unorthodox life of George Eliot would somehow explain and affirm her own. Having already sent Higginson a copy of *Daniel Deronda* in 1876, Dickinson appears to have conferred these "gifts" of Eliot's life and works on Higginson as a further, albeit subtle, means of criticizing, and distinguishing herself from, the group of more conventionally feminine writers, including Harriet Prescott Spofford and Helen Hunt Jackson, whom Higginson sponsored and admired.

But while Dickinson was drawn to and fascinated by Eliot's unconventional life, her "vulture" image also suggests some of the ambivalence and envy she experienced in relation to Eliot as the most powerful woman writer of her age. Commenting on the "formidable figure" of George Eliot in *A Literature of Their Own*, Elaine Showalter observes: "Her female contemporaries never faltered in their praise of her books, but they felt excluded from, and envious of, her world. Her very superiority depressed them" (107). For all her admiration of Eliot's work, Dickinson was not above taking personal snipes at her physical ugliness. In an 1881 letter to Elizabeth Holland, Dickinson commented on a picture of George Eliot that Dr. Holland promised to send: "Vinnie is eager to see the Face of George Eliot which the Doctor promised, and I wince in prospective, lest it be no more sweet. God chooses repellant settings, dont he, for his best Gems?" (*Letters* 3: 693) (Fig. 4).

If, on the one hand, Eliot provided a brilliant model of the female literary life, on the other, her professional success and the apparent fullness of her personal life made Dickinson's own very different life choices seem less certain by comparison. "Now, *my* George Eliot" (*Letters* 3: 700), Dickinson wrote to the Norcross sisters after reading the notice of her death, as if she could now introject Eliot as a kind of private patron saint. But while Dickinson's response expresses her paradoxical metaphysics of absence as presence—the idea that "Death sets a Thing significant" (*Poems* #360)—her response also suggests that as the most formidable woman writer and intellectual of her age, Eliot is easier to approach and to possess as a model once she is dead. In fact, Eliot's death makes it easier for Dickinson to constitute her as a legitimizing symbol of her own personal and artistic life.

In reading the biographies that began to appear after Eliot's death, Dickinson appeared to be looking "like a vulture" for signs not of Eliot's success and achievement but of her unhappiness and sorrow. Having devoured Mathilde Blind's *George Eliot*, which had been sent to her by the publisher Thomas Niles in 1883, Dickinson responded in a note to Niles, written only a few weeks after receiving the biography: "The Life of Marian Evans had much I never knew—a Doom of Fruit without the Bloom, like the Niger Fig" (*Letters* 3: 769). Like Dickinson's representation of her own lack of "Bloom" in relation to Sue in "Ourselves were wed one summer—dear—," her "Niger Fig" image presents an effective and somewhat sobering figure of the travail of the Victorian woman artist's life, suggesting at once creation as destiny (doom) and the privation, lack, and hunger in which female creation occurs. But as a response to Blind's biography, Dickinson's "Niger Fig" image also represents a seemingly willful misreading of Eliot's life, in which Dickinson deliberately reads against the legacy of artistic achievement, professional success, public acclaim, and personal happiness Blind stresses and celebrates in *George Eliot*.

Dickinson makes use of a similar figure—"Life's empty Pack"—in the poem on Eliot that she enclosed in her letter to Niles:

> Her Losses make our Gains ashamed—
> She bore Life's empty Pack
> As gallantly as if the East
> Were swinging at her Back.
> Life's empty Pack is heaviest,
> As every Porter knows—
> In vain to punish Honey—
> It only sweeter grows.
>
> (*Poems* #1562)

While the poem is about the heroism of the female artist life, here again, there is something almost willfully perverse about the stress Dickinson places on the motifs of emptiness, loss, and punishment in a poetic tribute to a woman writer whose artistic achievement Blind had compared to Shakespeare and the best writers of her age. Rather than being paradigmatic of the "Empty pack" conferred by Eliot on her literary daughters, as Sandra Gilbert has argued, Dickinson appears to be intent on emptying Eliot's historically "full" pack in order to make the "empty Pack" of her own life seem more full by comparison.[17] Reversing the economics of their actual historical situations, in which Eliot earned large financial "Gains" in the literary marketplace and Dickinson earned nothing, Dickinson emphasizes Eliot's "Losses"—perhaps the death of her mother, her failure to marry and bear children, and her lack of faith—in an ambiguous hyperbolic figure that foregrounds her own "Gains" and the ultimate value of her own seemingly unsuccessful, unproductive, and unremunerated life.

Although Blind had suggested Eliot's sorrow at the loss of her mother, her highly sensitive nature, and the spiritual struggles of her early years, the image of Eliot that Dickinson presents more closely mirrors the plight of one of Eliot's romantic heroines. Emptying out Eliot's historically successful life, Dickinson, in effect, fills it with the heroic sufferance of one of her fictive heroines—such as Armgart in the verse drama of the same name. This poem about a successful woman artist who loses her voice and is forced to "bear the yoke of thwarted life" (George Eliot, *Poems* 123) may in fact have suggested Dickinson's image of "Life's empty Pack." When Armgart contemplates suicide, her cousin, Walpurga, urges her to bear the "common load" of suffering with ordinary humanity:

> Noble rebellion lifts a common load;
> But what is he who flings his own load off
> And leaves his fellows toiling?
>
> (*Poems* 126)

Like the punishment that Eliot appears to visit on Armgart for her creative and worldly aspiration, Dickinson's poetic tribute to Eliot appears to be driven by a similar desire to punish Eliot for her success in the literary marketplace.

Rather than emphasizing Eliot's public and professional success, Dickinson feminizes her as a creature of common and womanly suffering, poetically translating her into "*my* George Eliot," a heroic figure of renunciation and Christ-like suffering who, in effect, embodies Dickinson's own discipline of art. While the first six lines of the poem, in which the image of "Life's empty Pack" is twice repeated, bear the inscription of female deprivation and lack under the law of the fathers, the final lines cast the poem outward toward the open space—the "Honey"—of female creation: "In vain to punish Honey— / It only sweeter grows." Despite the "empty Pack" dealt to the female, Eliot, Dickinson suggests, was able to pursue her transactions with eternity in time, turning privation into honey, punishment into creation; indeed the "Honey" of her artistic creation is paradoxically bound up with the extent of her punishment. Mythologizing Eliot as a martyr to the cause of female artistic creation, Dickinson not only (re)invents George Eliot as a version of herself; she also invents a literary precursor whose "Losses" ultimately legitimize the "Gains" of her own decision not to go to market.

In an essay entitled "My Personal Acquaintance with Emily Dickinson," Dickinson's niece, Clara Newman Pearl, describes her as "the modest little woman who deemed it 'unfeminine' to publish" (Sewall 274). Although Pearl's characterization of her aunt is sentimental and perhaps apocryphal, it does suggest one final dimension of Dickinson's relationship to George Eliot. When in 1826 Dickinson's father met Catharine Sedgwick, the popular author of *A New England Tale,* he commented on her countenance of "much thought, & rather masculine features" (qtd. in Sewall 49). Unable to reconcile the apparent contradiction between the terms woman and intellectual, critics frequently noted a similarly "masculine" quality in Eliot's physical demeanor. Whatever else Dickinson learned from the life and work of George Eliot, the crucial lesson she may have received was that if she was going to achieve the standard of literary excellence and critical success Eliot had, she would have to enter the marketplace not like a woman but like a man. Rather than do this, Dickinson chose to remain in the traditionally female space of the home, projecting her poetic power as a "Loaded Gun" whose agency was masculine and elsewhere.

Going to Market: Helen Hunt Jackson

In the final decade of her life, Dickinson found a flesh-and-blood model of the female literary life in the figure of Helen Fiske Hunt Jackson. They had known each other as children in Amherst, where for a brief period Jackson attended Amherst Academy. Years later, after the premature death of her husband and then her son in the early sixties, Jackson turned to writing as a source of livelihood. Sponsored in her enterprise by Thomas Higginson, her fellow boarder at Mrs. Hannah Dame's literary boardinghouse in Newport, Rhode Island, Jackson rose to national fame under the pseudonym "H. H." as an author of sentimental verse, popular fiction, and family and travel literature, much of which was originally published in the *New York Independent,* the *New York Post, Home and Hearth, Atlantic Monthly,* and *Scribner's Monthly Magazine.* Having gained acclaim as one of America's most popular and admired women writers of the post-Civil War period, in the final years of her life she came to see her works of protest against United States Indian policy, *A Century of Dishonor* (1881) and her novel *Ramona* (1884), as the most valuable work she had done. To Higginson she said: "My *Century of Dishonor* and *Ramona* are the only things I have done for which I am glad now. The rest is of no moment. They will live on and they will bear fruit. They already have" (qtd. in Banning 224).

Dickinson was familiar with Jackson's first volume of poems, *Verses* (1870), which she placed within a developing tradition of women poets: "Mrs Hunt's Poems are stronger than any written by Women since Mrs—Browning, with the exception of Mrs Lewes [George Eliot]—but truth like Ancestor's Brocades can stand alone," she wrote to Thomas Higginson in 1871 (*Letters* 2: 491).[18] Dickinson was also probably familiar with Jackson's *Saxe Holm* stories, which Dr. Josiah Holland began to publish in *Scribner's* in 1871. Later, Jackson sent Dickinson copies of her works, including *Bits of Travel at Home* (1878) and *Ramona.* "Pity me . . . I have finished Ramona," Dickinson wrote Jackson in 1885, comparing her to Shakespeare, but failing, typically, to make any allusion to Jackson's political cause (*Letters* 3: 866).

Jackson first came to know Dickinson's work through Higginson, who began sharing some of Dickinson's poems with her around 1866. She was immediately struck by the originality of Dickinson's verse. She made use of the theme of a cloistered female genius in her *Saxe Holm* short story "Esther Wynn's Love Letters" (1871) and in the novel *Mercy Philbrick's Choice* (1876). She also launched a campaign to persuade her sister poet in Amherst to "sing aloud" (*Letters* 2: 545)

The relationship between Jackson and Dickinson has usually been treated as an empowering meeting of female literary minds that encouraged and heartened Dickinson in the final decade of her life. Richard Sewall writes glowingly of Dickinson's relationship with Jackson: "What Higginson had given her was—at last—an uncomplicated friendship, free from anguish, open, frank, delightful. Here she was no one's Scholar or Daisy or 'Wife— without the Sign!' It was a relationship of equals" (592).[19] But while Dickinson's relationship with Jackson appears to be cordial and at times even fervent, Jackson also represented precisely the model of the popular poetess that Dickinson most abhorred. In fact, nowhere is Dickinson's ambivalent attitude toward successful women writers and the literary marketplace more evident than in her relationship with Helen Hunt Jackson.

Like other women writers of her time, Jackson began her literary career by placing herself under a male "mentor" and "teacher" in the person of Thomas Higginson, whom she regarded as the supreme literary craftsman. Higginson was, she wrote Charles Dudley Warner in 1873, "the one man to whom & to whose style, I chiefly owe what little I have done in literature (*Leyda* 2: 213). Seeking Higginson's advice on issues of rhyme and meter, and rigorously adhering to his first rule of literary composition in his "Letter to a Young Contributor" (1862)— "fight to render your statement clear and attractive" rather than "abstruse"—Jackson learned under Higginson's guidance to write simple, direct, and thoroughly conventional verse (Higginson, "Letter to a Young Contributor" 404). Producing poems of feminine feeling centered on the home, the hearth, the maternal affections, nature, death, grief, and the consolation of religion, she also learned to market herself as a thoroughly conventional woman writer who confirmed rather than challenged traditional gender bounds.

"Upon occasion she had defied the tradition and written as she pleased," writes her biographer Ruth Odell, "but her failure readily to place such pieces resulted in her abandoning them" (*Helen Hunt Jackson* 227). Like Aurora Leigh in the flush of her first success in London, Jackson quickly learned the art of writing for "hire" by writing to please the editors of popular journals and their readers. "The man who writes must, if he needs pay for his work, write what the man who prints will buy," she said (qtd. in Odell 112). Having risen to national fame by writing what "the man who prints will buy," Jackson was a shrewd businesswoman who knew how to market herself and her works. Although she valued publication in the more prestigious literary journals such as *Atlantic Monthly* and *Scribner's*, she also antagonized editors by insisting that she be paid the market price for her work. "I never write for money, I write for love, then after it is written, I *print* for money," she wrote to James Fields at the *Atlantic* in 1870 while she was negotiating the price for her "Valley of Gastein" travel letters (qtd. in Banning 90). When in 1876 she sent her novel *Mercy Philbrick's Choice* to *Scribner's*, she included the following note to Holland: "I have sent the next Saxe Holm story to you . . . Please send me at once eight hundred dollars of the ten hundred and eight that it is worth" (qtd. in Banning 124).[20]

Like other women writers of her time, Jackson was also split between the masculine assertion of her public career and traditional middle-class notions of true womanly virtue. While she earned a living writing and traveling throughout the United States and Europe, she was opposed and even hostile to the movement for women's rights. In an essay entitled "Wanted—A Home" in *Bits of Talk About Home Matters*, she wrote: "There is an evil fashion of speech which says it is narrowing and narrow life that a woman leads who cares only, works only for her husband and children; that a higher, more imperative thing is that she herself be developed to her utmost" (236). Unlike Dickinson who stayed at home and challenged traditional gender bounds in her life and writing, Jackson went abroad and developed herself to the utmost in a public career, and yet in her writings she insisted that a woman's place is in the home. The woman "who creates and sustains a home, and under whose hands children grow up to be strong and pure men and women, is a creator, second only to God" (236–37), she wrote, failing to note the contradiction between her maternal and pious platitudes and her own mobile and self-fulfilling life as a writing woman.

For her public conformity and private charm Jackson was rewarded with publication and praise by some of the major arbiters of literary taste in the United States, including Ralph Waldo Emerson, who published five of Jackson's poems in *Parnassus* (1874). Although Emerson singled out Jackson's poems for "rare merit of thought and expression," his anthology included no poem by Walt Whitman, whose work he had earlier championed as "the most extraordinary piece of wit and wisdom that America has yet contributed" (Whitman 731). Jackson had also succeeded in gaining literary recognition from three of the male editors and writers with whom Dickinson had failed to find a sympathetic audience for her verse. In the January 1, 1874, issue of the *Springfield Republican*, Samuel Bowles wrote: "Mrs Hunt stands on the threshold of the greatest literary triumphs ever won by an American woman" (Leyda 2: 215). When Josiah Holland became editor of *Scribner's* in 1870, the amount of verse Dickinson sent to the Hollands increased significantly, but in the eyes of Holland her verse was "too ethereal" for publication (Leyda 2: 193). And yet, it was through Holland that Jackson found her most lucrative work as the author of the "Saxe Holm" series of stories, which began appearing in *Scribner's* in 1871. While Higginson looked on Dickinson's poetry as "remarkable, though odd" and "too delicate" for publication, by 1868 he was already championing "H. H." as "one of the most gifted poetesses in America." When Jackson died in 1885, Higginson eulogized her as the "most brilliant, impetuous, and thoroughly individual woman of her time,—and one whose very temperament seemed mingled of sunshine and fire" (*Contemporaries* 142).

Some of Dickinson's anger at Jackson's literary success surfaces in a letter she wrote to Higginson in response to his *Short Studies of American Authors* (1879), which included critical sketches of Helen Hunt Jackson, Edgar Allan Poe, Nathaniel Hawthorne, Henry David Thoreau, William Dean Howells, and Henry James: "Mrs Jackson soars to your estimate as lawfully as a Bird, but of Howells and James, one hesitates—Your relentless Music dooms as it redeems—" (*Letters* 2: 649). Dickinson's words are typical of the doubleness of her response to Jackson, particularly in her correspondence with Higginson. Although she appears to endorse Higginson's high estimate of his protégée, she also suggests that Jackson has totally conformed to his literary laws. There is in fact an implicit contrast between the dynamics of Higginson's relationship with Jackson, who yields herself Galatea-like to his literary will, and Higginson's relationship with Dickinson, who, as he himself noted, could never be led "in the direction of rules and traditions" (*Carlyle's Laugh* 262).

A similar ambivalence informs the written exchanges between Jackson and Dickinson. The existing correspondence between them begins with a poem.[21] When Helen Hunt married William S. Jackson in October 1875, Dickinson sent her the following note:

> Have I a word but Joy?
>   E. Dickinson
>   Who fleeing from the Spring
>   The Spring avenging fling
>   To Dooms of Balms—
>   (*Letters* 2: 544)

Baffled and mystified by Dickinson's lines, which had been taken from her poem "Upon a Lilac Sea" (*Poems* #1337), Jackson returned them with a "request for interpretations": "I do wish I knew just what 'dooms' you meant," she wrote (*Letters* 2: 544). Dickinson may have intended to wish Jackson a destiny of marital bliss, but the image "Dooms of Balms" also suggests her notion of marriage as a "soft Eclipse" and the hostility to the marriage of her women friends that frequently marks her poems and correspondence. Whatever she intended, here as elsewhere in her exchanges with Jackson, Dickinson's multiply nuanced and metaphorically dense expression functions as a form of competition that shows up and ultimately defies the more simple, direct, and popular style of her "successful" literary friend.

Dickinson never explained herself, but the tension in this initial exchange between Helen Hunt Jackson as an eminently public figure—direct, candid, hearty, and at times overbearing—and Emily Dickinson as an insistently private woman—elusive, veiled, reserved, coy—is a tension that would continue to characterize the dynamics of the relationship between them. "So threads cross, even on the outermost edges of the web," Jackson wrote Dickinson in 1875. "I hope some day, somewhere I shall find you in a spot where we can know each other. I wish very much that you would write to me now and then, when it did not bore you." Jackson sought more than a renewed correspondence with Dickinson. As a secret admirer of the poems Higginson shared with her, she also sought to persuade her to publish. "I have a little manuscript volume with a few of your verses in it—and I read them very often—," Jackson wrote in the same letter. "You are a great poet—and it is wrong to the day you live in, that you will not sing aloud. When you are what men call dead, you will be sorry you were so stingy" (*Letters* 2: 544–45).

As the only writer of her age to recognize Dickinson's poetic worth, Jackson became a kind of self-appointed advocate and agent of Dickinson's work. "How can you print a piece of your soul?" Dickinson is said to have asked Jackson when she visited her in Amherst.[22] But the question once again suggests the fundamental difference between them. Although Dickinson may genuinely have wondered how to "print," her question also implicitly criticizes Jackson for marketing her "soul." In opposition to Jackson's willingness to print what the man "will buy," Dickinson sets her own high cultural and increasingly privatized notion of art as an affair of the "Human Spirit" that, as she says in "Publication—is the Auction," should not be reduced "To Disgrace of Price—" (*Poems* #709).

Convinced that a "great poet" should "sing aloud" and not completely cognizant of Dickinson's aristocratic aversion to the literary marketplace, Jackson was determined to show Dickinson *how* to publish her poems. While Thomas Higginson was still complaining about Dickinson's "spasmodic" and "uncontrolled" verse, Jackson sought to persuade her to publish her work in the No Name Series of books being planned by Roberts Brothers of Boston. "I enclose to you a circular which may interest you," she wrote Dickinson in August 1876. "When the volume of Verse is published in this series, I shall contribute to it: and I want to persuade you to. Surely, in the shelter of such *double* anonymousness as that will be, you need not shrink. I want to see some of your verses in print. Unless you forbid me, I will send some that I have. May I?" According to the circular, the No Name books, under the editorship of Thomas Niles, were each to be written by "a great unknown" (*Letters* 2: 563).

Jackson followed up her request with a personal visit to Dickinson in October of 1876. "You say you find great pleasure in reading my verses," she wrote shortly after her call. "Let somebody somewhere whom you do not know have the same pleasure in reading yours" (*Letters* 2: 565). As a woman poet who had herself hidden behind such pseudonyms as Marah, Saxe Holm, and Rip Van Winkle, Jackson understood Dickinson's need for what she called "*double* anonymousness." She tried to appeal to Dickinson's love of secrecy and play by presenting publication in the No Name series as a kind of literary conspiracy, a secret sharing among women. She wrote again in 1878:

> Would it be of any use to ask you once more for one or two of your poems, to come out in the volume of "no name" poetry which is to be published before long by Roberts Bros.? If you will give me permission I will copy them— sending them in my own handwriting—and promise never to tell any one, not even the publishers, whose the poems are. Could you not bear this much of publicity? Only you and I would recognize the poems. I wish very much you would do this—and I think you would have much amusement in seeing to whom the critics, those shrewd guessers would ascribe your verses.
>
> (*Letters* 2: 624–25)

After another personal visit to Dickinson in October 1878, Jackson continued to press her on the issue of publication: "Now—will you send me the poem? No—will you let me send the 'Success'—which I know by heart—to Roberts Bros for the Masque of Poets? If you will, it will give me a great pleasure. I ask it as a personal favor to myself—Can you refuse the only thing I perhaps shall ever ask at your hands?" (*Letters* 2: 625) The seeming desperation of Jackson's request is owing to the fact that in an act of rashness she had already submitted the "Success" to Thomas Niles, and the poem was about to appear in print whether or not Dickinson gave her consent. Jackson's exchanges with Dickinson over the publication of "Success" provide a fair sample of the willful and even overbearing manner for which she was known. Dickinson had at first refused to give Jackson permission to submit any of her poems for publication, even citing Higginson's disapproval as her reason. But the desperation of Jackson's final plea—"Can you refuse the only thing I perhaps shall ever ask at your hands?"—forced her to give her consent. While Jackson may have meant well in submitting "Success" for publication without Dickinson's consent, this violation of confidence at the outset of the renewed correspondence between them suggests that their relationship was not as "open" and "free from anguish" as Sewall and others have suggested.

As a woman writer who shared Higginson's notion of the potential "majesty" of a "literary career," Jackson clearly could not understand Dickinson's reasons for resisting publication (Higginson, "Letter to a Young Contributor" 403). Had Dickinson encountered Jackson fifteen years earlier, says Sewall, the course of her career might have been different (Sewall 592). But the fact that "Success" was submitted for publication without Dickinson's permission and then altered at the hands of Jackson and later Niles before it was printed raises questions about what would have happened if Dickinson *had* entered the literary marketplace. When Jackson submitted "Success" to Niles, she not only copied it over in her "own handwriting," she also quite literally wrote the poem over. She and Niles altered and added pronouns and articles, changed words, regularized the meter, and rewrote the final ambiguous lines—"Burst agonized and clear!"—to read "Break, agonizing clear." Although these changes were no doubt made in the interest of clarity and conventional taste, the total effect was to mutilate and efface Dickinson's own poetic signature. Printed anonymously in *A Masque of Poets* (1878), "Success is counted sweetest" was, in the eyes of what Jackson called the shrewd-guessing critics, commonly adjudged to be the work of Emerson.

It is ironic that Dickinson's experience in publishing a poem about the ultimate "triumph" of "those who ne'er succeed" in conventional American terms appears to have further steeled her will against pursuing "Success" in the literary marketplace when Niles approached her about the possibility of publishing a collection of her poems with Roberts Brothers. When in 1882 Dickinson inquired about the publication date of John Walter Cross's biography of George Eliot, Niles responded: " 'H. H.' once told me that she wished you could be induced to publish a volume of poems. I should not want to say how highly she praised them, but to such an extent that I wish also that you could" (*Letters* 3: 726). Dickinson thanked him for his praise, but indirectly turned down his invitation to publish by enclosing a copy of "How happy is the little Stone," a poem expressing a lack of "care about Careers" and fear of "Exigencies" (*Poems* #1510).

The following year, when Niles sent her a copy of Mathilde Blind's *George Eliot*, published that spring by Roberts Brothers, Dickinson sent him her own copy of the *Poems by Currer, Ellis, and Acton Bell*. The gesture was mysterious but not without precedent. Immediately after initiating her literary correspondence with Higginson in 1862, she had sent him a portrait of Elizabeth Barrett Browning; a few years later, she sent a copy of the Brontë poems to Samuel Bowles, who had published a few of her poems in the *Springfield Republican*. She may have intended these offerings of other writing women as a kind of literary armor that would facilitate her own advance on the masculine establishment by reminding them of a potent tradition of women writers. But Dickinson's gestures were ambivalent: *Poems by Currer, Ellis, and Acton Bell* also suggests the danger of female publication. The Brontë sisters veiled themselves in anonymity because, Charlotte Brontë wrote, "we did not like to declare ourselves women, because . . . we had a vague impression that authoresses are liable to be looked on with prejudice" ("Biographical Notice of Ellis and Acton Bell" 4).

Whatever the symbolism of Dickinson's gesture, Niles appears to have missed it entirely. "Surely you did not mean to present me with your copy—if you did, I thank you heartily, but in doing so I must add that I would not for the world rob you of this very rare book, of which this is such a nice copy." He uses the occasion to invite her to submit her own poems for consideration: "If I may presume to say so, I will take instead a M.S. collection of your poems, that is, if you want to give them to the world through the medium of a publisher" (*Letters* 3: 769). *Through the medium of a publisher*. It was precisely this problem of mediation—of reaching "the world" through the mediations and violations of well-meaning friends and editors—that was causing or had already caused Dickinson to demur.

As in her relationships with Higginson and Jackson, Dickinson appears to have enjoyed making contact with the literary world through Niles, for she sent him copies of a few of her poems, including "Further in Summer than the Birds," "It sifts from Leaden Sieves—," and "No Brigadier throughout the Year." But she never replied to his offer to publish. Nor did Niles, in his turn, pursue the project. In fact, when Higginson later approached him about the possibility of publishing Dickinson's poems posthumously, he expressed reservation: "It has always seemed to me that it would be unwise to perpetuate Miss Dickinson's poems. They are quite as remarkable for defects as for beauties & are generally devoid of true poetic qualities" (Bingham, *Ancestors' Brocades* 53). When in 1890 Dickinson's poems finally did reach the public "through the medium" of Niles, Higginson, Todd, and Roberts Brothers of Boston, many of their "defects" would in fact be mediated and erased in accord with the "true poetic qualities" of the time.

The irony of Dickinson's relationship with Jackson in the final decade of her life is that while Jackson's fame did not live beyond her time, she has in some sense been immortalized in the life and work of Emily Dickinson. As Dickinson's most attentive audience after their meeting in 1876, Jackson was the recipient, source, and inspiration for several poems, including "Spurn the temerity—," "Before you thought of Spring," "One of the ones that Midas touched," "A Route of Evanescence," "Upon his Saddle sprung a Bird," "Pursuing you in your transitions," "Take all away from me, but leave me Ecstasy," and "Of God we ask one favor." The existing correspondence between Jackson and Dickinson is scant, but what this correspondence indicates is that these poems were often called forth by Jackson's enthusiastic response to Dickinson's work. After Dickinson had apparently sent her a copy of "Before you thought of Spring," Jackson wrote:

My dear friend,

   I know your "Blue bird" by heart—and that is more than I do of any of my own verses.—

I also want your permission to sent it to Col. Higginson to read. These two things are my testimonial to its merit.

We have blue birds here—I might have had the sense to write something about one myself, but I never did: and now I never can. *For which I am inclined to envy, and perhaps hate you. . . .*

What should you think of trying your hand on the oriole? He will be along presently.

(*Letters* 2: 639; emphasis added)

Coming from one of America's most revered writers, Jackson's "testimonial," which communicated the sense of a common subject matter and a shared craft, moved Dickinson to write two more bird poems: the first on the oriole, "One of the ones that Midas touched" and another on the hummingbird, "A Route of Evanescence," which was destined to become one of Dickinson's most anthologized poems. "To the Oriole you suggested I add a Humming Bird and hope they are not untrue—," Dickinson wrote (*Letters* 2: 639). But while this exchange suggests the role that Jackson played as muse and audience for Dickinson's work in the final decade of her life, Jackson's teasing words, "I am inclined to envy, and perhaps hate you," also suggest the competitive spirit that animated their relationship and inspired Dickinson to write not *one* but *two* poems. In fact, what Jackson's "testimonial" suggests is that Dickinson's "Blue bird" poem has in effect silenced her and caused her to recognize the limits of her own talent.

"What portfolios of verses you must have," Jackson wrote Dickinson in 1884, requesting that she be made her literary executor:

It is a cruel wrong to your "day & generation" that you will not give them light.—If such a thing should happen as that I should outlive you, I wish you would make me your literary legatee & executor. Surely, after you are what is called "dead," you will be willing that the poor ghosts you have left behind, should be cheered and pleased by your verses, will you not?—You ought to be—.

(*Letters* 3: 841–42)

Suffering herself from "Nervous prostration" since the death of her nephew Gilbert in 1883, Dickinson was flattered by Jackson's unflagging devotion and impressed by her continued high spirits, despite the fact that she had broken her leg and was unable to walk. "I shall watch your passage from Crutch to Cane with jealous affection," she wrote. "From there to your Wings is but a stride—as was said of the convalescing Bird,

> And then he lifted up his Throat
> And squandered such a Note—
> A Universe that overheard
> Is stricken by it yet—

(*Letters* 3: 840)

This quatrain, taken from the poem "Upon his Saddle sprung a Bird," pays tribute both to Jackson's duress under hardship and the uplifting effect of her winged "Notes" on Dickinson's life. But Dickinson never directly responded to Jackson's request to be her "literary legatee & executor." Perhaps embarrassed by Jackson's presumption, she may have responded indirectly in another poem she included in her letter:

> Pursuing you in your transitions,
> In other Motes—
> Of other Myths
> Your requisition be.
> The Prism never held the Hues,
> It only heard them play—
>> Loyally,
>> E. Dickinson—
>> (*Letters* 3: 841)

The lines are cryptic, suggesting the possibility of other worlds—"other Motes" and "other Myths"—opened by Jackson's mercurial and multifaceted presence. But the lines also suggest the distance and difference between them. What the poem finally seems to say is that Jackson is an outsider, a representative of the "Motes" and "Myths" and "Hues" of a totally other literary world. As such, her "requisition"—her literary requirements, her demand that Dickinson publish, her request to be Dickinson's "literary legatee"—is out of the question.

After Jackson visited Dickinson in Amherst in 1876, she wrote an article for the New York *Independent* entitled "Wanted in New England: An Apostle for Sunshine," in which she criticized New Englanders for their gloomy and sunless lives. Like Higginson, Jackson was a proponent of optimism, sunshine, and good cheer in literature and in life. It was these qualities that she emphasized and sought to call forth in her correspondence with Dickinson, as she urged her to help and please and cheer the world by publishing her verse. Although Dickinson tried to be cheerful and at times even ecstatic in the poems she sent to Jackson, Jackson continued to be mystified by much of what Dickinson wrote. "I like your simplest and most direct lines best," she wrote, after puzzling over and finally decoding one of Dickinson's poems (*Letters* 2: 565). Possessed of a "darker spirit," Dickinson could not finally be one of Jackson's "Apostles of Sunshine" nor could she subscribe to her aesthetics of brightness and good cheer. After her experience with "the Success" and after a decade of "cheerful" poetic exchanges with Jackson, Dickinson must surely have recognized that if she made Jackson her "literary legatee & executor" her work was in danger of being quite literally executed.

"Helen of Troy will die, but Helen of Colorado, never," Dickinson wrote to Jackson's husband immediately following her death in the summer of 1885.

She described the empowering effect that Jackson's winged presence had on her life. "Dear friend, can you walk, were the last words that I wrote her. Dear friend, I can fly—her immortal (soaring) reply. I never saw Mrs Jackson but twice, but those twice are indelible, and one Day more I am deified, was the only impression she ever left on any Heart (House) she entered—" (*Letters* 3: 889). She also wrote to Thomas Niles, requesting a photograph of Jackson, perhaps intending to place it beside the portraits of Eliot and Browning that already hung in her room.

More than any other writer of the time, Jackson gave Dickinson a responsive audience, bolstered her self-esteem, and taught her to believe in the value and immortality of her own poetic creation. But while Dickinson was drawn to and even "deified" by Jackson's vibrant personality, and while she composed poems in appreciation of the rejuvenating effect that Jackson's buoyant spirit and persistent literary interest had on her life, the two verse elegies that she sent Higginson on Jackson's death bear traces of the peculiar tension and doubleness of their relationship as Dickinson appears both to celebrate and to take away the "immortality" of Jackson's life and work. In the first of these elegies, Dickinson appears to express gratitude for the gift of "Human Love" and "immortality" that Jackson gave:

> The immortality she gave
> We borrowed at her Grave—
> For just one Plaudit famishing,
> The Might of Human Love—
> (*Poems* #1648)

As in her other poems in praise of literary women, Dickinson's lines are ambiguous. Although Jackson is represented as a heavenly figure, the ray of light that brought the "one Plaudit" and "Might of Human Love" for which Dickinson had been "famishing," the lines also suggest that Dickinson has inherited or at least "borrowed" the "immortality" that Jackson had given up in her bid for success and popularity in the marketplace.

In the second elegy, Dickinson associates Jackson with a luminous force of nature, living on after her death. As site and source of glory and light, she is apotheosized in a star:

> Of Glory not a Beam is left
> But her Eternal House—
> The Asterisk is for the Dead,
> The Living, for the Stars—
> (*Poems* #1647)

Here again, however, Jackson's immortality is in question. Although she appears to be apotheosized in a star, Dickinson's poetic eulogy also suggests that for all Jackson's earthly "Glory" as an "Apostle of Sunshine," "not a Beam is left" after her death. Having never given up her own immortalizing work for earthly "Glory," Dickinson may in fact be suggesting that she herself is the only "Living" and true "Star" left after Jackson's death.

"No 'Sonnet' had George Eliot," Dickinson wrote in a draft of the letter she sent to Higginson containing her verse elegies on Jackson. Although this comment in response to Higginson's 1886 sonnet "To the Memory of H. H." was never sent, it does reveal some of Dickinson's anger and jealousy at the fact that Higginson had clearly preferred and sponsored Jackson's work rather than her own. Dickinson's seemingly innocent comment suggests that while Higginson has been singing the praises of Helen Hunt Jackson, he has failed to recognize the work of a truly immortal artist like George Eliot—and, by implication, like herself. No sonnet had Emily Dickinson either when she died.

Dickinson's mixed and at times even hostile reaction to Jackson as Higginson's true "Star" is evident in a letter she sent to him at about the same time she composed her verse elegies. "When she came the last time she had in her Hand as I entered, the 'Choir invisible,'" she wrote of Jackson's visit to Amherst in 1878. "'Superb,' she said as she shut the Book, stooping to receive me, but fervor suffocates me" (*Letters* 3: 903). What Dickinson seems to say is that in remembering Jackson's last visit she is overcome by fervid emotion for her. But Dickinson's words might also be read oppositely to suggest a fundamental difference between them. The fervor and passion that Higginson and others so admired in Jackson are in fact overwhelming and indeed even suffocating. For all Jackson's high spirits and charm, Dickinson appears to have been put off by her affected, condescending, and overbearing manner.

Having, as Sue later said, "withstood even the fascinations of Mrs. Helen Jackson" (Leyda 2: 473), Dickinson had, for the final time, avoided the suppression and violation that would have occurred had she chosen to give her work to the world "through the medium of a publisher." What is perhaps most striking about Dickinson's exchanges with Jackson in the final decade of her life is her growing confidence in the value and "absolute Decree" of her own work. Having already experienced the "surgery" of Higginson and the corrections of editors and friends, including Jackson herself, eager to straighten her "slant" style, Dickinson prefers to remain "independent as the Sun / . . . Fulfilling absolute Decree," as she says in the "Pebble" poem she sent to Jackson, as well as to Higginson and Thomas Niles (*Poems* #1510). She refuses to publish not because her poems are not good enough, but because she believes her poems are too good to be violated by the conventional taste of the time.

Her belief in herself and the value of her work was no doubt strengthened
by the attention and admiration she received from Helen Hunt Jackson. But as
the very embodiment of the public career woman, Jackson also served paradoxically to strengthen Dickinson's determination not to go to market. For all
her national reputation as one of the most acclaimed writers of her time,
Jackson was also in some sense both the product and the victim of popular
taste. After her first visit to Dickinson in 1876, Jackson confessed her uneasiness:

> I feel as if I had been very impertinent that day in speaking to you as I did,—
> accusing you of living away from the sunlight—and telling you that you looked
> ill . . . but really you looked so white and moth-like! Your hand felt like such a
> wisp in mine that you frightened me. I felt like a great ox talking to a white
> moth, and begging it to come and eat grass with me to see if it could not turn
> itself into a beef! How stupid.—
>
> *(Letters* 2: 565)

Jackson's words reveal as much about her own career choices as they do about
Dickinson's. Representing herself as a great ox, a beef who has grown fat on
popular acclaim, Jackson appears to have sensed that the white moth, who
chose to live "away from the sunlight" and refused to go graze on the public
field, might be the ultimate victor.

While Dickinson was gratified by the recognition she received from Jackson, Jackson in her turn was made insecure by her contact with Dickinson.
Their relationship was not, as Sewall argues, "a relationship of equals." They
both knew that Dickinson was, if not a popular poet, then at least a smarter
and wittier poet whose work was less simple, less sunny, and less subject to
the demands of the literary marketplace. In fact, having made contact with
Dickinson when her own works were beginning to receive negative reviews
and just before she turned her main energies to the Indian cause, Jackson was
made increasingly conscious through her relationship with Dickinson of her
own questionable status as marketable commodity. Whereas Dickinson continued to pursue her "absolute Decree," imagining the Christ-like and immortalizing "expanse" of her self and her work from her room in Amherst,
Jackson, in one of the last poems she wrote before her death, registered her
sense that she had somehow lost her direction on the way to market: "Fool to
be dumb, and to dissemble! / Alas, for the song I never wrote!" (*Poems*
#266)

4

Differences That Kill: Elizabeth Bishop and Marianne Moore

> darkened and tarnished
> by the warm touch
> of the warm breath,
> maculate, cherished,
> rejoice! For a later
> era will differ.
> (O difference that kills,
> or intimidates, much
> of all our small shadowy
> life!)
>   —Elizabeth Bishop
>   "Song for the Rainy Season"

As a student at Vassar in the early thirties, Elizabeth Bishop and several other women, among them Mary McCarthy, Muriel Rukeyser, and Eleanor Clark, founded a literary magazine to protest the policies of the *Vassar Review*. "The regular literary magazine was dull and old-fashioned," Bishop remembered. "Mary and Eleanor and I and several others decided to start one in competition. It was to be anonymous. We used to meet in a speakeasy and drink dreadful red wine and get slightly high. . . . We called the magazine *Conspirito*. We got out only three numbers, I think, but we prevailed" (Ashley Brown 7–8). The title *Conspirito* was, as sister conspirator Eunice Clark noted, "an almost Joycean palimpsest of meanings," suggesting not only wine and spirits but also conspiracy, heady defiance, and the vigorous impulse with which this most distinguished group of women writers sought to oppose the dull conventionality and Arnoldian pieties of the *Vassar Review* (Jessup 17).

In the image of women breathing together in creative power and women conspiring against the conventional policies of the *Vassar Review*, the name *Conspirito* suggests the ways some women writers have historically turned to each other as sources of empowerment against the pressures of a predominantly masculine tradition. What is striking about this particular bond among women, however, is that it is a bond formed not against the fathers, but against and "in competition" with other women: it was a *conspiracy* formed by an exclusive and high-toned group of avant-garde women against what they considered the more ordinary and "old-fashioned" Vassar girls who ran the *Vassar Review*. As such, *Conspirito* provides a useful corrective to feminist representations of the natural bonds of reciprocity and sisterhood that link women across social, race, and class lines. As a conspiracy among women against other women, *Conspirito* also provides a fitting introduction to the problems of exclusivity, struggle, and difference as they are played out in Bishop's celebrated relationship with Marianne Moore and in her own literary career.

For all the sense of conspiratorial power that Bishop found among writing women at Vassar, she was a literary loner who would never allow her work to be published in a magazine or anthology devoted exclusively to women. "When I was in college and started publishing, even then, and in the following few years, there were women's anthologies, and all-women issues of magazines, but I always refused to be in them." Although the emphasis among some feminists on the necessarily empowering bonds among women might lead one to interpret Bishop's refusal as an antifemale gesture, Bishop herself looked upon her refusal as an act grounded in feminist principle: "I felt it was a lot of nonsense, separating the sexes," she said; "I suppose this feeling came from feminist principles, perhaps stronger than I was aware of" (Starbuck 21).

In a 1938 article entitled "The Poet as Woman," John Crowe Ransom described the antipathy "provoked in him by generic woman in the flesh, as well as by the literary remains of Emily Dickinson, Elizabeth Barrett, Christina Rosetti, and doubtless, if we only had enough of her, Sappho herself" (77). Cognizant of the ways contemporary male poets and critics used the category "Woman Writer" to marginalize, trivialize, and limit women's artistic creation, Bishop not only resisted "women's anthologies" as the literary equivalent of separate spheres. She also resisted and in some sense sought to detach herself from the historical category "Woman." "One gets so used, very young, to being 'put down' that if you have normal intelligence and have any sense of humor you very early develop a tough, ironic attitude" (Starbuck 22). In her writing, this "tough, ironic attitude" placed Bishop in the self-divided and self-contradictory position of simultaneously denying the categories Woman and Woman Writer even as she struggled to affirm her historical experience as a writing woman. Her refusal to be categorized and fixed by the critics as a "woman writer" is in fact at odds with Bishop's central concern with the historical experience of women and their relationships across race, class, and national bounds that marks all her work from the poems of *North & South* (1946) to *Geography III* (1976). "I've always considered myself a strong feminist," she said in the late seventies when a woman reporter for the *Chicago Tribune* sought to "play [her] off" against Adrienne Rich and Erica Jong as "old-fashioned" and unfeminist. "I finally asked her if she'd ever read any of my poems" (Spires 383).

Bishop's desire *not to be* identified and placed as a woman writer seems particularly contradictory, given the fact that her lifelong personal and literary friendship with Marianne Moore was, by Bishop's own admission, "possibly to influence the whole course of my life" (Bishop, *The Collected Prose* 122, hereafter referred to as *Collected Prose*). Moreover, while Bishop sought to avoid a specifically feminine identity as a writer, she was a lesbian who spent much of her adult life living in intimate companionship with other women. But these contradictions in the sexual and textual politics of Bishop's life and work are, I would argue, contradictions that are at the very center of the gender politics of literary modernism and postmodernism and of feminism itself. They are also contradictions that inform Bishop's lifelong, complex, and embattled relationship with Marianne Moore. This chapter examines the relationship between Elizabeth Bishop and Marianne Moore not so much as an instance of literary influence but as an instance of literary difference that reveals at once the complex interplay of gender, writing, and social struggle among twentieth-century writers and the very real difficulties women poets have experienced in seeking to possess each other as mothers, mentors, ancestors, and muses.

Gender and Modernism

In a 1977 interview with George Starbuck, Bishop was asked if as a young writer it seemed important to notice what other women poets were doing. "No," she responded emphatically; "I never made any distinction; I never make any distinction" (Starbuck 21). It was not Moore's gender but her practice of writing—her modernist craft—that initially drew Bishop to Moore's work, which she had read in the small experimental magazines of the time. "I hadn't known poetry could be like that; I took to it immediately" (*Collected Prose* 121). She met Moore through the college librarian, Fanny Borden, who had lent her a copy of Moore's *Observations* (1924) and arranged a meeting with Moore in 1934, when Bishop was a senior at Vassar. Although Moore's *Selected Poems* did not appear until the following year, by 1934, through her radically experimental verse and her work as editor of *The Dial* between 1926 and 1929, she had already acquired a high reputation among the writers and producers of literary modernism, including Ezra Pound, William Carlos Williams, Wallace Stevens, T. S. Eliot, and H. D. (Hilda Doolittle).

As a kind of empress of high modernism, Moore was herself a study in contradictions. Her technically dazzling poems were conjoined with a neo-Victorian, archly feminine public persona that verged on masquerade. Her seemingly ladylike timidity and modesty masked an ambition to invent herself as an American original. She found her precursors among men rather than women, among prose writers rather than poets. She considered the very name Walt Whitman unmentionable, and, unlike Amy Lowell, she had no desire to place herself in the literary tradition of Emily Dickinson.[1] In fact, she appears to have been troubled by the specter of self-absorption, dark "interiorization," and unhealth that had come to be associated with Dickinson's "secret" life. "In studying the letters one seems to feel an anxiety lifted," she wrote in a review of Mabel Loomis Todd's *Letters of Emily Dickinson* (1931), breathing an almost audible sigh of relief as she praised Todd's "reticence" in establishing "a seclusive, wholly non-notorious personality" and "the wholesomeness of the life" (*The Complete Prose of Marianne Moore* 290–91, hereafter referred to as *Complete Prose*).

Moore's determination to rescue Dickinson's "wholesomeness" and virtue from "the voracity of the wolfish" reveals something of her own complex status as *the* modernist woman poet male modernists chose to sponsor and admire (*Prose* 290). "Marianne was our saint—if we had one—in whom we all instinctively felt our purpose come together to form a stream. Everyone loved her," wrote William Carlos Williams in his *Autobiography* (146). But while male modernists praised Moore's craft, intellect, irony, and originality, they also appear to have been relieved that she did not assault them with her emotions, her sexuality, or her body. "Thank God, I think you can be trusted not to pour out flood (in the manner of dear Amy and poor Masters)," Ezra Pound wrote her in 1918 (Willis 1). After noting that Moore's poems were "too good . . . to be appreciated anywhere," T. S. Eliot concluded his review of *Poems* (1921) with what he called "one final, and 'magnificent' compliment": "Miss Moore's poetry is as 'feminine' as Christina Rosetti's, one never forgets that it is written by a woman; but with both one never thinks of this particularly as anything but a positive virtue" (597). Both sexually and aesthetically Moore could be counted on to observe a ladylike decorum—and her male critics were grateful.

For all the radicalism of her formal experiments, Moore, was, in effect, a modernist anomaly whose work represented an extension into the twentieth century—and into the very midst of the literary avant-garde—of what Ann Douglas calls "the feminization of American culture." Through the influence exerted on her life and art by her morally pious mother and her Presbyterian minister brother, Moore sought to enter the American marketplace armed with the traditionally feminine and Christ-like virtues of love, humility, self-abnegation, and piety. Like her nineteenth-century forbears, she sought to challenge and transform the traditionally masculine values of greed, aggression, and violence that had come to dominate American public culture with an essentially feminine ethos of love, domesticity, and nurturance.

Modernism Moore's way was fundamentally about the feminization of American culture. The ease with which Moore's notion of the "feminine" and the Christian elides with modernist aesthetics and an entire vision of the moral being of the universe is evident in her famous lines in "To a Snail":

> If "compression is the first grace of style,"
> you have it. Contractility is a virtue
> as modesty is a virtue.
> (*The Complete Poems of Marianne Moore* 85,
> hereafter referred to as *Complete Poems*)

These lines draw a moral equation between modernist virtue and feminine virtue in a putatively objective statement about the nature of things. In Moore's version of modernism, "compression" and economy as "the first grace of style" are an aesthetic correlate of feminine modesty and constraint. The impersonality of the artist figures a ladylike sense of humility and self-abnegation, and the modernist emphasis on the object rather than the overflow of powerful feelings embodies traditional notions of feminine virtue and reticence.

But while Moore fostered traditional notions of the feminine in her life and in her work, male modernists and recent feminist critics have in some sense been misled by her seemingly modest persona. "Being 'one of the boys,' in the case of Marianne Moore," says Suzanne Juhasz, "resulted in a concentration upon technical brilliance coupled with a marked exclusion of feminine experience from art" (*Naked and Fiery Forms* 35). What Juhasz appears to mean by "feminine experience" is the direct expression of the "self" through a "central and exposed" *I*—the kind of verse written by Emily Dickinson. However, if Moore set herself apart from the tradition of female lyricism represented in her time by Sara Teasdale, Edna St. Vincent Millay, and Elinor Wylie, as her poem "O To Be a Dragon" suggests, her seemingly "objective" persona masked a powerful moral will that became increasingly evident in the forties and fifties when the armored strategies and technical difficulties of her poems began to give way to direct statement.[2] "My wish," Moore wrote:

> O to be a dragon,
> a symbol of the power of Heaven—of silkworm

>   size or immense; at times invisible.
>   Felicitous phenomenon!
>   (*Complete Poems* 177)

As symbolic enactments of the "power of Heaven," Moore's poems represent
a contradictory embodiment of humility and strength—of what she called
"Humility, Concentration, and Gusto" (*Complete Prose* 426). On the one
hand, her endless proliferation of animals, objects, and other peoples' words
appears to be a shield that she constantly hides behind. On the other hand, the
seemingly "feminine" modesty of her style is a sign of her "at times invisible" and heavenly power. Locating her poetic authority in objects and texts
outside herself, she collects, catalogues, and recuperates all things, making
the entire world speak herself. Her personal point of view is ultimately objec-
tified and naturalized as fact, textuality, and spiritual truth.

    If Moore was, on some level, Eliot's "hyacinth girl," she was the "hya-
cinth girl" with a mind, a voice, and a moral mission. "But after all, what is
this enviable apparatus for? if not to change our mortal psycho-structure," she
said of poetry in a letter to Bishop that dismisses Yeats's writing as the work of
a eunuch with a "genius for word-sounds and sentences" (Bishop, *Collected
Prose* 146). From her critique of masculine presumption and the bounds of
patriarchy in "Marriage" (1923), to her vision, in "He Digesteth Harde Yron"
(1941), of a nurturant male bird who "watches his chicks with / a maternal
concentration" and defies man's vanity, greed, and violence through time, to
her representation of "humility" as the shield of Presbyter John in "His
Shield" (1951), Moore was herself "battle-dressed," engaged in a struggle to
transform men, modernism, and history itself along feminine and ultimately
Christ-like lines (*Complete Poems* 99).

As a kind of moral keeper at the gate of literary modernism, Moore not only
faulted her fellow modernists for their ego, moral failings, and lack of a larger
spiritual vision, she also vigorously sponsored the work of women writers
who appeared to embody transforming, but nevertheless proper, notions of the
feminine. Moore's literary friendship with Elizabeth Bishop was in fact part
of an entire network of relationships among women writers that Moore had
cultivated in her life. But it is important to keep in mind that this network did
not represent a natural or spontaneous meeting of female literary minds. For
one thing, it represented a specific historical response to the marginality of
women writers in the landscape of literary modernism. For another, it represented a highly exclusive and selective network of women writers that privileged the specifically feminine ethics and poetics that Moore admired. If
modernism was the scene of a "battle of the sexes," as Sandra Gilbert and

Susan Gubar argue (*No Man's Land* 1: 3–62), it was a battle not only between men and women; it was a battle that was also waged between and within women themselves.

In her reviews for *The Dial* and other small magazines in the twenties, Moore was just as exclusive and political as her male modernist counterparts were in selecting which women writers she would single out for attention and praise. Thus, she reviewed the work of H. D., Bryher, and Gertrude Stein, but not the work of Amy Lowell, Edna St. Vincent Millay, or Djuna Barnes. In a 1923 review of H. D.'s *Hymen* for *Broom,* Moore represents H. D. as a feminist modernist warrior who substitutes an essentially feminine ethics and poetics for the traditionally masculine values of aggression and violence. Noting the "martial" and "apparently masculine tone" of H. D.'s writing, Moore argues that she breaks down traditional categories of the "feminine": "preeminently in the case of H. D., we have the intellectual, social woman, non-public and 'feminine.' " What Moore finds in H. D. is a compelling instance of her own transforming vision of femininity as power wielded against the "brute force" of masculinity. In H. D.'s work, says Moore, the relationship between "weapons and beauty" is characterized by "the absence of subterfuge, cowardice and the ambition to dominate by brute force, we have heroics which do not confuse transcendence with domination and which in their indestructibleness, are the core of tranquility and of intellectual equilibrium" (*Complete Prose* 82).

A few years earlier Bryher and H. D. had arranged for the publication of Moore's *Poems* (1921) out of a similar sense that Moore's work was part of their common struggle for modernist and female artistic creation. H. D. and Moore had in fact been classmates at Bryn Mawr where, under the energetic leadership of M. Carey Thomas, they had learned some of the warrior-like sense of determination and commitment they would later bring to the cause of women and art (Fig. 5). When the *Egoist* first published Moore's poems in 1915, H. D. appears to have recognized—or at least wanted to recognize—a modernist woman warrior like herself: "I know, more or less, what you are up against, though I escaped some five years ago! . . . I felt so terribly when I was in U. S. A., the putty that met my whetted lance . . . You will forgive me? I am speaking to a you which I am more or less re-constructing from my own experience!" (Rosenbach Museum and Library, August 21, 1915:V:23:32; hereafter referred to as *R*).

Representing World War I as the scene of a kind of cultural struggle between the sexes, H. D. deploys a similar language of feminist and modernist militancy in a review of Moore's poems for *The Egoist* in 1916. Moore is the "perfect swordsman, the perfect technician" in the battle for art and beauty amid the destructiveness of war. "Her perfect craft" in the "direct presenta-

Figure 5. Photograph of Hilda Doolittle (third from left in back row) and Marianne Moore (second from right) at Bryn Mawr College, 1909, from the album of Mildred Pressinger von Kienbusch. "I know, more or less, what you are up against, though I escaped some five years ago," H. D. wrote Moore from England, when the *Egoist* first published Moore's poems in 1915. (Courtesy of Bryn Mawr College Library)

tion of beauty" is "destined to endure longer, far longer than the toppling sky-scrapers, and the world of shrapnel and machine-guns in which we live." If Pound, Eliot, and Williams did not recognize Moore's battle dress—not her "shield" but her "sword"—H. D. did. Moore's weapon was language, wrote H. D., "wielded playfully, ironically, with all the fine shades of thrust and counter-thrust"; she wrote "with absolute surety and with absolute disdain," as if to say, " 'my sword is very much keener than your sword, my hand surer than your hand—but you shall not know that I know you are beaten' " (118). These mutual reviews and exchanges suggest that Moore and H. D. saw themselves engaged in a common struggle on two fronts: their pens were swords wielded not only in the modernist battle against what H. D. calls the "squalor and commercialism" of the age but in a specifically female battle to save both art and civilization from the destructiveness of men. "At least, let us have courage!," H. D. wrote Moore privately in 1916—"Your satire is a breast-work of our age" (*R* April 15, 1916:V:23:32).

The Dynamics of Influence

Moore's relationship with Bishop was grounded in a similar ethics and poetics of the feminine and a similar politics of exclusion practiced in relation to other women writers who did not qualify. When Bishop first met Moore, she was conscious of having been preceded by a number of other young women writers who "hadn't passed muster." "Miss Borden had sent several Vassar girls to meet Miss Moore and sometimes her mother as well, and every one had somehow failed to please" (Bishop, *Collected Prose* 123). To gain Moore's affection and the benefits of her literary mentorship, Bishop, who had always been temperamentally shy and insecure, had to defer to Moore's moral will and literary authority. As the relationship progressed, Moore became increasingly eager to conscript Bishop as one of her own feminine soldiers.

Their first meeting took place outside the Reading Room at the New York Public Library, where, if someone "failed to please," Moore could make a quick getaway. A few weeks later Bishop wrote to Moore inviting her to the Ringling Brothers circus. The letter, which was postmarked March 19, 1934, was the first in what was to be a lifelong correspondence between the two women poets; it was also the first of a number of invitations that Bishop regularly sent to Moore as she moved, paradoxically, farther and farther away from her. At the circus, Bishop was officially initiated into Moore's seemingly magical and otherworldly company when she was asked to assist in the operation of diverting a mother elephant with bread crumbs while Moore clipped a hair from a baby elephant for her elephant hair bracelet (Bishop, *Collected Prose* 126). Even in these first encounters, however, Moore's potentially controlling will is evident: it is Moore who lays down the "conditions" of their meetings as Bishop willingly gives herself up to the mannered and slightly offbeat rituals of Moore's world.[3]

The relationship between Elizabeth Bishop and Marianne Moore is usually celebrated as an empowering personal and literary friendship between what Bonnie Costello calls two "kindred spirits." "Not the oedipal verb 'struggle' which dominates our Bloomian notion of literary influence, but the centrally female verb 'nurture' characterizes their relationship," says Costello ("Marianne Moore and Elizabeth Bishop" 131). Placing a similar emphasis on female nurturance, David Kalstone finds that Moore provided a "sustaining maternal world" that "nourished Bishop's writing life" (*Becoming a Poet* 5).[4] This emphasis on nurturance in the relationship between Moore and Bishop not only assumes that nurture is a "centrally female verb," and thus something all women naturally do. It also suggests that a mother/daughter relationship between two women writers will somehow be more free from struggle than the Bloomian relationship between fathers and sons. What the relationship between Moore and Bishop in fact suggests is that the bond between them, particularly in its early mother/daughter configuration, had its potential dangers as well as its benefits to both writers. While the mother/daughter configuration initially strengthened the bond between them, it was also the site of their most intense struggle, and it eventually drove them apart.

The mother/daughter inflection of the Moore/Bishop relationship was intensified by the fact that Bishop was herself an orphan. Her father died when she was eight months old, and her mother, who was hospitalized for mental illness throughout Bishop's childhood, died in 1934, the same year that Bishop made contact with Moore for the first time. Raised by grandparents in Nova Scotia and later by an aunt in Boston, Bishop early experienced the sense of exile and dispossession that was to figure centrally in her life and writing. "My relationship with my relatives—I was always a sort of guest, and I think I've always felt like that," she said (Spires 379). In "At the Fishhouses," Bishop's experience of herself as an exile from home, family, and traditional notions of maternal nurturance is transfigured into "what we imagine knowledge to be":

> dark, salt, clear, moving, utterly free,
> drawn from the cold hard mouth
> of the world, derived from the rocky breasts
> forever, flowing and drawn, and since
> our knowledge is historical, flowing, and flown.
> (Bishop, *The Complete Poems. 1927–1979* 66,
>   hereafter referred to as *Complete Poems*)

The experience of separation and exile—signified by the maternally suggestive but nonnurturant figure of the "rocky breasts / forever, flowing and drawn"—becomes the base of an entire metaphysics, an entire way of being and seeing in a world that has no stable center, saving order, or forever-nurturant mother. This epistemological vision of separation and radical otherness also becomes bound up with Bishop's sense of marginality as a woman, a poet, a lesbian, and later as a foreigner—a middle-class white woman—who lived for many years in Brazil.

Bishop's needs as a literal and spiritual orphan played an important role in the early configuration of her relationship with Marianne Moore. Moore, who had spent her entire life living with and caring for her mother, came to represent the old-fashioned values of family, home, and domesticity that Bishop had lost. In fact, to Bishop, Moore and her mother seemed like ancestral beings unmarked by the messiness of twentieth-century history. "The atmosphere of 260 Cumberland Street was of course 'old-fashioned,' " Bishop wrote, "but even more, otherworldly—as if one were living in a diving bell from a different world, let down through the crass atmosphere of the twentieth century." When Bishop left this "diving bell," she was continually jolted by the stark contrast between the "exquisitely prolonged etiquette" of the Moore household and the "row of indifferent faces" she encountered on her ride back to Manhattan on the subway. And yet, Bishop said, "I never left Cumberland Street, without feeling happier: uplifted, even inspired, determined to be good, to work harder, not to worry about what other people thought, never to try to publish anything until I thought I'd done my best with it, no matter how many years it took—or never publish at all" (*Collected Prose* 137).

Bishop's description of the Moore household effectively suggests the personal, moral, and literary qualities that initially drew her to Moore; the high standards Moore set for writing and publication; and the empowering role she played as both mentor and model of the successful literary career. Moore's morally and aesthetically ordered world provided a temporary escape from Bishop's own grim perception of twentieth-century history, an escape that uplifts and inspires her to pursue her poetic work without regard to the opinions of others. But, just as Moore's relationship with her own mother was both empowering and inhibiting, so Bishop's words suggest the ways Moore may have encouraged her sense of personal inadequacy and inhibition as a poet.[5] If she could not attain the rigorous moral and artistic standards demanded by Moore and her mother—if she could not "be good"—Bishop might, indeed, "never publish at all." Although Moore did not finally silence Bishop, their correspondence suggests that Moore's insistence on the values of modesty, reticence, manners, and a particular construction of the feminine may have kept Bishop from the personal and historical subject matter that became a major source of her inspiration and reputation as Bishop began to move away from Moore both physically and artistically in the forties and the fifties.

In playing a kind of dutiful daughter role in the early stages of her relationship with Moore, Bishop had to suppress and silence important dimensions of her historical experience and areas of potential contest between them. Like the poems that Bishop wrote under Moore's most direct influence, their letters are polite, formal, and reticent, both personally and emotionally.

Bishop's visits to Moore are characterized by a similar reticence. Under the moral gaze of Moore and her mother, Bishop felt compelled to police her behavior. Thus, although Moore provided cigarettes and alcohol, Bishop always felt uneasy either smoking or drinking on her visits: "I tried to smoke no more than one or two cigarettes a visit, or none at all. I felt that Mrs. Moore disapproved" (*Collected Prose* 128).

In her memoir of Marianne Moore, Bishop also notes that on one occasion Moore expressed anxiety about the religious "fate" of a male friend whose sexual preference for men "had always seemed quite obvious" to Bishop: " 'What are we going to do about X . . . ? Why, sometimes I think he may even be in the clutches of a *sodomite!*' " "One could almost smell the brimstone," Bishop said, in words that clearly mark the fundamental difference between Moore as a religiously devout and sexually chaste Presbyterian and Bishop as a politically radical—and lesbian—"Unbeliever" (*Collected Prose* 130). The fact that Bishop remembered this particular incident with its accompanying moral weight of brimstone and damnation suggests the early and potentially repressive role Moore played in encouraging her to mask and mute, particularly in her writing, her own wicked and *sodomite* desire as a woman who sexually loved other women.

Bishop and Moore met during the Depression, when as Bishop recalled "a great many people were communist, or would-be communist," the "atmosphere at Vassar was left-wing," and it was becoming increasingly fashionable among poets to write with political consciousness (Starbuck 20; Ashley Brown 8). Bishop was herself a socialist—and at one time an anarchist—a political position that set her in diametrical opposition to Moore, who was and would remain a political conservative and stalwart supporter of the Republican Party even during the worst years of the Depression. "America is pestered at present by a man named Franklin D. Roosevelt, as Germany has been with Hitler, but I think Mr. Hoover will 'win,' as our neo-Hitler would put it," she wrote Bryher before the election in 1932 (*R,* October 3, 1932:V:8:6).

When Bishop was asked which poets she had to come to terms with in the generation that preceded her, it was W. H. Auden rather than Marianne Moore who came immediately to her mind: "I don't think I ever thought of it that way, but perhaps that was Auden. All through my college years, Auden was publishing his early books, and I and my friends, a few of us, were very much interested in him. His first books made a tremendous impression on me" (Starbuck 18). What Bishop admired in particular was Auden's ability to write politically knowledgeable poetry with "dazzling" technical skill; she also admired his "sexual courage," at a time when, as she herself knew, it was far more difficult to "come out" as a homosexual writer: "His then leftist politics, his ominous landscape, his intimations of betrayed loves, war on its way, disasters and death, matched exactly the mood of our late-depression and post-depression youth. We admired his apparent toughness, his sexual courage—actually more honest than Ginsberg's, say, is now, while still giving expression to technically dazzling poetry" (Schwartz and Estess 308).

But while Bishop admired Auden as "someone who *knew*" and made her "feel tough, ready, and in the know, too," she also noted, in words that reveal her own desire for distinction: "I think I tried not to write like him then, because everybody did" (Schwartz and Estess 308; Starbuck 19). Despite her radical politics, she was uneasy with what she called " 'social conscious' writing," particularly of the more propagandistic and doctrinaire sort. "I was always opposed to political thinking as such for writers," she said in a 1966 interview with Ashley Brown. "I stood up for T. S. Eliot when everybody was talking about James T. Farrell" (Ashley Brown 8).

Bishop's turn toward Moore in 1934 was part of her attempt not to write like Auden, not to write politically, and, albeit paradoxically, not to write like a woman. Moore's poems in *Observations*—particularly "Marriage," "The Octopus," and "Peter"—struck her as "miracles of language and construction. Why had no one ever written about things in this clear and dazzling way before?" (Bishop, *Collected Prose* 123). Seemingly objective and nonpolitical, Moore represented precisely those values of craft and imagination, word magic and wit, irony and understatement that Bishop admired in other modernist writers, including T. S. Eliot, Wallace Stevens, and Jules Laforgue. For a time, at least, she appeared to believe in new critical fashion that her technical practice as a poet could be separated from her personal and historical experience as a woman, a lesbian, and a leftist. In the course of her relationship with Moore, this uneasy division between poetry and politics, craft and sexuality, form and history would become harder and harder to maintain until finally the pressure of Bishop's personal and political difference from Moore would trigger an artistic break and transformation in her life and work.

When Bishop first met Moore in 1934 she was extraordinarily shy and extraordinarily lacking in self-confidence. Although she was already a skilled poetic technician who had published several poems in high school and college magazines, she was hampered by the sense that she lacked the (male) experience, knowledge, and ego necessary for serious poetry. Like other women poets seeking to enter a predominantly male literary tradition, Bishop was torn between her sense of personal insignificance and modesty as a woman and the power and ego she associated with the role of poet. As a student at Vassar, she was "embarrassed" to admit that she had published poetry in a national magazine. "I'd just hold my tongue," she confessed in a 1978 interview. "I was embarrassed by it. And still am. There's nothing more embarrassing than being a poet, really. . . . No matter how modest you think you feel or how minor you think you are, there must be an awful core of ego somewhere for you to set yourself up to write poetry. I've never *felt* it, but it must be there" (Spires 383). Bishop never lost this feeling of embarrassment. At a crucial stage in her poetic career, however, the example of Moore's work suggested a subject matter that she might use in seeking to avoid any overt self-representation as a woman. Bishop wrote to Moore:

> [W]hen I began to read your poetry at college, I think it immediately opened up my eyes to the possibility of the subject-matter that I could use and might never have thought of using if it hadn't been for you.—(I might not have written any poems at all, I suppose.) I think my approach is so much vaguer and less-defined and certainly more old-fashioned—sometimes I'm amazed at people's comparing me to you when all I'm doing is some kind of blank-verse—can't they *see* how different it is? But they can't, apparently.
>
> (*R,* October 24, 1954:V:5:4)

By revealing the possibility of the natural world as a poetic subject, Moore gave Bishop some of the confidence she needed to draw on her own powers of observation and description in making the ordinary and the immediate the subject of her poems. Bishop would never cease to acknowledge this sense of primal indebtedness to Moore: "I have always been observant, I think—at least they tell me so—, but I might not have put this gift to use as much if it hadn't been for Marianne," she wrote to Lynn Keller shortly before her death in 1979 (Keller 408). However, as their relationship developed, Bishop's desire to honor Moore's originary influence ("I might not have written any poems at all," "I might not have put this gift to use as much") came into conflict with her increasing desire for poetic distinction ("Can't they *see* how different it is?").

It was Moore, too, who introduced Bishop to the American reading public when in 1935 several of her poems—"The Reprimand," "Three Valentines," and "The Map"—were published in an anthology entitled *Trial Balances.* The volume is interesting because it represents Bishop's first appearance in book form among several other pairings of younger and more established poets, including Louise Bogan and Theodore Roethke, Stephen Vincent Benet and Muriel Rukeyser. It also suggests the ways Moore, even at this early date, undertook to manage and control Bishop's writing career. There is, indeed, a certain strain in Moore's commentary as she seeks simultaneously to introduce, to instruct, to correct, and in some sense to produce Bishop as a decorously feminine poet. "Some feminine poets of the present day seem to have grown horns and to like to be frightful and dainty by turns," Moore says, as she underscores Bishop's more ladylike inscription of the values of humility, deference, and propriety. "We look at imitation askance," she says, noting

Bishop's debt to John Donne and Gerard Manley Hopkins, "but like the shell which the hermit-crab selects for itself, it has value—the avowed humility, and the protection." And yet, even as Moore seeks to construct Bishop as a properly "feminine" and reticent version of herself, she is also troubled by a certain excess and lack of "vigilance" in Bishop's use of language. "Miss Bishop's sparrows (*Valentine I*) are not revolting, merely disaffecting," Moore wrote, apparently disapproving of Bishop's use of the word *lust* to rhyme with *dust* ("Archaically New" 82–83).[6]

The title *Trial Balances* is itself an apt one for the first public appearance of Bishop and Moore together as a kind of literary pair, for it suggests the lifelong "trial" of their relationship as they both struggled to maintain a balance between affection and autonomy, influence and possession. The strain that marks Moore's first public commentary on Bishop—between Moore's desire for control and Bishop's potential excess, between Bishop's difference and Moore's desire to contain her within conventional definitions of the feminine—is a strain that would intensify in the late thirties as the balance in their relationship began to shift from instruction to intervention, from mentorship to proprietorship. In 1936, certain that she had failed in her trial period as a poet, Bishop was considering dropping poetry to study medicine: "I cannot, cannot decide what to do," she wrote to Moore. "I am even considering studying medicine or bio-chemistry, and have procured all sorts of catalogues, etc. I feel that I have given myself more than a fair trial, and the accomplishment has been nothing at all" (*R*, August 21, 1936:V:4:30). Moore responded immediately, assuring Bishop of her unique poetic ability:

> What you say about studying medicine does not disturb me at all; for interesting as medicine is, I feel you would not be able to give up writing, with the ability for it that you have; but it does disturb me that you should have the *feeling* that it might be well to give it up. To have produced what you have—either verse or prose is enviable, and you certainly could not suppose that such method as goes with a precise and proportioning ear, is "contemporary" or usual.
>
> (Vassar College Library, August 28, 1936:10:128;
> hereafter referred to as *V*)

Moore offered more than encouraging words; she also began to take charge of Bishop's work. Between 1936 and 1940, she revised, edited, commented on, and sometimes even typed final drafts of the work that Bishop sent to her.

In the first years of their literary friendship, Bishop was deferrent, gracious, earnest, and frequently self-effacing in response to Moore's advice and encouragement. She was also conscious of the mother/daughter dimensions of their relationship. "[Y]ou have a very generous and protective apron and I am not sure how much of it I should seize upon," she wrote to Moore in 1937, in words that register the reserve and caution that would continue to mark

Bishop's relationship with Moore. In 1940 she wrote: "I have several poems almost completed as well—I am wondering about *The Southern Review*. But I should like to show them to you first, unless you are beginning to feel like a *baby-walker*. . . . I'm afraid I take up so much of your time" (*R,* March 6, 1937:V:4:31; March 14, 1940:V:5:2).

In an article entitled "What Do Women (Poets) Want? H. D. and Marianne Moore as Poetic Ancestresses," Alicia Ostriker asks what women poets want in "poetic ancestresses": "My belief is that we want strong mothers," she responds, arguing that in the relationship among women poets the model of oedipal struggle is replaced by the myth of Demeter and Kore, "only it is the daughter who descends to Hades, groping in the dark, to retrieve and revive her mother" (479). Within this model, Ostriker sees Moore and H. D. as "key ancestresses for the woman poet . . . not least because they were poets who were able to accept the mothering of other women and despite their differences, to mother each other" (479). In seeking Moore out at the beginning of her poetic career and in the same year that her own mother died, Bishop made contact not with the ghost of a poetic mother, as does Amy Lowell in "The Sisters" or Adrienne Rich in "The Spirit of Place," but with a flesh-and-blood figure of female power whose personal support and exacting critical standards would have a profound influence on her personal and poetic development. What the relationship between them suggests, however, is that strong mothers can be empowering as well as dangerous; if they can nourish, they can also inhibit, silence, and kill.

While Moore had, as Bishop said, shown her the "possibility of a subject-matter" she might use in pursuing her career as a poet, Moore's emphasis on the values of craft, observation, description, and personal reticence had also turned Bishop away from the personal and historical subject that she regarded as distinctively her own. In a notebook dated 1934–1937—the very years of the most intense correspondence between Bishop and Moore—Bishop mused on the possibilities of herself, her past, and her "family monuments" as literary subjects:

> A set of apparently disconnected, unchronological incidents out of the past have been re-appearing. I suppose there must be some string running them altogether, some spring watering them all. Some things will never disappear, but rather clear up, send out roots, as time goes on. They are my family monuments, sinking a little more into the earth year by year, boring slightly, but becoming only more firm, and inscribed with meanings gradually legible, like letters written in "Magic Ink" (only 5 metaphors)
> (*V,* Notebook 1934–1935–1936–1937)

It would take Bishop many years and many moves away from Moore's sphere of influence before she would return to these "family monuments"—the rupture, pain, and loss that marked her personal past, the "tears" that filled her grandmother's house in Nova Scotia, the "scream" of her crazed mother that hung "in the past, in the present, and those years in between"—as the "Magic" letter and most potent subject of her own work.

In the early stages of her relationship with Bishop, Moore seemed conscious of the potentially negative and inhibiting influence she might have on Bishop's development, and sought to exercise caution in offering advice. Responding to several poems that Bishop sent to her immediately following her crisis of poetic faith, Moore observed:

> The poems are so fine, and dart-proof in every way,—especially THE WEED and PARIS 7 A.M.—that they shiver my impulsive offers of helpfulness. This exteriorizing of the interior, and the aliveness all through, it seems to me are the essential sincerity that unsatisfactory surrealism struggles toward. Yet the sobriety and weight and impact of the past are also here. The great amount of care, the reach of imagination, and the pleasure conveyed, make it hard for me not to say a great deal; but I fear to make suggestions lest I hamper you.
>
> (*V*, September 20, 1936:10:128)

By emphasizing the particular strengths of Bishop's poems and seeking to steer her in the direction of what she considered her greatest power—"this exteriorizing of the interior, and the aliveness all through"—Moore helped Bishop define and place herself amid the conflicting impulses of literary modernism.

But because Bishop's work never quite fit within the ethical-aesthetic bounds of modernism Moore's way, Moore also encouraged Bishop's feeling of inadequacy as a writer. By Moore's standards, Bishop's work lacked ultimate significance and value. "You are menaced by the goodness of your mechanics," she wrote to Bishop in 1937. "One should, of course, have the feeling—this is ingeniously contrived—but a thing should make one feel after reading it, that one's life has been altered or added to. . . . I wish to say, above all, that I am sure good treatment is a handicap unless along with it, significant values come out with an essential baldness" (*V*, March 7, 1937:10:129). Moore was particularly concerned about the lack of any underlying set of moral or religious values in Bishop's life and work: "I can't help wishing you would sometime in some way, risk some unprotected profundity of experience; or since noone admits profundity of experience, some characteristic private defiance of the significantly detestable. . . . I feel a responsibility against anything that might threaten you; yet fear to admit such anxiety, lest I influence you away from an essential necessity or particular strength. The golden eggs can't be dealt with theoretically, by presumptious mass salvation formulae. But I do feel that *tentativeness and interiorizing are your danger as well as your strength*" (*R*, May 1, 1938:V:5:1; emphasis added).

The doubleness of Moore's response to Bishop and its potentially damaging effects on her poetic development are particularly evident in this exchange. Moore recognizes that Bishop's uncertainty and subjectivity are a source of her danger and her power. She also recognizes that Bishop's refusal to assert and moralize represents a major difference from herself: "The wrought excellence and infectious continuity of your thinkings—the abashingly as I said above—formidable demureness, disgust me with my own bald performances" (*R*, May 1, 1938:V:5:1). But while Moore acknowledges Bishop's difference as a poet, she cannot resist the urge to correct and judge her, and to find her lacking in relation to her own moral, religious, and aesthetic codes. Rather than build Bishop's confidence in a tentative, interiorizing, and ultimately postmodern subject, who refuses to subscribe to any grand and saving master narrative, Moore undermines her poetic authority and the power of her refusal by suggesting that her poems are "ingeniously contrived" registers of pure feminine sensibility and ultimately lacking in profundity, significance, and value. Bishop's poems are in fact so "potent" in their "retiringness" and so "formidable" in their "demureness" that they make the "undermining modesty" of Moore's own poems look like "bald performances."

For all Moore's "anxiety" not to "influence" Bishop away from the particular sources of her power, as a strong, powerful, and original poetic mother, she ended by enforcing Bishop's sense of inadequacy and belatedness as a poet. This sense of belatedness in relation to Moore and in relation to a world of pure textuality in which there appears to be nothing new or true to say is the subject of "The Sea & Its Shore" (1937), one of the stories Bishop sent to Moore. In this story, Edward Boomer is assigned the task of clearing the "public beaches" of other people's words. "The more papers he picked up and the more he read, the less he felt he understood. In a sense he depended on 'their imagination,' and was even its slave, but at the same time he thought of it as a kind of disease" (Bishop, *Collected Prose* 178–79). The story registers a postmodern sense of exhaustion, not only about the possibilities of the "literary life" but also about the possibility of meaning and knowledge in a world that "came before many years to seem printed, too" (*Collected Prose* 178). In a world that already bears the signature of others, Bishop appears to fear that as an artist, she, like Boomer (which suggests Bishop's maternal family name, Bulmer), can be no more than a reader, an endless consumer of the words of others rather than an originator of her own texts.

Not coincidentally, this story about the problem of belatedness appears to bear the mark of Moore's influence. After sending the story to Moore, Bishop wrote her:

> This morning I have been working on THE SEA & ITS SHORE—or rather, making use of your and your mother's work—and I am suddenly afraid that at

the end I have stolen something from THE FRIGATE PELICAN. I say: "Large flakes of blackened paper, still sparkling red at the edges, flew into the sky. While his eyes could follow them, he had never seen such clever, quivering manoeuvres." *It was not until I began seeing pelicans that my true source ocurred* [*sic*] *to me.* I know you speak of the flight like "charred paper", and use the word manoeuvres. I am afraid it is almost criminal. I haven't the book here and I wonder if you will tell me just how guilty I am and forgive what was really unconscious.

(*R*, January 5, 1937:V:4:31; emphasis added)

Bishop's words suggest her increasing anxiety about the ways her work was beginning to interface with the work of Moore and her mother. But they also suggest something potentially more terrifying to Bishop: that Moore's original description of pelicans in "The Frigate Pelican" has entered into and shaped her perception of pelicans *before* she has actually seen them herself: "It was not until I began seeing pelicans that my true source ocurred to me." This anxiety about her "unconscious" borrowings from Moore's work and about a universe that, in effect, has already been written upon and signed by Moore would continue to haunt Bishop even as she sought to move farther away from her in her own life and work.[7]

In "In Prison" (1938), Bishop seeks to work through this problem of belatedness and knowledge in a world in which, in the words of Paul Valéry's M. Teste, "our thoughts are reflected back to us, too much so, through expressions made by others" (*Collected Prose* 188). Through a Poesque narrator, she plots a fantasy of self-imprisonment in a cell of "whitewashed" walls which will enable her to "place" herself in a world with no exit, to establish her "point of view," and "fully to realize" her "faculties" by defining herself in relation to "one very dull book" (186–87). But while this fantasy of removal and isolation from the world registers Bishop's acceptance of her "place" within and among what she calls the "inscriptions already there," it also registers her desire for distinction, originality, and difference. Interpreting her one dull book, "not at all according to its intent," she says, "I shall be able to form my own examples of surrealist art!—something I should never know how to do outside, where the sources are so bewildering" (188). She will read the "Writing on the Wall" of the prison "very carefully." "Then," she says, "I shall adapt my own compositions, in order that they may not conflict with those written by the prisoner before me. The voice of a new inmate will be noticeable, but there will be no contradictions or criticisms of what has already been laid down, rather a 'commentary' " (188). Looking "just a little different" in her uniform "from the rest of the prisoners," she will "be unconventional, rebellious perhaps, but in shades and shadows" (189).

This fantasy of rebellion "in shades and shadows" enacts Bishop's own desire to "place" and differentiate herself in a world of potentially "bewildering" texts already signed by others. It also registers her desire to leave her mark—her "legacy of thoughts"—to "become an *influence*." Through "my carefully subdued, reserved manner," the narrator says, in words that suggest a more self-conscious and demonic dimension of her relationship with Marianne Moore, "I shall attract to myself one intimate friend whom I shall influence deeply. This friend, already an important member of the prison society, will be of great assistance to me in establishing myself as an authority, recognized but unofficial, on the conduct of prison life. It will take years before I become an *influence*, and possibly—this is what I dare to hope for, to find the prison in such a period of its evolution that it will be unavoidable to be thought of as an *evil influence*" (*Collected Prose* 190).

Although the precise nature of this "evil influence" is unclear, Bishop's fantasy of satanic power suggests an early and surprising self-consciousness about what was at stake, not only in her parable of the world as prison with no "outside" but also in her relationship to Moore, modernism, American national ideology, and an entire Western philosophical tradition grounded in the notion of a rational and stable self living in a correspondingly ordered universe of plan, design, and ultimate value. Beneath the flat surfaces and "carefully subdued, reserved manner" of her work, Bishop was, in effect, undoing the traditional dualisms of good and evil, subject and object, masculine and feminine, inside and outside, and any transcendent notion of absolute design and value—political, religious, aesthetic, or otherwise. In the words of the seemingly mad narrator of "In Prison": "One must be *in;* that is the primary condition" (*Collected Prose* 182).

If Bishop's tale of belatedness in "The Sea & Its Shore" became an occasion for uneasiness about her own "guilty" borrowings from Moore, her tale of aspiration for "place," difference, and the exertion of "evil influence" in "In Prison" became the scene of a struggle and a reversal in Bishop's relationship with Moore as her rebellion in "shades and shadows" became more open. "You should let me see all you do," Moore wrote to Bishop in 1937 (*R*, February 9, 1937:V:04:31), and for the remainder of the year, Bishop continued to send her work to Moore. But when Bishop finished "In Prison" in January 1938, she bypassed Moore, and sent it directly to the *Partisan Review*, where she also submitted it to a contest for a 100-dollar prize. Perhaps Bishop sensed that this story of "evil influence" would not please Moore; perhaps, she did not want her story of wickedness and rebellion in "shades and shadows" to be written over by Moore and her mother; and perhaps, too, she was embarrassed by the story's not so covert references to her relationship with Moore.

Moore was not pleased with Bishop's act of rebellion. "It was very independent of you to submit your prize story without letting me see it," she wrote Bishop in February 1938. "If it is returned with a printed slip, that will be why" (*R*, February 10, 1938:V:5:1). Moore's commanding and imperious tone suggests some of the difficulty she was having letting go as Bishop began to assert her independence. "In Prison" was in fact accepted and published in the March issue of the *Partisan Review*—without the benefits of Moore's mediation. And, perhaps not surprisingly, it was precisely this story that provoked her anxiety about the "danger" of Bishop's "tentativeness and interiorizing." "Never have I . . . seen a more insidiously innocent and artless artifice of innuendo than in your prison meditations," she wrote, complimenting Bishop on her technical skill, but urging her to read Dr. Niebuhr on Christianity and to adopt a "more comprehensive, more lastingly deep and dependable" view of things (*R*, May 1, 1938:V:5:1).

"Can't They *See* How Different It Is?"

In 1939 Bishop, like the narrator of "In Prison," made her own move toward seclusion and isolation when she bought a house and settled in Key West, Florida, with her classmate from Vassar, Louise Crane. The move represented at once a move away from the literary scene in the United States (which she always found pretentious) and an attempt to distance herself both physically and artistically from Moore's sphere of influence. Although Bishop's emphasis on the strategies of description and observation continued, her center of vision shifted from a Moore-like focus on objects to the social world and the intimate but also strained and distanced relations among races and classes—blacks, whites, and hispanics, servants and masters—that are the subject of such Key West poems as "Jerónimo's House" and "Cootchie." But while Bishop began to move toward what she called the "more earnest" subject matter she found in the social landscape of Florida, even in Key West she continued to be pursued by Moore's signature and her potentially overwhelming power of description and observation: "I don't know how, without seeing Key West, you managed to do it, but what you said about its being a 'kind of ten commandments in vegetable dye power color-printing' is the best description yet," Bishop wrote her in February 1940. "I find it alternately inspirational and depressing—to think that I should come so far and try so hard and achieve nothing but approximations, while you stay at home and hit the Key West lighthouse right on the head" (*R*, February 19, 1940:V:5:2).

"I am sometimes appalled to think how much I may have unconsciously stolen from her," Bishop wrote in her memoir of Marianne Moore. "Perhaps we are all magpies" (*Collected Prose* 141). But for all Bishop's sense of indebtedness, belatedness, and inadequacy in relationship to Moore, she might well say of her work, "Can't they *see* how different it is," for even in the poems written under Moore's direct "influence," the differences between them are apparent. Whereas Moore's use of syllabic verse, hidden rhymes, and intricate stanza design is experimental, Bishop is more conventional— more "old-fashioned" as she said—in her use of rhyme, meter, and poetic structure, and she makes frequent use of traditional forms such as the ballad, sonnet, villanelle, sestina, and nursery rhyme. But if Bishop's use of form is "old-fashioned," her vision is fundamentally postmodern. Whereas Moore uses aesthetic form to figure a higher moral and spiritual order, Bishop uses traditional form expressively to set off and simultaneously control the scenes of desolation, unbelief, and exhaustion that are the subject of her poems.

Moore's poems state, affirm, moralize, and assume all things as part of a spiritual scheme. Bishop's poems question, challenge, doubt, and destabilize in ways that undermine the modernist and humanist faith in the coherence of self and world and the very possibility of meaning, value, and the imagination itself. In Bishop's poems the sordid facts of modern existence remain unrecuperated and unredeemed. If Moore envisions the city and technology as signs of human creativity and progress through time, Bishop's poems resist any easy faith in the advance of humanity or civilization. Whereas Moore's "New York" celebrates the city as the site of "accessibility to experience," in "From the Country to the City," Bishop's harlequin utters the word "Subside." Moore is, in effect, a patriot and a prophet in the tradition of what Sacvan Bercovitch describes as the American Jeremiad, (re)calling Americans to their national, moral, and spiritual destiny. Bishop is an American alien, who ultimately leaves the land, refusing allegiance to all master narratives— national, ideological, religious, or metaphysical.

Although Bishop's early poems speak with Moore-like reticence and restraint, unlike Moore, who emphasized reticence as a form of aesthetic and feminine virtue, Bishop experienced her temperamental shyness and reticence as gender limitations—and social constructs—she would have to struggle against as she moved toward the assertion of a historically specific, gendered, and lesbian "I." Whereas Moore masks herself behind and within objects, Bishop places herself as a traveler at the perceptual center of her poems. If the "I" of Bishop's early poems seems genderless and lacking in historical specificity, the splitting that marks such poems as "The Weed" and "The Gentleman of Shalott" may, as Adrienne Rich suggests, register some of the self-division and pain she experienced as a "lesbian writing under the false universal of heterosexuality" (*Blood, Bread, and Poetry* 127). Unlike Moore who believed in an essential—and essentially nurturant—female identity that could transform the world and traditional masculine orders of dominance and submission, Bishop was personally and erotically drawn to other women, but she never translated her sexual preference into any saving narrative of feminine or feminist transformation. As in "Cootchie" and "Songs for a Colored Singer," women are from the first at the center of her poems, but they are complicit in the systems that oppress them, and their relationships are sites of struggle as well as affection across race, class, and gender lines.

The differences between Moore and Bishop are particularly evident when they focus on the same physical object, as in their respective poems on "The Fish." As Moore herself once said, "Her FISH and my FISH have in common, an interesting verisimilitude but are by no means 'a pair' " (*V*, June 21, 1959:11:148). Moore's poem lifts the fish to the level of the imagination, creating an imaginary order with real fish in it. The title, like the fish themselves, is incorporated into a poetic (re)ordering of the physical world:

The Fish

wade
through black jade.
    Of the crow-blue mussel-shells, one keeps
    adjusting the ash-heaps;
        opening and shutting itself like

an
injured fan.
    The barnacles which encrust the side
    of the wave, cannot hide
        there for the submerged shafts of the
            (*Complete Poems* 30)

Through a self-consciously literary patterning of rhyme, syllable, line, and stanza unit, Moore fractures the normal orders of language and typography, calling attention to the aesthetic order through which the fish wade. For all the apparent motion of the undersea world, this world is ultimately fixed and aestheticized as an emblem of meaning, design, and absolute value.

Whereas Moore's poem incorporates the fish into an aesthetic and ultimately ethical ordering of the natural world, Bishop's poem takes place at the point of contact between subject and object, self and world. Moore does not speak as a personal "I" in the poem; her focus is on the object rather than the subject of perception. Bishop is at the perceptual center of her poem; her evocation of the fish is framed by her perceiving "I":

I caught a tremendous fish
and held him beside the boat
half out of water, with my hook
fast in a corner of his mouth.
        (*Complete Poems* 42)

Unable to separate her experience of the fish from the fish itself, Bishop is more tentative and less self-consciously literary in her presentation. Moore's poem is emblematic and moves toward "objective" statement:

> All
> external
> > marks of abuse are present on this
> > defiant edifice—
> > > all the physical features of
> >
> ac-
> cident—lack
> > of cornice, dynamite grooves, burns and
> > hatchet strokes, these things stand
> > > out on it; the chasm side is
> >
> dead.
> Repeated
> > evidence has proved that it can live
> > on what can not revive
> > > its youth. The sea grows old in it.
> > > > (*Complete Poems* 32–33)

Bishop's poem is symbolistic and moves toward subjective vision:

> I stared and stared
> and victory filled up
> the little rented boat,
> from the pool of bilge
> where oil had spread a rainbow
> around the rusted engine
> to the bailer rusted orange,
> the sun-cracked thwarts,
> the oarlocks on their strings,
> the gunnels—until everything
> was rainbow, rainbow, rainbow!
> and I let the fish go.
> > (*Complete Poems* 43–44)

Whereas Moore's "Fish" emphasizes the product and meaning of observation, Bishop's "Fish" foregrounds the process of observation and the essential gap between subject, representation, and world. Moore appropriates the fish into an imaginative order that gives rise to ethical insight; Bishop begins with an act of appropriation—"I caught a tremendous fish"—but ends by returning the fish to the experiential flux from which the fish, her "vision," and the poem arise. The ultimate focus of Moore's poem is aesthetic and moral, revealing a natural providential order of permanence and value. The focus of

Bishop's poem is epistemological and visionary, suggesting temporality, transcience, and the subjectivity of value. If Moore's poem is "about" the values of adaptability, endurance, and natural heroism, Bishop's poem is "about" the experience of living in an alien, mutable, and ultimately mystifying world. Like her vision of Darwin—"his eyes fixed on facts and minute details, sinking or sliding giddily off into the unknown" (Stevenson 66)—Bishop's Moore-like concentration on the object slips "giddily" off into the unknown, the strange, the surreal, unfixing traditional notions of a bounded self and world and collapsing the traditional distinction between conscious and unconscious, subject and object, self and world.

And yet, if Bishop's "The Fish" is a profoundly subjective and philosophical poem that marks her difference from Moore, at the time that she composed it, at least, she experienced this difference as an artistic lack—a sign of her slightness and failure of profundity in comparison with Moore. Having incorporated some of Moore's suggestions about "The Fish," Bishop sent her the revised version on February 19, 1940: "If you think this poem too hopelessly slight and wrong—please don't bother to think about it. I am working at several more earnest things that I hope you will like better" (*R*). As she moved in Key West toward the social and racial subjects that would further distance her from Moore, she feared that even these "more earnest" things might be lacking in depth. Along with "The Fish," she enclosed "Jose's House" ["Jerónimo's House"], but feared that it "isn't very good" (*R*, February 19, 1940:V:5:2); and the following week, she sent "Cootchie" to Moore, noting that it "may be banal, I can't decide" (*R*, February 26, 1940:V:5:2).

At about this time Bishop sent Moore a paper nautilus. This gift, which Bishop considered one of her "most successful," became the subject of one of Moore's own poems "A Glass-Ribbed Nest" (later "The Paper Nautilus"). On the broadest level the poem is about the relationship between motherhood and artistic creation as it is figured in the "thin glass shell" constructed by the paper nautilus to hatch her eggs from within. But the poem also appears to be an attempt by Moore to come to terms with her relationship with Bishop at a time when both women were attempting to break out of the potential constraints of the mother/daughter bond. Against "authorities whose hopes / are shaped by mercenaries" and the merely material "comforts" of a literary life, Moore sets the creation of the paper nautilus as a form of artistic work and a form of mothering that balances the values of nurturance and autonomy, gentleness and strength, love and freedom. Watchful and protective, the paper nautilus hides but does not crush the "cradled freight" that she carries within, and when the eggs are hatched the shell is freed:

> the intensively
> watched eggs coming from

the shell free it when they are freed,—
leaving its wasp-nest flaws
of white on white, and close-

laid Ionic chiton-folds
like the lines in the mane of
a Parthenon horse,
round which the arms had
wound themselves as if they knew love
is the only fortress
strong enough to trust to.
                          (*Complete Poems* 122)

But for all Moore's desire to counter a traditionally masculine and mercenary
ethos of power, domination, and greed with a maternal ethos of love, nurturance, and mutual freedom, her actual relationship with Bishop was manifesting the difficulty of putting this ideal into effect. Rather than freeing the
"intensively watched" creation of Bishop as she grew to poetic maturity,
Moore was tightening her hold and revealing an increasing urge to determine
what Bishop's self-definition and artistic creation would be. Having constructed herself as the dutiful daughter of a powerful and original literary
mother, Bishop, in her turn, was being at once "hid" and "crushed" by the
"Ionic chiton-folds" of Moore's art, even as she sought to free herself from
Moore's potentially debilitating hold. In response to Moore's "A Glass-
Ribbed Nest," Bishop wrote: "The whole poem is like a rebuke to me, it
suggests so many of the plans for the things I want to say about Key West and
have scarcely hinted at in 'Jose's House' for example. But I will try very hard,
and won't write again until I have something of the proper length and depth to
send you" (*R*, May 21, 1940:V:5:2).

In her correspondence with Moore, Bishop's identity as a poet is always on
the verge of annihilation. "I scarcely know why I persist at all," she wrote to
Moore in the late summer of 1940:

> It is really fantastic to place so much on the fact that I have written a half-dozen
> *phrases* that I can still bear to re-read without too much embarassment [*sic*]. But
> I have that continuous uncomfortable feeling of "things" in the head, like
> icebergs or rocks or awkwardly-shaped pieces of furniture—and it's as if all the
> nouns were there but the verbs were lacking—if you know what I mean. And I
> can't help having the theory that if they are joggled around hard enough and
> long enough some kind of electricity will occur, just by friction, and will
> arrange everything—.
>   (*R*, September 11, 1940:V:5:2)

Like Moore, Bishop has the "nouns"—the objects and "things" Moore has
suggested as the subject matter of her poems—but she lacks the verbs—the

activating frame of belief or value—to make her nouns do or say something of ultimate significance and value.

Within the next month Bishop had joggled her subjects and verbs hard enough to compose "Roosters." In this poem, which she considered "the most ambitious I had up to then attempted," Bishop finally chose to stand on her own personal, political, and poetic ground. The poem did not please either Moore or her mother; in fact, it stirred them to what Bishop called "an immediate flurry of criticism." The two sat up all night rewriting the poem, and the next day a retyped version was sent to Bishop with her lines reworked, her language reworded, and several revisions suggested, including a change in the poem's redundant rhythm and the deletion of the word *water-closet* and other vulgarisms from the poem. Moore also retitled the poem "The Cock," perhaps thinking of the historical etymology of the word and completely missing its more contemporary and blatant sexual reference.

In her cover letter, she urged Bishop to practice "the heroisms of abstinence" and to resist the example of "Dylan Thomas, W. C. Williams, E. E. Cummings, and others," who "feel that they are avoiding a duty if they balk at anything like unprudishness." Moore argued that while she might use a vulgarism in personal conversation with her mother, she would not dare risk saying in her work that her mother had a feather on her rump (*V*, October 16, 1940:10:130). As in her earlier exchanges with H. D., Moore insists on her own feminine brand of modernism. She clearly sets herself against what she considers the excess and vulgarity of the male modernists, and she wants Bishop to set herself against them too by adopting her own moral, decorous, and ladylike aesthetic posture. Until this time, Bishop had, for the most part, yielded to Moore's "better" judgment in revising and editing her poems for publication. With the composition of "Roosters," however, Bishop had acquired a poetic maturity that enabled her to turn down Moore's suggestions and in so doing to define clearly her own poetic priorities.

Bishop's response to Moore amounts to a declaration of poetic independence. "What I'm about to say, I'm afraid, will sound like ELIZABETH KNOWS BEST," wrote Bishop. "However, I *have* changed to small initial letters!" Insisting on her own poetic intention, which was to depict the violence and sordidness of contemporary militarism in images and colors similar to Picasso's "Guernica," Bishop refused to mask her effects by practicing the ladylike "heroisms of abstinence" advocated by Moore. "I cherish my 'water-closet' and the other sordidities," she said, "because I want to emphasize the essential baseness of militarism. In the 1st part I was thinking of Key West, and also of those aerial views of dismal little towns in Finland & Norway, where the Germans took over, and their atmosphere of poverty" (*R*, October 17, 1940:V:5:2).

In the context of Bishop's poetic career, "Roosters" represents a decisive move away from the "imaginary Islands" of such early poems as "The Map," "The Imaginary Iceberg," and "The Man-Moth" toward the personal and historical subject matter that would become the focus of her later poems. The poem is at once a stark and unsparing evocation of the impulses toward brutality, domination, and colonial conquest that motivated World War II, and, like Virginia Woolf's *Three Guineas* and H. D.'s *Trilogy*, an angry protest against the patriarchal orders in which war, militarism, fascism, and violence are grounded. Crowing "uncontrolled, traditional cries" in the blue dawn, Bishop's cocks

> planned to command and terrorize the rest,
>
> the many wives
> who lead hens' lives
> of being courted and despised;
>
> deep from raw throats
> a senseless order floats
> all over town. A rooster gloats
>
> over our beds
> from rusty iron sheds
> and fences made from old bedsteads,
>
> over our churches
> where the tin rooster perches,
> over our little wooden northern houses
> (*Complete Poems* 35–36)

Unlike Moore, whose "imaginary gardens" and fundamental Protestant faith set her apart, aesthetically and morally, from the sordidities of the times, Bishop focuses on the contemporary world with such pained and keen-eyed awareness that her poem appears to prophecy the racial and nuclear holocaust of World War II.

But there are other and more private ways that the poem sets itself apart from Moore. As a poem that insists on the relationship between the personal and the political, between the cocks who "command and terrorize" women in the private sphere and the "senseless order" of war, militarism, and violence in the public sphere, "Roosters" is also a kind of veiled "coming out" poem in which Bishop registers her personal protest against the "senseless order" of marriage and heterosexuality that "floats / all over town" and "gloats" over the bed of lesbian love. "Roosters, what are you projecting?" the speaker asks:

> what right have you to give
> commands and tell us how to live,

> cry "Here!" and "Here!"
> and wake us here where are
> unwanted love, conceit and war?
>
> (36)

The speaker's questions are at once personal and political, registering her protest against the scenes of private and public violation—of "unwanted love, conceit and war"—to which she is awakened by the heterosexual order of the rooster as cock or phallus.

At this point, there is an abrupt break in the poem, as the speaker turns away from the more angry and personal protest against male violation of women in the first section toward the more meditative tone of the second section in which the rooster's cry of "denial" is linked with the "inescapable hope" signified by Peter's denial and later forgiveness by Christ:

> There is inescapable hope, the pivot;
>
> yes, and there's Peter's tears
> run down our chanticleer's
> sides and gem his spurs.
>
> (38)

The poem has usually been read as a meditation on the two sides of humanity emblematized by the dual symbolism of the roosters as figures of denial and affirmation, despair and hope. "Carven roosters, emblems of brutality, cowardice, *and* forgiveness, provide a quietly enduring response to the 'senseless order,' " writes Thomas Travisano (81). But the gemmed spurs of the "Roosters" may, in fact, suggest just the opposite: that the redemptive possibility signified by the Church, Christianity, and "Peter's tears" has served historically to "gem" the "spurs" of the cocks—and a political ideology of regeneration through violence—by sacralizing and justifying the very orders of masculine aggression and heterosexual dominance that Bishop protested in the first part of the poem. Whatever redemptive possibility "Roosters" suggests is indeed undercut by the poem's ambiguous and unregenerate conclusion: "The sun climbs in / following 'to see the end,' / faithful as enemy, or friend" (39).

Moore did not disapprove of Bishop's contemporary focus or her critique of patriarchy—a critique that she herself had undertaken in "Marriage." But the "immediate flurry of criticism" that caused her to overstep the bounds of mentorship by rewriting "Roosters" on her own terms suggests that she may have sensed the deeper levels of personal, sexual, and antireligious revelation in the poem. What troubled Moore in particular was a certain blatancy and vulgarity in language and rhythm that seemed to swerve from the subtle and understated effects she had encouraged in Bishop's work. In "Roosters," however, Bishop was seeking the more violent and expressionistic effects of

Picasso's "Guernica" and Paul Klee's "Man of Confusion." While she granted Moore's aesthetic correctness, she felt that her "rattle trap rhythm" and sordidities of language and imagery were part of the poem's idiom of contemporary discordance: "I know that esthetically you are quite right," she said, "but I can't bring myself to sacrifice what (I think) is a very important 'violence' of tone—which I feel to be helped by what *you* must feel to be just a bad case of the *threes*. It makes me feel like a wonderful Klee picture I saw at his show the other day, 'The Man of Confusion.' I wonder if you could be mesmerized across the bridges to see it again with me?" (*R*, October 17, 1940:V:5:2)

"May I keep *your poem?*" Bishop wrote, barely concealing her resentment at Moore's attempt to rewrite and in effect possess her work. "It is very interesting, what *you have done*" (*R*, October 20, 1940:V:5:2; emphasis added). Although Bishop's struggle with Moore over "Roosters" did not end their relationship, it did alter the nature of the bond between them. "After that," Bishop told Lynn Keller, "I decided to write entirely on my own, because I realized how very different we were" (424). While they continued as friends, their correspondence thinned from several letters a month to, for the most part, only one or two a year, and Bishop almost never sent Moore copies of her work in progress.

But for all Bishop's attempt to write entirely on her own, as her critical reputation developed, she would continue to be cast in the shadow of Moore. Reviewers of Bishop's first volume of poems, *North & South* (1946), consistently located and defined her as a subsidiary in the school of Marianne Moore, who had come to represent the very terms on which a woman could be taken seriously as a poet. "When you read Miss Bishop's 'Florida,' " wrote Randall Jarrell, "you don't need to be told that the poetry of Marianne Moore was, in the beginning, an appropriately selected foundation for Miss Bishop's work." Completely missing the fact that "Florida" is not at all like Moore in its unromanticized representation of nature as violent, predatory, and deadly, Jarrell goes on to emphasize the "unassuming," "pleasant," "charming," and essentially Moore-ish qualities of Bishop's work: "Miss Bishop's poems are almost never forced. . . . In her best work restraint, calm, and proportion are implicit in every detail of organization and workmanship" ("The Poet and His Public" 499). Robert Lowell similarly locates and limits Bishop as a woman poet writing in the tradition of Moore. "It is obvious that her most important model is Marianne Moore," he says. "On the surface, her poems are observations—surpassingly accurate, witty and well-arranged, but nothing more." While he notes Bishop's differences from Moore, he also finds her lacking in comparison with Moore: "She is softer, dreamier, more human and more personal; she is less idiosyncratic, and less magnificent. She is probably slighter; of course, being much younger, she does not have nearly so many extraordinarily good poems" ("Thomas, Bishop, and Williams" 497–98).

These early critical readings of Bishop through the lens of Moore tended to misrepresent her work and fix her literary reputation as a quiet, calm, and technically expert poet of mere surface description and observation. They also tended to fix and marginalize her work in the category "woman poet," emphasizing the essentially feminine qualities of her work—modesty, reticence, sympathy, dreaminess, softness, and charm—and circumscribing the extent of her achievement within specifically female bounds. Compared with male writers, Bishop's work is "modest," says Lowell. "Her admirers are not likely to hail her as a giant among the moderns, or to compare anything that she will ever write with Shakespeare or Donne." In comparison with the work of women writers, however, he finds " 'Roosters' and 'The Fish,' large and perfect, and, outside of Marianne Moore, the best poems that I know of written by a woman in this century" ("Thomas, Bishop, and Williams" 499). Given the way even well-meaning critics like Jarrell and Lowell had used her gender and her relationship with other women poets as a critical weapon against her, it is no wonder that Bishop came to see the notion of a woman's tradition not as a source of empowerment but as a categorical limit and a bound that would be used ultimately to diminish and dismiss the work of women. Perhaps with Lowell's review in mind, Bishop later said: "At the very end they often say 'The best poetry by a woman in this decade, or year, or month.' Well, what's that worth? You know?" (Starbuck 23)

The early critical emphasis on the quiet, understated, and essentially feminine qualities of Bishop's work was also encouraged by Moore herself, who published a review of *North & South* in *The Nation* entitled "The Modest Expert." Apparently choosing to forget publicly the very real differences that emerged in their struggle over "Roosters," in her review Moore continues to sign Bishop with her own "modest" and moral signature. "Elizabeth Bishop is spectacular in being unspectacular," said Moore. "Why has no one ever thought of this, one asks oneself; why not be accurate and modest?" (Mis)representing Bishop's work as a "small-large book of beautifully formulated aesthetic-moral mathematics," she emphasizes the mechanics and morality of Bishop's poems, and scolds her for her periodic lapses from poetic decorum. She also ascribes to Bishop's verse—and to "Roosters" in particular—a moral purpose and "religious faith" that is completely at odds with Bishop's refusal to assert moral, epistemological, or religious absolutes: "Art which 'cuts its facets from within' can mitigate suffering, can even be an instrument of happiness; as also forgiveness, symbolized in Miss Bishop's meditation on St. Peter by the cock, seems essential to happiness." Refusing to accept Bishop's "tentativeness" as the lack of "underlying knowledges" it is, Moore seems intent on redefining it on her own terms as a form of moral persuasion that "knows" and convinces by "uninsistence": "With poetry as with homiletics, tentativeness can be more positive than positiveness; and in 'North & South,' a much instructed persuasiveness is emphasized by uninsistence. At last we have someone who knows, who is not didactic" ("A Modest Expert" 354). Although Moore's review appears to reveal a new sense of artistic distance from Bishop, it is in fact written as a kind of critical damage control in which Moore seeks to recontain all that she finds most dangerous and disturbing in Bishop's work.

"I am very tired of sounding so quiet," Bishop wrote Robert Lowell in 1948, in a letter that included her poem "Over 2,000 Illustrations and a Complete Concordance" (Houghton Library). In the context of the critical reception of *North & South,* Bishop's comment sounds like a reaction against both the ethics and poetics of feminine reticence propounded by Moore and the critical tendency to read her work as a modest exemplar of Moore's influence and a particularly female kind of writing. Bishop's protest against "sounding so quiet" marks an important moment in her poetic career, a moment when she began to make a more self-conscious break away from Moore in order to repossess the personal subject matter and the autobiographical subject that had in some sense been silenced—or at least muted—under Moore's regime of poetic reticence.

This break is already evident in "Over 2,000 Illustrations," a poem in which Bishop seeks to link her travels and her descriptions with a more personal autobiographical content, associated in particular with her childhood, her family history, and her lesbian identity. In this poem, Bishop names her presence in the lesbian brothels of Marrakesh, where "the little pockmarked prostitutes / . . . did their belly dances" and "flung themselves / naked and giggling against our knees / asking for cigarettes"; and she associates her lack of saving religious vision—"Everything only connected by 'and' and 'and' "—with the rupture and disorder of her own "Nativity" and family history. As Bishop's scenes of travel, description, and natural observation become increasingly the locus for articulating her personal experience of pain, loss, and instability as the autobiographical subject of her work, her poems begin to gain that "unprotected profundity of experience" toward which Moore had beckoned her. But it is a deepening that Bishop achieves by resisting Moore's moral orders and standing on her own tentative, subjective, and ultimately unregenerate ground.

If Moore had helped Bishop define herself as a poet, it was Robert Lowell, whom she met in 1946, who helped Bishop discover herself and her past as her most potent subject. As David Kalstone writes: "They were mischievous as children about the figures they most held in awe—Lowell about Jarrell and Tate, Bishop about Moore—and their curiosity about each other helped wean them away from their earlier literary attachments" (*Becoming a Poet* 112). In their friendship and correspondence, which lasted until Lowell's death in 1977, Lowell aided Bishop in the process of placing her autobiographical "I" and her family history at the center of her verse, and, at a crucial stage in Lowell's poetic career, the example of Bishop's work helped him gain distance from his tendency toward self-absorption and self-pity through formal control and a more descriptive focus on the external world.

Bishop's attempt to retrieve her personal history as the subject of her work was also aided by her return to Nova Scotia and Cape Breton in the summers of 1946 and 1947. These scenes from her childhood became the subject of several poems in *A Cold Spring* (1955), including "At the Fishhouses" and "A Summer's Dream." Her bus trip back to the United States from Nova Scotia also became the subject of "The Moose," a personal meditation— "half groan, half acceptance"—on loss, dissolution, and the momentary release into "otherworldly" vision signified by a "she" Moose—which Bishop began writing in 1946 but did not complete until 1976 when it was published in *Geography III*.

Witchcraft

It is one of the ironies of Bishop's relationship with Moore that her most public affirmation of Moore's influence and power, "Invitation to Miss Marianne Moore," appeared at the very moment when she was making her most self-conscious effort to distance and differentiate herself from Moore personally and artistically. Bishop began working on the poem shortly after their exchange over "Roosters." "I wish I could think of such nice things to say as you can," Bishop wrote to Moore in December 1940; "but, anyway, I am writing a poem with you in mind and if it turns out well I'll send it—a very cheerful poem!" (*R*, December 9, 1940:V:5:2). Bishop may have intended the poem as a peace offering to smooth over any ill feeling that remained after their disagreement over "Roosters." But an early version of the poem, which is among Bishop's unpublished manuscripts in the Vassar Library, suggests that the process of coming to terms with her indebtedness to Moore and their differences was not at all easy—even in a "very cheerful poem." Titled "To the Admirable Miss Moore," the poem expresses a mixture of reverence, gratitude, and resentment in a rattletrap rhythm and triple rhyme that appears to play on their disagreement over "Roosters":

> To the Admirable Miss Moore,
> Of whom we're absolutely sure,
>
> knowing that through the longest night
> her syllables will come out right,
> her similes will all flash bright
>
> what can we give, yet not be rude
> to show the proper gratitude
>
> (*V*)

The final version of the poem registers a similar mixture of attitudes toward Moore, but Bishop's self-parody is translated into a brilliant and comic imitation of Moore herself. The poem, which was originally titled "For M. M.," was first published in 1948 in a special issue of the *Quarterly Review of Literature,* in honor of Marianne Moore's sixtieth birthday. It was followed by a laudatory essay on Moore entitled "As We Like It."

Like Alberto Rojas Jimenez in Pablo Neruda's "Alberto Rojas Jimenez Viene Volando," which served as a model for "Invitation to Miss Marianne Moore," Moore is invoked and invited as a figure of magical and otherworldly power who flies over, above, and beyond the "accidents" and "injustices" of the world "at large." But while the poem is comic and high-spirited, its humor also masks Bishop's determination to name and proclaim publicly her own sense of difference and distance from Moore. Enacting the major dimensions of their relationship, the poem is finally an attempt on Bishop's part to honor Moore without allowing herself to be destroyed by her.

Bishop begins the poem, as she began their relationship, with an invitation:

> From Brooklyn, over Brooklyn Bridge, on this fine morning,
>   please come flying.
> In a cloud of fiery pale chemicals,
>   please come flying,
> to the rapid rolling of thousands of small blue drums
> descending out of the mackerel sky
> over the glittering grandstand of harbor-water,
>   please come flying.
>
> (*Complete Poems* 82)

From her first letter to Moore in 1934, in which she invited her to the circus, to later invitations to depart for Nova Scotia, Key West, or Brazil, Bishop regularly urged Moore to share her adventurous and roving life as "a believer" in what she called "total immersion" ("At the Fishhouses," *Complete Poems* 65). But Moore, the poem implies, chooses to stay at home, both literally and figuratively, within the safety of her own domestic, moral, and imaginative orders.

Drawing on the fantasy that closes her "ELIZABETH KNOWS BEST" letter—"I wonder if you could be mesmerized across the bridges"—Bishop seeks to match and indeed mirror Moore's own magical and transforming power in an effort to make New York "safe" and ready to receive her:

> Whistles, pennants and smoke are blowing. The ships
> are signaling cordially with multitudes of flags
> rising and falling like birds all over the harbor.
> Enter: two rivers, gracefully bearing
> countless little pellucid jellies
> in cut-glass epergnes dragging with silver chains.
> The flight is safe; the weather is all arranged.
> The waves are running in verses this fine morning.
>   Please come flying.
>
>   (82)

In the image of the river bearing "countless little pellucid jellies / in cut-glass epergnes dragging with silver chains," Bishop effectively imitates Moore's own poetic transfigurations of worldly turbulence. The world into which she invites Moore is, like Moore's own poetic universe, cordial, decorous, safe, and artistically ordered. It is a world in which waves run, however implausibly, "in verses."

The poem turns on the comedy generated by the clash between the formality of the public image of Miss Marianne Moore and the fabulous fairy-tale figure who emerges in the poem. Moore's well-known dress—black pointed shoes, cape, and tricornered hat—are transformed into the costume of a fairy godmother or good witch; and her proverbial reserve and formality are released in images of motion and flight.

> Come with the pointed toe of each black shoe
> trailing a sapphire highlight,
> with a black capeful of butterfly wings and bon-mots,
> with heaven knows how many angels all riding
> on the broad black brim of your hat,
>   please come flying.
>
>   (82)

But for all her magical and witch-like power, the figure Bishop invites, with her pointed shoes and "black capeful of butterfly wings and bon-mots" seems slightly ridiculous and out of place in the world. And it is precisely Moore's removal from the world that becomes a site of trouble and difference in Bishop's poetic tribute.

"I have a vague theory that one learns most—I have learned most—from having someone suddenly make fun of something one has taken seriously up until then," Bishop wrote Anne Stevenson (Washington University Library, January 8, 1964). In "Invitation" laughter and humor are turned to similar purposes as Bishop seeks, in effect, to make fun of something she "has taken seriously up until then." Humor serves to deflect some of Bishop's hostility to Moore, to diffuse the tensions in their relationship, and finally to distance Bishop from Moore personally and publicly by dispelling her potentially overwhelming influence. Moore's fastidious attention to syllable count, her censorious critical eye, and her exacting moral vision—qualities that were at the very sources of the "serious" differences between them—are presented in comic perspective:

> Bearing a musical inaudible abacus,
> a slight censorious frown, and blue ribbons,
>   please come flying.
> Facts and skyscrapers glint in the tide; Manhattan
> is all awash with morals this fine morning,
>   so please come flying.
>
>   (82)

The passage pokes fun at Moore's attempt to make the universe beat to the rhythm of her own "inaudible abacus." Moore's poetic flights are performed in a providential and artistically ordered universe in which "Manhattan / is all awash with morals." These moral and imaginary orders and flights of poetic fancy set her apart from the sordidities of the world:

> Mounting the sky with natural heroism,
> above the accidents, above the malignant movies,
> the taxicabs and injustices at large,
> while horns are resounding in your beautiful ears
> that simultaneously listen to
> a soft uninvented music, fit for the musk deer,
>   please come flying.
>
>   (83)

Moore's flight separates her not only from the discordance and noise of the modern world but from the more desolate and unrecuperated vision of Bishop herself. Whereas Moore listens to a timeless music, "fit for the musk deer," Bishop's poems are embedded in the very dissonances, "accidents," and "injustices" of the world "at large" that Moore seeks to mount above and transcend.

But while Moore seems rather comically out of touch with the wickedness and evils of the world, even as a good witch, she has the witch's power of enchantment and control: things and people yield themselves to her enchanting spell. She is a woman

> For whom the grim museums will behave
> like courteous male bower-birds,
> for whom the agreeable lions lie in wait
> on the steps of the Public Library,
> eager to rise and follow through the doors
> up into the reading rooms,
>   please come flying.
>
> (83)

By implication, Bishop, too, yielded herself up to Moore's spellbinding power as she—like "the agreeable lions"—followed Moore "up into the reading rooms" of the New York Public Library. And it is here, in the place of their first meeting, that Bishop enters the poem for the first time, imagining an encounter with Moore that reenacts the scenes of their relationship:

> We can sit down and weep; we can go shopping,
> or play at a game of constantly being wrong
> with a priceless set of vocabularies,
> or we can bravely deplore, but please
>   please come flying.
>
> (83)

The relationship Bishop describes seems cramped, cloyingly "feminine," and removed from the world. With its shopping and tears, its word games that are constantly wrong, and its brave, but seemingly ineffectual, moral judgments, Bishop's imaginary encounter with Moore suggests the limits of their relationship as a site at once of enchantment and entrapment. In fact, the relationship Bishop describes seems so ambiguous and at odds with the more public and celebratory tone of the poem that the entire base of her invitation— and her comic and cheerful poem—seem on the verge of collapse.

In the final passages of the poem, Bishop pushes away from this site of entrapment and trouble in a gesture of celebration that pays tribute to Moore's transforming power of imagination and her life-affirming vision:

> With dynasties of negative constructions
> darkening and dying around you,
> with grammar that suddenly turns and shines
> like flocks of sandpipers flying,
>   please come flying.
>
> (83)

Just as in her poems Moore's double negatives become positive, so her power of language transforms "dynasties of negative constructions" into artistic constructs of order and grace, "like flocks of sandpipers flying." But even in this final gesture of celebration, the passage suggests the limits of Moore's power of transformation in words that inscribe the difference of Bishop's own more desolate vision. "Like flocks of sandpipers flying," or, as Bishop says in her final metaphoric representation of Moore, "like a daytime comet," Moore's luminous moral and imaginative orders are only temporary and fleeting constructions of light and affirmation set against "dynasties of negative contructions" and Bishop's own bleak vision of a "darkening and dying" world. If Bishop celebrates and invites Moore as a celestial figure whose luminous imagination and "long unnebulous train of words" have inspired her own poetic creation, it is an invitation issued from afar and on Bishop's terms, written in full knowledge of the fact that had she remained under the enchanting spell of Moore's influence she would have been destroyed as a poet.

"As We Like It," the essay that follows Bishop's poetic invitation, is marked by similar reservations about Moore's imaginative power. While she praises Moore as "The World's Greatest Living Observer," comparing her with Shakespeare, Poe, and Hopkins, she ends by suggesting that her observations are fabulously seductive but finally untrue: "With all its inseparable combinations of the formally fabulous with the factual, and the artifical with the perfectly natural, her animal poetry seduces one to dream of some realm of reciprocity, a true *lingua unicornis*" ("As We Like It" 135). What remains unsaid but implicit in Bishop's final judgment of Moore is that her dream of "reciprocity, a true *lingua unicornis*" is ultimately inadequate to Bishop's own more pessimistic vision of the fundamental difference and distance that separate subject and object, observer and nature, imaginary orders and a radically other and nonreciprocal world. In Moore's poems all the animals are good animals, whereas in Bishop's "The Prodigal" the mother sow eats her young.

Moore responded enthusiastically to Bishop's poem and essay:

> Your magic poem—every word a living wonder—with an unfoldment that does not ever go back on itself, and the colors! beyond compare in the small blue drums and the mackerel sky and the jelly-colored epergnes. What of your unabashed "awash with morals?"! What would Bernard De Voto say! (who hates preachers) Then the suicidal courage of your treatise! as based on Shakespeare and Poe and G. M. Hopkins.
>
> (*V*, August 24, 1948:10:137)

As usual Moore focuses on the style of Bishop's poem, apparently recognizing the pieces of her own word magic translated into such images as the "small blue drums," the "mackerel sky," the "little pellucid jellies," and the "cut-glass epergnes." About the content, however, Moore seems less sure. Although her response is polite and even playful, she must surely have recognized that, like Bishop's "unabashed" association of her with a world "awash with morals," the poem was not entirely complimentary. In fact, in her "magic poem," Bishop seems so determined to come to terms with the problem of Moore's influence by representing her as a comic, fairy-tale figure that she may inadvertently have helped produce and foster the image of Moore as a rather eccentric and overfastidious spinster—an image that would ultimately tend to simplify the complexity of her work and diminish her critical reputation as a poet in the fifties and sixties.[8] As Moore herself wrote in "Voracities and Verities Sometimes Are Interacting," perhaps with Bishop in mind: "Some kinds of gratitude are trying" (*Complete Poems* 148).

"Driving to the Interior"

"Invitation to Miss Marianne Moore" appears at the end of *A Cold Spring* (1955), a volume that marks a transition in Bishop's work between the early poems written under Moore's influence and the later poems in which Bishop moved more emphatically toward the personal and autobiographical material that had been repressed under Moore's regime of poetic reticence. Like all future volumes of Bishop's poems, *A Cold Spring* is dedicated to a woman, Dr. Anny Baumann (Bishop's physician). Women and the relations of affection and struggle between them also dominate the volume, from the eroticized female body of nature figured in "A Cold Spring," to the representation of race and class conflict between women in "Faustina, or Rock Roses," to the intensely private and at times pained expressions of love in "Insomnia," "Varick Street," "Four Poems," "Argument," and "The Shampoo." The poems in this volume bear the traces of a period of personal and poetic crisis in the late forties as Bishop struggled to come to terms with an unhappy love affair with a woman and to reconcile the conflict between gender and creativity—between a more confessional impulse to name the erotic relationships with women that were at the emotional center of her life and a more formalist impulse to efface the specifically female and lesbian dimensions of her experience for fear of being marginalized and dismissed as a woman writer and a pervert.

Under the pressure not to speak her lesbian desire in the love poems of *A Cold Spring,* Bishop seems simultaneously to engage and to distance, to confess and to conceal, that desire in an eroticized female landscape, a language coded to the point of obscurity, and passionate addresses to a non-specified and neutered you. In "Insomnia" Bishop's desire and her anger seem closer to the surface as she seeks for the first time to name and figure her experience as lesbian and outsider in images of the moon, mirrors, bodies of water, and inversion:

> By the Universe deserted,
> *she'd* tell it to go to hell,

and she'd find a body of water,
or a mirror, on which to dwell.
So wrap up care in a cobweb
and drop it down the well

into that world inverted
where left is always right,
where the shadows are really the body,
where we stay awake all night,
where the heavens are shallow as the sea
is now deep, and you love me.

                                   (*Complete Poems* 70)

Not surprisingly, Moore was "very opposed" to "Insomnia"; it was, she told Bishop, "a cheap love poem" (Spires 375). Moore's judgment represented at once a moral and an aesthetic condemnation. Not only was Bishop in some sense behaving like a hussy; she was also failing to observe Moore's ladylike code of aesthetic reticence. "I don't think she ever believed in talking about the emotions much," Bishop said, in words that suggest some of the aesthetic pressure Moore put on Bishop, either voiced or unvoiced, not to talk about her feelings, especially her feelings for women.

But Moore was not alone in objecting to the more personal dimension of Bishop's new work. Having achieved a reputation as a protégée of Moore and a set piece poet of high modernist impersonality and descriptive accuracy, Bishop was censored by the critics for lapsing into mere feminine feeling. John Ashberry was disappointed with *A Cold Spring* because, he said, in several poems, "the poet's life threatened to intrude on the poetry in a way that didn't suit it. One accepted without question the neutral 'we' in earlier poems as the necessary plural of 'I,' but a couple of the new ones veered dangerously close to the sentimental ballad of the Millay-Teasdale-Wylie school, to one's considerable surprise" (25).[9]

As Bishop's most cheerful and Moore-like poem, "Invitation to Miss Marianne Moore" seems curiously out of place among the troubled love poems of *A Cold Spring;* yet its very appearance there suggests the extent to which that relationship partook of the "gentle battleground" of female relations Bishop describes in the volume. In fact, the placement of "Invitation" just before "Arrival at Santos," Bishop's poem about her move to Brazil in 1951, and "The Shampoo," a poem that celebrates her love relationship with Lota Macedo Soares, marks the dual—and ambivalent—status of the poem as both invitation and farewell, artistic homage and personal break, as Bishop departs for Brazil, where she would live for sixteen years with Soares (Fig. 7). "We

Figure 6. Photograph of Elizabeth Bishop in Petrópolis, Brazil, in 1955, by Rollie McKenna. "What I'm really up to," Bishop said of her residence in Petrópolis, "is recreating a sort of deluxe Nova Scotia all over again in Brazil. And now I'm my own grandmother." (copyright Rollie McKenna)

are driving to the interior," Bishop says in "Arrival at Santos," in words that announce the drive to the interior of Brazil that would correspond with her creation of a home with Lota Soares and her return to the interior of her own past.

In taking up residence in Brazil, Bishop distanced herself personally and geographically not only from Moore and the centers of literary power in the United States but from American Cold War ideology, "The gathered brasses" that "want to go / *boom—boom*," as she says in "View of the Capitol from the Library of Congress," a poem she wrote while she was serving as Consultant in Poetry at the Library of Congress in 1949–50 (*Complete Poems* 69). Her self-exile became a means in some sense of realizing the lesbian fantasy

Figure 7. Photograph of Elizabeth Bishop's intimate companion in Brazil, Lota Soares, at about 40 years old. (Courtesy, Vassar College Library)

of "Insomnia": "By the Universe deserted, / *She'd* tell it to go to hell" (70). "What I'm really up to," Bishop said of her residence in Petrópolis, "is recreating a sort of deluxe Nova Scotia all over again in Brazil. And now I'm my own grandmother" (Kalstone, *Becoming a Poet* 152).

Within the relative safety of her reconstituted family and as a kind of grandmother to herself, Bishop began to write about the losses of her child-hood in two short stories, both published in 1953: in "In the Village" Bishop represents the insanity and early loss of her mother as an initial "scream" that hangs over both past and present; in "Gwendolyn" she explores the unresolved feelings associated with her love and loss of a childhood girlfriend. These two stories appear to have helped Bishop gain the sense of clarity and control that would eventually enable her to retrieve what she had earlier called the "Magic Ink" of her "family monuments" as the subject of her poems. "Do please write an autobiography—or sketches for one," she wrote Lowell after completing "In the Village" and "Gwendolyn"; "the two or three stories I've managed to do have been a great satisfaction somehow—that desire to get things straight and tell the truth" (Houghton Library, May 20, 1955).

But while Bishop began in Brazil to drive toward the interior of her childhood losses, the process of placing her past and an historically located "I" at the center of her poems would not be easy. In fact, after the crisis years of the late forties, she began to move away from the emotionally volatile personal subject of *A Cold Spring* toward the external world and the seemingly promising potential of Brazil as a subject of her poems. During her first years in Brazil, however, she wrote almost no poems at all. "Since I cannot seem to write much poetry about Brazil—you must come & do it," Bishop wrote Moore in 1953. "I read over *Costa Rica* & can just vaguely imagine—& dimly see it on the page—what you would do here!" (*R*, December 8, 1953:V:5:4). At one point, Bishop dreamed Moore's presence into the Brazilian landscape: "Last night I dreamed I found a specimen of your handwriting on a rock out in the garden which must mean something, I'm sure" (*R*, October 15, 1954:V:5:4). The "meaning" of Bishop's dream, like the meaning of her invitation, is in some sense double. On the one hand, Moore's handwriting in the landscape suggests Bishop's sense of indebtedness to Moore for revealing the possibility of the physical world as a subject of her poems and for providing a point of stasis, a kind of "rock" foundation of moral and artistic order, in a world that was, as Bishop said in "At the Fishhouses," forever "flowing, and flown." On the other hand, as in "The Sea & Its Shore," Bishop's dream registers her continued sense of belatedness and inadequacy, particularly in relation to Moore. In a world that already bears Moore's handwriting, Bishop's work as a poet can be at best supplementary, merely to write over what has already been written upon by Moore.

This is not to say that Bishop's relationship with Moore did not remain cordial during her Brazilian years. In fact, pictures of both Moore (Fig. 8) and Lowell hung over Bishop's work table in Brazil, and in the early fifties she began writing another poem to Moore, which she planned to include along with "Invitation" in *A Cold Spring*. "I still hope to have the 2nd poem on the subject of *you* in this next book—I have started in on it again and soon I may

Figure 8. Photograph of Marianne Moore, taken in 1953 by George Platt Lynes, that hung over Elizabeth Bishop's work desk in Brazil. "I am turning the pages of an illuminated manuscript and seeing that initial letter again and again: Marianne's monogram; mother; manners; morals," Bishop wrote of her lifelong relationship with Marianne Moore. (Courtesy of George Platt Lynes Estate and Vassar College Library)

dare to send it on," Bishop wrote Moore in December 1953 (*R,* December 8, 1953:V:5:4). Apparently Bishop never completed the poem, for it was not published in her *Complete Poems 1927–1979,* nor does it appear among her unpublished manuscripts at Vassar. However, there is among her manuscripts a poetic fragment addressed to both Moore and Lowell. This fragment has none of the humor and distance that marked Bishop's earlier poetic invitation; it is, in effect, a cry for help:

and I am sick of myself
and sometime during the night
the poem I was trying to write
has turned into prepositions:
ins and aboves and upons

what am I trying to do?
Change places in a canoe?
            method of composition—

                . . .

Marianne, loan me a noun!
Cal, please cable a verb?
Or simply propulse through the ether
some more powerful meter
The radio battery is dead

                                                (V)

This fragment registers a sense of self-disgust that is linked with her lack of productivity as a poet and her sense that Moore and Lowell can succeed at the role of poet better than she can. Whereas in her earlier letter to Moore, Bishop had the nouns but not the verbs, here she has neither a subject nor anything significant to say about it. She has become merely a deft manipulator of prepositions within the limited space of a canoe.

Although Bishop urged and influenced Lowell in the direction of *Life Studies* when she suggested that he try to write stories about his personal past, she continued to be reluctant to place her own autobiographical "I" at the center of her poems. Bishop appeared to feel that Lowell's personal experience as a male "I" with a fascinating family history would count and be of interest to the public in ways that her autobiographical female "I" would not. "I must confess," she wrote Lowell in 1957, "that I am green with envy of your kind of assurance. I feel that I could write in as much detail about my uncle Artie, say—but what would be the significance? Nothing at all. . . . Whereas all you have to do is put down the names! And the fact that it seems significant, illustrative, American, etc. gives you, I think, the confidence you display about tackling any idea or theme, *seriously,* in both writing and conversation" (Houghton Library, December 14, 1957).

Feeling that she lacked Lowell's self-assurance and Moore's moral certitude, Bishop would continue to be hampered by the sense that she had no place or position to speak from—that she could be no more than a precious poet.

> Because of my era, sex, situation, education, etc. I have written, so far, what I feel is a rather "precious" kind of poetry, although I am very much opposed to the precious. One wishes things were different, that one could begin all over again. One almost envies those Russian poets a bit—who feel they are so

important, and perhaps are. At least the party seems afraid of them, whereas I doubt that any American poet (except poor wretched Pound) ever bothered our government much.

(Letter to Anne Stevenson, Washington University Library,
January 8, 1964)

Although Bishop recognized that in the contemporary world the poet in general lacked a sense of significance and power, she was also aware of the ways her socialization as a woman had limited her creation as a poet: "Sometimes I think if I had been born a man I probably would have written more. Dared more, or been able to spend more time at it," she said toward the close of her life (Starbuck 329).

In the poems that Bishop wrote in Brazil, which were published in *Questions of Travel* (1965), she appears to be seeking a way out of mere preciosity and her sense of personal and historical limitation as a poet by turning to a more pronounced emphasis on social and political themes. *Questions of Travel* opens with a section of poems entitled "Brazil," in which Bishop's personal identity as alien and outsider is linked with the differences, distances, and struggles between rich and poor, white and black, ruler and ruled in the political landscape of Brazil. These more public poems, which are followed in the original edition by her story "In the Village," provide the larger historical context within which to read the family history poems in the second section, entitled "Elsewhere." Unlike Lowell, who could assume that his personal history was "significant, illustrative, American, etc.," Bishop had to forge and create the relation between the political and the personal—between herself in history in the "Brazil" poems and history in herself in the "Elsewhere" poems.

In "Brazil, January 1, 1502," which appears at the outset of *Questions of Travel*, immediately following "Arrival at Santos," Bishop sets the context for herself in history in scenes of patriarchal violation in the New World. At the very time that Marianne Moore was asserting the need for renewed "faith" in America's political and spiritual destiny in "Enough: Jamestown, 1607–1957," Bishop exposes the actual practice of sexual and racial violation that underlay the political and religious conquest of America:

> Directly after Mass, humming perhaps
> *L'Homme armé* or some such tune,
> they ripped away into the hanging fabric,
> each out to catch an Indian for himself—
> those maddening little women who kept calling,
> calling to each other (or had the birds waked up?)
> and retreating, always retreating, behind it.
>
> (*Complete Poems* 92)

The image of armed Christian patriarchs ripping "away into" a "hanging fabric" that is at once both Indian woman and land suggests the relation between the conquest of the New World and the violation of the Indian woman as sexual and racial other. But the poem also suggests that for all the violent and violating design and desire of the Christian patriarchs, "those maddening little women," who kept "retreating, always retreating, behind" the "hanging fabric," remain finally *other* and *elsewhere* to the political and religious orders that are "out to catch" and possess them.

In the image of "those maddening little women who kept calling, / calling to each other" as they flee patriarchal violation, Bishop also inscribes her own embattled status as lesbian and *other* seeking to retreat from the heterosexual order of *l'homme armé*. In fact, like the Indian women who retreat behind the "hanging fabric" of the land, Bishop's life and her work in Brazil seem to drive toward an interior of protective enclosure, associated with the domestic and the female. This drive toward domestic enclosure is evident in her attempt to reconstitute a familial order in her love relationship with Lota Soares. It is also inscribed in the poems and stories of her Brazil years, as well as in her prose translation of *Minha Vida de Menina (The Diary of "Helena Morley")*, which was published in 1957. The main point of her story, wrote Helena Morley, was that "happiness does not consist in worldly goods but in a peaceful home, in family affection, in a simple life without ambition—things that fortune cannot bring and often takes away" (*Diary* xxxvii).

But in her love relationship with Lota Soares and in her desire for domestic order, Bishop—unlike more explicitly feminist writers including H. D., Adrienne Rich, and Alice Walker—would never be led to romanticize the home, relations between mothers and daughters, or relations among women as a blissfully loving, nurturant, and mutual haven against the oppressive designs of patriarchy. On the contrary, in Bishop's work the home is always a site of radical instability, separation, and difference, and the quest for domestic order is always countered by an equally compelling desire to immerse herself in the flux and mutability of a wildly disordered world. In "Varick Street," lesbian love is locked in the same systems of commerce, exploitation, and oppression as the industrial factory: *"And I shall sell you sell you / sell you of course, my dear, and you'll sell me"* (*Complete Poems* 75). It is not her mother's love but her mother's "scream" that is at the center of Bishop's quest to return home in "In the Village"; and in "Sestina" her grandmother's "chilly" house is marked by the pain of loss, separation, and "equinoctial tears" (123).

Even "Song for the Rainy Season," Bishop's most moving love poem on her relationship with Lota Soares, is "darkened and tarnished" with the realization that their relationship is at best temporary and passing:

> darkened and tarnished
> by the warm touch
> of the warm breath,
> maculate, cherished,
> rejoice! For a later
> era will differ.
> (O difference that kills,
> or intimidates, much
> of all our small shadowy
> life!)
> (*Complete Poems* 102)

Like the house that they designed and rebuilt together in Petrópolis, Bishop's love relationship with Lota Soares is at once "cherished" and "maculate," stained with the knowledge of inevitable decay and death—and the "difference that kills" in self, in others, and in the world.

Bishop's relationship with Marianne Moore became part of her drive toward familial enclosure when in 1969 she decided to name her Brazilian house "Casa Mariana," in honor of Moore. "[I]t is a nice name," Bishop wrote to Moore, "and also the house happens to be on the road to Mariana, a lovely smaller place about seven miles away" (*R*, August 5, 1969:V:5:5). When she discovered that the Daughters of Mariana was a Catholic Women's Club, she wrote Moore of the sign "Casa Mariana" that she placed at the entrance to her house: "Oh dear—but I shall keep it up forever even if someone thinks something worse—" (*R*, June 17, 1970) (Fig. 9). By naming her house Casa Mariana only a few years before Moore's death in 1972, Bishop in effect consecrates what Moore had always meant to her as a figure of moral and religious certitude and old-fashioned family values who offered a temporary haven against a world of difference and dissolution that lacked any essential design, whether maternal or paternal, spiritual or material. Ultimately, however, not even the sign "Casa Mariana" would remain "up forever." Like Bishop's "crypto-dream-house" in "The End of March" and like Moore's own imaginary orders, Casa Mariana would also prove to be "perfect! But— impossible." After the suicide of Lota Soares in 1967, Bishop sold the house they had shared together in Brazil and returned permanently to the United States in the early seventies (*Complete Poems* 180–81).

"You Are an *Elizabeth*"

At about the same time that Bishop named her house Casa Mariana she also began working on a memoir of Moore, entitled "Efforts of Affection," which

Figure 9. Line drawing by Elizabeth Bishop of "Casa Mariana," the house in Ouro Prêto that Bishop named in honor of Marianne Moore. (Courtesy of the Rosenbach Museum and Library)

was published posthumously in 1983. The title responds to Moore's poem "Efforts of Affection" (1948), which may have been Moore's own effort to come to terms with her relationship with Bishop. In this poem, love is represented as a relationship of struggle, an effort to integrate the conflicting demands of individuation and union into the "wholeness" of love. By giving her memoir of Moore the same title, Bishop suggests the similar "efforts" she had to make to come to terms with Moore's influence and the problem of their personal, political, and artistic differences. Bishop pays tribute to Moore and seeks to explore the basis of her affection for her, at the same time that she notes, often half-humorously, the sources of contest and struggle that informed the relationship between them. She is obviously trying to maintain a balance between homage and critical distance that will acknowledge Moore's influence and yet enable her to exist independently as a poet and a person ultimately very different from Moore. At times, however, the balance is lost, and we can hear Bishop's anger and rebellion in "shades and shadows," which is perhaps why she never published the essay.

During the period of her personal crisis in the forties, Bishop remembers, they almost had "a falling out" because Bishop was seeing a psychoanalyst: "She disapproved quite violently and said that psychoanalysts taught that 'Evil is not *evil*. But we know it *is*.' " "We didn't speak of it again," Bishop says, in words that once again suggest how much she had to silence in order to maintain her relationship with Moore. "We never talked about Presbyterianism, or religion in general, nor did I ever dare more than tease her a little when she occasionally said she believed there was something *in* astrology" (*Collected Prose* 155). If in the early stages of their relationship Bishop was in some sense infantilized by Moore, her memoir suggests a reversal of roles, as Bishop assumes the position of the adult and the realist and Moore is represented as an artist who, for all the "rarity" of her "true originality," maintained a childlike moral innocence against and in spite of the violence, pain, and disaster of twentieth-century history. After seeing a Walt Disney short before the film *Potemkin,* Bishop recalls, Moore "talked at length and in detail about the ingenuity of the Disney film," but said of *Potemkin:* "Life is not like that" (*Collected Prose* 151).

"I have a sort of subliminal glimpse of the capital letter *M* multiplying," Bishop writes in the final paragraph of her memoir of Moore. "I am turning the pages of an illuminated manuscript and seeing that initial letter again and again: Marianne's monogram: mother; manners; morals." Bishop's words pay tribute to Moore as the "initial letter" and "illuminated" presence written across the pages of her own life and work. But in the course of her essay, as in the course of their relationship, each of the terms of Moore's monogram— "mother," "manners," "morals"—has threatened to disable as much as enable Bishop as a poet. Still pursued by the determining design and desire of Moore's signature, Bishop ends by asserting her own dreamy tentativeness and inability to "draw conclusions" about a world that only *seems* to make sense: "Manners and morals; manners *as* morals? Or is it morals *as* manners?," she asks, in words that seem to mimic Moore's own overfastidious manner with language. Bishop cannot answer the riddle. Her response is subjective, tentative, and inconclusive in ways that mark—one last time—her aesthetic and philosophical difference from Moore: "Since like Alice, 'in a dreamy sort of way,' I can't answer either question, it doesn't matter which way I put it; it *seems* to be making sense" (*Collected Prose* 156).

It was in *Geography III* (1976) that Bishop finally succeeded in lifting herself out from under Moore's signature. In these poems, which were for the most part written after Moore's death in 1972, Bishop turned toward her own "letters written in 'Magic Ink' " as the autobiographical subject of her work. As David Kalstone observes: "The time and the space these poems lay claim to are more peculiarly Elizabeth Bishop's own—less geological, less historical, less vastly natural; her poems are more openly inner landscapes than ever before" (*Five Temperaments* 31). But while Bishop places her private history, particularly her childhood in Nova Scotia, at the center of these poems, she would never move in the direction of what she called the "School of Anguish" poets—represented by Robert Lowell, Theodore Roethke, John Berryman, Anne Sexton, and Sylvia Plath. "I *hate* confessional poetry, and so many people are writing it these days," she told one of her students at the University of Washington in 1966. "Besides, they seldom have anything interesting to 'confess' anyway. Mostly they write about a lot of things which I should think were best left unsaid" (Wehr 327).

In the personal poems of *Geography III*, Bishop actively resisted what she considered the more morbid, self-absorbed, and self-pitying dimensions of confessional writing. Her private and public scenes of disaster are modulated and managed through formal control, understatement, irony, and humor. "My outlook is pessimistic," Bishop wrote to Anne Stevenson, in words that sum up the underlying vision of her work. "I think we are still barbarians, barbarians who commit a hundred indecencies and cruelties every day of our lives." "But," she added, "I think we should be gay in spite of it, sometimes even giddy,—to make life endurable and to keep ourselves 'new, tender, quick' " (Washington University Library, January 8, 1964).

It is in the opening poem of *Geography III*, "In the Waiting Room," that Bishop for the first time names herself as the autobiographical subject of her verse. "You are an *I* / you are an *Elizabeth*," she says, in a poem that evokes the terror she experienced as a child when she realizes that her "foolish" and "timid" aunt's "*oh!* of pain" in the dentist's office is in fact hers:

> Without thinking at all
> I was my foolish aunt,
> I—we—were falling, falling.
>
>   . . .
>
> But I felt: you are an *I*,
> you are an *Elizabeth*,
> you are one of *them*.
> *Why* should you be one, too?
> I scarcely dared to look
> to see what it was I was.
>   (*Complete Poems* 160)

On the broadest level, "In the Waiting Room," like other Bishop poems, inscribes the terrifying instability of the "I" and individual identity as the traditional bounds between inside and outside, self and world collapse into mere boundlessness and flux: "Why should I be my aunt, / or me, or anyone?," the child asks, as the waiting room begins "sliding / beneath a big black wave, / another, and another" (*Complete Poems* 161). But the poem also registers the girlchild's terror and resistance as she experiences her identification with *other women* as a fall into the oppression and constraints of gender—signified by her "foolish aunt" and "those awful hanging breasts" she sees in the *National Geographic* as she reads and waits in the dentist's office. In words that adumbrate Bishop's later refusal to be categorized and anthologized as a woman poet and her lifelong friendship and struggle with Marianne Moore, the child's terror registers Bishop's own desire for distinction and difference and her simultaneous fear of having her historically specific "I" lost and absorbed in the sexual identity she shared with other women— including Marianne Moore.

The family history poems and the autobiographical "I" of *Geography III* were in some sense so powerful and so compelling that they have, over the last decade, precipitated a critical rereading and reevaluation of Bishop's entire work that has tended to sharpen her distance, difference, and distinction from Moore. "Unlike the poetry of her predecessor," writes Patricia Wallace, "Bishop's work is fundamentally personal and is so in ways we have yet to acknowledge" (97). Whereas earlier critics tended to emphasize the Moore-like qualities of Bishop's work—its impersonality, surface exactitude, and formal elegance—and feminist critics tended to dismiss Bishop's work in favor of more explicitly personal and confessional women poets, recent critics, under the influence of *Geography III*, have begun to offer revisionary readings of Bishop's work, noting that it is, as Thomas Travisano says, "permeated by controlled subjectivity" and an exploration of "the border ground conjoining imagination and fact" (10); and that, as Robert Dale Parker argues, "in addition to Bishop's famous descriptions quiet and clear, her poems are full of confusion and wonder about things, she never can make quiet or clear—about sexuality, politics, the burdens of imagination, the fate of the self" (ix).

What these revisionary readings suggest is that there was from the first at the center of Bishop's work "an *I*," "an *Elizabeth*"—mutable, unregenerate, and tentative to the end—who was, like the narrator of "In Prison," exerting "an *evil influence*" as she wrote against and wickedly undid not only the mannered, moral, and modernist vision of her literary ancestor but all master narratives—American or otherwise—that would make the essential disparateness and mystery of self and world cohere. These revisionary readings may be pushed even farther as we begin to recognize the ways Bishop's rebellion "in shades and shadows" was bound up with her sense of otherness and self-division as a lesbian woman writer. In fact, Bishop herself pushes us toward these rereadings of her work when, in the last lines of the last poem that she published before her death in 1979, this "creature divided" breaks the "bubble" of constraint and names what had formerly been said and not said in her poems: "flying wherever / it feels like, gay!" ("Sonnet," *Complete Poems* 192)

5

Adrienne Rich, Emily Dickinson, and the Limits of Sisterhood

> When my dreams showed signs
> of becoming
> politically correct
> no unruly images
> escaping beyond borders
> when walking in the street I found my
> themes cut out for me
> knew what I would not report
> for fear of enemies' usage
> then I began to wonder
> —Adrienne Rich
"North American Time"

In an essay on Elizabeth Bishop entitled "The Eye of the Outsider" (1983), Adrienne Rich comments on her quest as a young woman writer for a specifically female literary genealogy: "I was looking for a clear female tradition; the tradition I was discovering was diffuse, elusive, often cryptic" (*Blood, Bread, and Poetry* 125). In part because Rich was looking for a particular kind of women's writing and in part because of Bishop's literary reputation as a high modernist poet of wit, objectivity, and formal control, Bishop seemed at once inaccessible and unavailable to Rich as a literary model. "Women poets searching for older contemporaries in that period," says Rich, "were supposed to look to 'Miss' Marianne Moore as the paradigm of what a woman poet might accomplish, and after her, to 'Miss' Bishop. Both had been selected and certified by the literary establishment, which was, as now, white, male, and at least ostensibly heterosexual" (125). Rich herself "felt drawn but also repelled, by Bishop's early work," finding it "impenetrable: intellectualized to the point of obliquity" (125). It was only later that Rich's increasing sense of outsiderhood and marginality as a lesbian poet and her increased emphasis on the intersecting oppressions of race, class, and gender led her to a new appreciation of Bishop's own "struggles for self-definition and her sense of difference." "Especially given the times and customs of the 1940s and 1950s," Rich wrote in her 1983 essay, "Bishop's work now seems to me remarkably honest and courageous" (125).

What Rich's dynamic and changing relationship with Bishop suggests is, first, the reality of diffuseness, difference, and change beneath the seemingly static fictions of the "woman writer" and the "women's tradition"; and, second, the ways particular (re)constructions of the female literary tradition and the ways we read, interpret, and value particular women writers can be altered by changes in our social and political perspective. Indeed, the woman writer, relations among and between women writers, and what has come to be known as the "female literary tradition" are multiple, fluid, and continually self-transforming in ways we have yet to explore.

This chapter examines Rich's similarly changing relationship with Emily Dickinson as it foregrounds the problems of difference, change, and struggle not only in Rich's life and work but in the feminist movement itself. Speaking of Virginia Woolf's complex and passionate portrayal of the mother/daughter relationship in *To The Lighthouse,* Rich says: "Mrs. Ramsay is a kaleidoscopic character, and in successive readings of the novel, she changes, almost as our own mothers alter in perspective as we ourselves are changing" (*Of Woman Born* 227). Rich's words perfectly characterize the dynamics of her relationship with Emily Dickinson. Like Mrs. Ramsay, Dickinson is a kaleidoscopic character in the text of Rich's life and work. In seeking to repossess her as a literary precursor and foremother, Rich not only discovers new readings of Dickinson. Her successive readings of Dickinson also register changes in Rich's attitude toward women, motherhood, women's literary history, and the women's movement itself as she evolved toward a female-centered and lesbian feminist ethics, poetics, and politics.

Like Rich's changing response to Elizabeth Bishop, these changes and differences in Rich's readings of Dickinson over many years are important because they reveal the acts of reading, constructing, and interpreting the female poetic tradition as socially and politically constituted acts. They are also important because Rich herself has played such a central role in naming and in some sense producing what feminist writing, feminist criticism, feminist literary history, and the feminist movement would be in the United States. "Re-vision—the act of looking back, of seeing with fresh eyes, of entering an old text from a new critical direction—is for women more than a chapter in cultural history: it is an act of survival," Rich wrote in her now famous 1971 essay "When We Dead Awaken: Writing as Re-Vision." "A radical critique of literature," she said, "feminist in its impulse, would take the work first of all as a clue to how we live, how we have been living, how we have been led to imagine ourselves, how our language has trapped as well as liberated us, how the very act of naming has been till now a male prerogative, and how we can begin to see and name—and therefore live—afresh" (*On Lies, Secrets, and Silence* 35). Rich's empowering words have played a commanding role in authorizing and calling forth the essentially political work of excavating, rereading, and reinterpreting women's texts and women's writing that has been the main project of American feminist criticism over the last two decades.[1]

But in pursuing this work, Rich, and along with her many American feminist literary critics, would become increasingly essentialist in their revisions and reconstructions of the female literary tradition. Thus, in *An American Triptych: Anne Bradstreet, Emily Dickinson, Adrienne Rich* (1984), Wendy Martin argues that American women poets represent a particularly "female aesthetic-ethic" of love, nurturance, mutuality, and community. "Building on the tradition of such women poets as H. D., Millay, Moore, Plath, and Levertov as well as Bradstreet and Dickinson," writes Martin, "Rich has evolved a female aesthetic-ethic based on shared relationship, emotional reciprocity, and empathetic identification—concerns that Carol Gilligan has recently argued are characteristic of women's development" (234). Like Martin, most of Rich's critics have tended to accept rather than to question or problematize the potentially totalizing terms of Rich's transhistorical and essentially white female–centered "aesthetic-ethic."[2]

Thus, a kind of double standard has emerged in recent American criticism. Whereas the new historicists and new Americanists who came of age during the sixties have undertaken a massive questioning of the values, assumptions, and ideological complicity of white male canonical writers, feminist critics who emerged during the same period have tended to be appreciative and more or less celebratory in their critical representations of women writers and women's literary history. Rather than continuing to endorse and reenact Rich's construction of the woman writer, women's writing, and the women's literary tradition at a particular stage in her poetic career, in this chapter on Rich, Dickinson, and the limits of sisterhood, I shall examine the fluid and changing problematics of Rich's feminist theory and practice as they map out conflicts, contradictions, and changes in the feminist movement itself. I shall argue that, ironically, as Rich became increasingly conscious of her own contradictory location as a Southern Jewish, lesbian, feminist poet in the United States, she moved against and beyond the white, Eurocentric, feminist theory and practice she herself did so much to call forth. Just as Rich's readings of Dickinson changed at different stages in her poetic career, so Rich's feminist theory has become different from itself, even as her earlier white female–centered "aesthetic-ethic" has settled in the American academy into a particular kind of feminist practice—a practice that is now under attack as a putatively unified, monolithic, and naive American feminism signified by the work of Adrienne Rich herself.

Breaking the Mold

Rich came to Dickinson early, but for her, as for several other women writers, the Dickinson legend got in the way of her being repossessed as a poetic mother: "I know that for me, reading her poems as a child and then as a young girl already seriously writing poetry, she was a problematic figure. I first read her in the selection heavily edited by her niece which appeared in 1937; a later and fuller edition appeared in 1945 when I was sixteen, and the complete, unbowdlerized edition by Johnson did not appear until fifteen years later." In fact, says Rich, "the publication of each of these editions was crucial to me in successive decades of my life" (*On Lies, Secrets, and Silence* 167–68).

Before she learned to mask her personal experience in imitations of the male poets she read as an undergraduate, Rich kept private notebooks of poems imitating Dickinson and Edna St. Vincent Millay: "I spent months, at sixteen," Rich says, "memorizing and writing imitations of Millay's sonnets; and in notebooks of that period I find what are obviously attempts to imitate Dickinson's metrics and verbal compression" (*On Lies, Secrets, and Silence* 40). Rich was struck by the language and meter of Dickinson's verse and by her precise notation of psychic states. At the same time, however, Rich, like Amy Lowell and Marianne Moore, was troubled by the legend of Dickinson's life, which seemed to whisper that "a woman who undertook such explorations must pay with renunciations, isolation, and incorporeality" (*On Lies, Secrets, and Silence* 168).

Rich was particularly struck by the apparent split between the power of the woman poet and the powerlessness of the legendary child-woman, a split she found embodied in the poem from which *Bolts of Melody* (1945) drew its title. "I would not paint—a picture—," the poem begins, as Dickinson proceeds paradoxically both to use and to refuse her creative powers:

> Nor would I be a Poet—
> It's finer—own the Ear—
> Enamored—impotent—content—
> The License to revere,
> A privilege so awful
> What would the Dower be,
> Had I the Art to stun myself
> With Bolts of Melody!
>   (*Poems* #505)

At a time when Rich was beginning to write poetry seriously, she came to see in Dickinson's split between actor and acted-upon, power and powerlessness, the division she herself was experiencing between the potency of the girl who wrote poems and the passivity of the girl who—enamored, impotent, content—had resigned herself to playing a more orthodox feminine role.

In her first volume of poems, *A Change of World,* Rich wore a similar mask of passivity and containment—a mask that helped her gain immediate acceptance by the male literary establishment. But in their response to Rich, as in their response to Dickinson, the critics mistook the mask for the thing itself. In the foreword to *A Change of World,* W. H. Auden patronizingly observed: "The poems a reader will encounter in this book are neatly and modestly dressed, speak quietly but do not mumble, respect their elders but are not cowed by them, and do not tell fibs: that, for a first volume is a good deal" (11). Thus, Rich became another in the long line of women poets, including Anne Bradstreet, Jane Turell, Phillis Wheatley, Emily Dickinson, and Sylvia Plath, whose works were first presented to the American public via the perceptions and misperceptions of their male relatives, rulers, mentors, or teachers.[3] Responding to the volume as if it were the body of fifties' womanhood, W. H. Auden misperceived the nature of Rich, just as Thomas Higginson had misperceived Dickinson, and Robert Lowell would misperceive Plath. He missed the fact that beneath the neat and modest dress of the poems lurked "storm warnings," "murmurings of missile-throwers," and an atmosphere of physical and psychological violence that endangered men, women, and the future of the world.

Only occasionally in these early poems—in the startling juxtapositions and childlike tone of "A View of the Terrace" or in the cosmic riddles of "What Ghosts Can Say" and "Purely Local"—do we find evidence of Rich's private apprenticeship to Dickinson. Whereas Dickinson's poems are imagistic, metaphysical, and stylistically "slant," Rich's poems, at this stage, are discursive, social, and stylistically balanced. Unlike Dickinson's experimental form, Rich's craft is a sign of her formalist detachment from, rather than her engagement of, her personal psychic experience. Eager to be sufficiently universal, and thus nonfemale, Rich imitated the style of her male masters, who included at that time Robert Frost, T. S. Eliot, William Butler Yeats, and Wallace Stevens. She had not yet discovered her female experience as a subject for poetry and a potential source of poetic power. In accord with the modernist emphasis on the impersonality of the artist, Rich's personal and historical experience as a woman was contained and controlled by the craft of her formalist verse, and any conflict she might feel between woman and poet was projected through male personae and the objective masks of female artist figures like Aunt Jennifer, who was "Still ringed with ordeals she was mastered by" (*A Change of World* 19).

The masking evident in Rich's first volume of poems corresponds with the masking that characterized her life in the early fifties. Having married a graduate student in Economics at Harvard University in 1953 and given birth to three sons, in 1955, 1957, and 1959, respectively, Rich was split between the role she was expected to play as a wife and mother and the script she was trying to write for herself. After the publication of her second book of poems, *The Diamond Cutters* (1955), Rich stopped writing poetry. She wrote in a 1956 notebook:

> Whether it's the extreme lassitude of early pregnancy or something more funda-
> mental, I don't know; but of late I've felt, toward poetry,—both reading and
> writing it—nothing but boredom and indifference. Especially toward my own
> and that of my immediate contemporaries. When I receive a letter soliciting
> mss., or someone alludes to my "career", I have a strong sense of wanting to
> deny all responsibility for and interest in that person who writes—or who wrote.
>
> *(Of Woman Born* 26–27)

Between 1955 and the publication of *Snapshots of a Daughter-in-Law* in 1963, Rich struggled to unite the divided energies of body and mind, woman and poet, relation and creation in order, as she said in a 1958 notebook, "to give birth to—a recognizable, autonomous self, a creation in poetry and in life" (*Of Woman Born* 29).

Rich was aided in the process of placing herself at the center of her verse by a renewed contact with Emily Dickinson, whom she read in the late fifties in Thomas Johnson's unbowdlerized 1955 edition of *The Complete Poems*. Rich was impressed by "the unquestionable power and importance of the mind revealed there"; she also found in Dickinson's verse a means of linking her personal experience as a woman with a more public sphere. "More than any other poet," says Rich, "Emily Dickinson seemed to tell me that the intense inner event, the personal and psychological, was inseparable from the univer-sal; that there was a range for psychological poetry beyond mere self-ex-pression" (*On Lies, Secrets, and Silence* 168). Rather than reading Dickin-son's poems as the register of a specifically female psychology or sensibility, Rich appears to look on such readings as part of the problem rather than the solution of female poetic expression. It is because Dickinson appears to redeem and validate women's psychic experience for "universal" purposes that Rich is drawn to and enabled by her work at this point in her poetic career. For if the "intense inner [female] event" is not part of a separate sphere but of a "universal" sphere, then there is a "range" for the female poet "beyond mere self-expression." Rejecting her 1955 volume of poems, *The Diamond Cutters,* as "mere exercises for poems I hadn't written," in the late fifties Rich was able, as she says, "to write, for the first time, directly about experiencing myself as a woman" (*On Lies, Secrets, and Silence* 42, 44).

Rich's experience as a woman is at the structural and thematic center of her next volume of poems, *Snapshots of a Daughter-in-Law,* but it is an experience marked by a deep sense of ambivalence about other women, women writers, women's history, and mothers in particular. "We groan beneath your weight," Rich says of the mother in "A Woman Mourned by Daughters":

> And all this universe
> dares us to lay a finger
> anywhere, save exactly
> as you would wish it done
>   (35)

While the poems have some of the contemporary tone of Robert Lowell's *Life Studies* (1959), Rich's focus, as the title suggests, is on a woman's way of seeing and being in a world circumscribed by the laws of the fathers. Her words at the outset of *Snapshots,* "Now knowledge finds me out; / in all its risible untidiness" (12), sum up the impulse behind the break with traditional poetic and social forms that took place in the eight years between *The Diamond Cutters* and *Snapshots.* As knowledge found Rich out as a woman poet in fifties America, she began a quest for the historical sources of women's oppression that led her to the work of other women writers, including Emily Dickinson, Mary Wollstonecraft, Simone de Beauvoir, and her contemporary, Denise Levertov.

What is striking about this early effort to locate and place herself in relation to the historical experience of women is Rich's refusal to posit an essential female nature, her impatience with traditional masculine representations that had embedded female nature in the body and maternity, and her corresponding uneasiness with women and women writers who appeared to embody the limits imposed by men on women historically. Rich's own representations of women in *Snapshots of a Daughter-in-Law* are marked by a refusal to idealize and romanticize either women or the relationships between them. Mary Wollstonecraft was "a woman, partly brave and partly good, / who fought with what she partly understood" (23). And women are capable of monstrousness not only within but among themselves:

> Two handsome women, gripped in argument,
> each proud, acute, subtle, I hear scream
> across the cut glass and majolica
> Like Furies cornered from their prey:
> The argument *ad feminam,* all the old knives
> that have rusted in my back, I drive in yours,
> *ma semblable, ma soeur!*
>   (22)

Although the "argument *ad feminam*" suggests that patriarchal violation is the historical determinant of hostility among women, at this stage, at least, the problems of difference and even violence among women are not recuperated by any romantic vision of a naturally loving and nurturant sisterhood that will come to life as patriarchy is destroyed. In fact, Rich's *Snapshots* seem critical of the very polarity between male aggression and female nurturance that she would later generalize into a universal principle.

Rich's attempt to place her experience as a woman at the center of *Snapshots of a Daughter-in-Law* also corresponded with a transformation in the voice and form of her poetry. This transformation is particularly evident in the title poem, "Snapshots of a Daughter-in-Law," a poem in which the "ghost" of Dickinson is also evident. As Rich discovers a form commensurate with the "risible untidiness" of her knowledge as a woman—a daughter-in-law—defined and bound by the laws of the fathers, her style and vision begin to approximate the unfinished, fragmented quality of Dickinson's verse. For Rich, as for Dickinson, the fracture of image and syntax becomes not only a poetic strategy but an emblem of her subject position as woman in a world split by the polarities of masculine and feminine, mind and body, self and other, transcendence and immanence.

"The poem," says Rich, "was jotted in fragments during children's naps, brief hours in a library, or at 3:00 A.M. after rising with a wakeful child. I despaired of doing any continuous work at the time. Yet I began to feel that my fragments and scraps had a common consciousness and a common theme, one which I would have been very unwilling to put on paper at an earlier time because I had been taught that poetry should be 'universal,' which meant, of course, nonfemale" (*On Lies, Secrets, and Silence* 44). Through the precise, imagistic notation of personal states of mind, Rich achieves some of the psychic intensity and range that she admired in Dickinson's verse. At the same time, through the juxtaposition of these images in a sequence of mental snapshots, Rich collapses the traditional bounds of lyric poetry into the looser and more experimental poetics of the long poem, a form that had been, in the West at least, a traditionally male domain.

If Rich moved closer to Dickinson's fractured style as she moved away from the neatly and modestly dressed lyrics she had learned to write under her male mentors, she also moved closer to Dickinson's life as she meditated on the experience of daughters in the kingdom of the fathers. What she finds, however, is not an empowering mother, but a victim and a neurotic. In fact, Dickinson's life and writing become part of a more general critique of patriarchy in "Snapshots of a Daughter-in-Law," as Rich reflects on the ways female energies have been warped and thwarted by the rigidly defined codes that circumscribe female lives:

> Knowing themselves too well in one another:
> their gifts no pure fruition, but a thorn,
> the prick filed sharp against a hint of scorn . . .
> Reading while waiting
> for the iron to heat,
> writing, *My Life had stood—a Loaded Gun—*
> in that Amherst pantry while the jellies boil and scum,
> or, more often,
> iron-eyed and beaked and purposed as a bird,
> dusting everything on the whatnot every day of life.
>
> (22)

The oppositions between gifts/thorns, reading/waiting, writing/pantry stress the conflict between creative energy and destructive confinement embodied in Dickinson's lines, "My Life had stood—a Loaded Gun—."[4] Sandwiched between the wall of her Amherst pantry and the boil and scum of jellies, Dickinson becomes for Rich a troubling exemplar of all those women who, like herself, experience their potency as an instrument of destruction or as a form of demonic possession.

As Rich's allusion to Dickinson in "Snapshots" suggests, her renewed contact with Dickinson in the fifties was full of ambivalence. On the one hand, as a woman poet struggling to define herself within and against a traditionally masculine poetic tradition, Rich experiences a sense of empathy and identification with Dickinson; on the other hand, as in Lowell's "The Sisters," Rich experiences her relationship with Dickinson as a site of entrapment and limitation. The image of Dickinson in "Snapshots," like the images of women throughout the volume, projects a negative and destructive dimension of the mother, both literal and figurative, from which the free-spirited daughter seeks to release herself.

The liberation Rich conceives at the end of "Snapshots of a Daughter-in-Law" comes not from bonding with but from rising above women's lives:

> Well,
>   she's long about her coming who must be
>   more merciless to herself than history.
>   Her mind full to the wind, I see her plunge
>   breasted and glancing through the currents,
>   taking the light upon her
>   at least as beautiful as any boy
>   or helicopter,
>   poised, still coming,
>   her fine blades making the air wince
>   but her cargo

> no promise then:
> delivered
> palpable
> ours.
>
>   (24–25)

"At least as beautiful as any boy / or helicopter," Rich's new woman is defined not in relation to her matrilineal heritage, but in relation to a masculine figure—a boy child—who is linked with the mobile and propulsive energies of modern technology that Rich would later associate with the violations of patriarchy.

Rich's image of the helicopter is in fact borrowed from Simone de Beauvoir, who also saw female biology as the source not of female power but of "the enslavement of the female to the species" (*The Second Sex* 33). Arguing against traditional historical constructions of female nature, de Beauvoir wrote: "Woman is not a completed reality, but rather a becoming, and it is in her becoming that she should be compared with man; that is to say, her *possibilities* should be defined. What gives rise to much of the debate is the tendency to reduce her to what she has been" (30). Like de Beauvoir, Rich does not view the "coming" of the new woman at the end of "Snapshots" as a return to "what she has been" historically: the new woman is "still coming," and thus not a fixed identity or a "completed reality" but rather a figure of openness, movement, and possibility. Even the lines, images, and syntax of this final passage are broken in a manner that suggests the ways the fracture and reconstitution of language become integral to Rich's struggle to name this creature in the process of becoming.

The final poem of *Snapshots of a Daughter-in-Law* represents a similar flight from traditional constructions of the female. Here, Rich's stylistic model is not Dickinson, but Denise Levertov, to whom the poem is dedicated. Imitating Levertov's verse notation by duplicating the process of thought in the arrangement of line and image, Rich envisions herself as "The Roofwalker," breaking away from a half-finished house:

> A life I didn't choose
> chose me: even
> my tools are the wrong ones
> for what I have to do.
> I'm naked, ignorant,
> a naked man fleeing
> across the roofs
>
>   (63)

Here again, the house, like Dickinson's pantry, is the locus of destructive rather than creative energies. It is by bonding not with Levertov but with a naked male figure that Rich achieves her imaginative release.

Snapshots of a Daughter-in-Law sums up Rich's attitude toward the female and the feminine at this point in her poetic career. She dwells on the female figure as a victim rather than a creator; she emphasizes destructive rather than creative female energies; she conceives of liberation as a breaking away from rather than a bonding with women's lives; and she figures her imaginative release as the liberation of a masculine rather than a feminine power. It is only by breaking out of traditional constructions of the maternal and eternal feminine—by smashing "the mold straight off"—that Rich imagines the possibility of a new "creation in poetry and in life."

Feminism and Poetry

Rich's next volume of poems, *Necessities of Life*, was published in 1966, the same year that the National Organization for Women (NOW) was founded. The poems of *Necessities of Life* reverse the final vision of *Snapshots of a Daughter-in-Law:* the new theme of this volume is survival, or the "necessities of life," as Rich turns inward toward a sustained meditation on her personal resources before the advance into the world and toward the more active political engagement that would characterize her work in the late sixties and seventies. In the title poem, which opens the volume, Rich records the process of rebirth that comes from repossessing herself and women's culture. Having been "wolfed almost to shreds" by defining herself in relation to others, the poet rediscovers the inner resources of herself that will enable her to "dare inhabit the world":

> I learned to make myself
>
> unappetizing. Scaly as a dry bulb
> thrown into a cellar
>
> I used myself, let nothing use me.
> Like being on a private dole,
>
> sometimes more like kneading bricks in Egypt.
> What life was there, was mine.
>
> *(Necessities of Life* 9–10)

Rather than fleeing the half-built house, she undertakes to rebuild the house, brick by brick, out of herself. The future she imagines is inhabited not by naked men fleeing houses, but by women in houses, waiting breathlessly to tell their tales:

I have invitations:
a curl of mist steams upward

from a field, visible as my breath,
houses along a road stand waiting

like old women knitting, breathless
to tell their tales.

(10)

The new emphasis here on herself and women's lives as a source of creation and transformation is the dominant note of *Necessities of Life*. The final image of "old women knitting, breathless / to tell their tales" also prepares for the return to the female as a figure of power that would mark future volumes of Rich's work.

This new emphasis on houses and women as possible sites of creative power coincides with the unification and concentration of energies Rich was attempting to achieve in her personal life at this time. In a 1965 notebook entry, Rich recorded the following direction to herself:

> Necessity for a more unyielding discipline in my life.
> Recognize the uselessness of blind anger.
> Limit society.
> Use children's school hours better, for work & solitude.
> Refuse to be distracted from own style of life.
> Less waste.
> Be harder & harder on poems.
>
> (*Of Woman Born* 31)

As Rich sought to unify the energy of relation and the energy of creation, she came to see Dickinson not as a victim but as a survivor, whose discipline, seclusion, and isolation made her a countervailing figure—a spirit-sister—in her struggle against the culture of domesticity represented by her biological mother and her own motherhood. "Given her vocation," said Rich of Dickinson, "she was neither eccentric nor quaint; she was determined to survive, to use her powers, to practice necessary economies" (*On Lies, Secrets, and Silence* 160).

It is as a figure of "necessary economies" that Dickinson reentered Rich's life and work during the sixties and seventies. In Dickinson's choice for herself and her art, Rich saw not only a model of female survival in patriarchal culture but also a figure of female poetic power, creating herself and recreating the world through the power of language. As a woman poet who was herself struggling to challenge and dislodge the phallogocentric assumptions embedded in language and culture, Rich found in the slant style, paradoxical vision, and fractured rhythm of Dickinson's verse a clue to the ways patriarchal language might be used as a vehicle of female creation and transformation. In fact, Rich's rediscovery of Dickinson as a source of linguistic renewal corresponded with a transformation in her poetics. In 1965 Rich wrote "I Am in Danger—Sir—," in which she celebrates Dickinson's creative potency; in the same year, in "Poetry and Experience," she declared her break with her earlier concept of poetry as a predetermined arrangement of ideas and feelings and her move toward a new concept of poetry as a means of renaming, reknowing, and reconstituting the world: "In my earlier poems," says Rich, "I told you, as precisely and eloquently as I knew how, about something; in the more recent poems something is happening, something has happened to me and, if I have been a good parent to the poem, something will happen to you who read it" (*Adrienne Rich's Poetry* 89).[5]

As in Dickinson's poems, the drama of Rich's new poems is created not by logical development or narrative line, but by verbal compression and the dynamic tension generated by the splitting of syntax, image, line, and unit. Thus, Dickinson was an early model for the poetics of process that Rich pursued in *Leaflets* (1969) and *The Will to Change* (1971) in which, through the ghazal couplets of Mirza Ghalib, the projective verse of Charles Olson, and the new wave cinema of Jean-Luc Godard, Rich sought a form commensurate with an age of cultural and political breakup and collapse. In fact, Rich's two-space rhythm, which she employed for the first time in *Leaflets* to achieve fracture, pause, and emphasis, was probably a descendant of Dickinson's dash.

"I Am in Danger—Sir—," which appears at midpoint in *Necessities of Life,* underscores Dickinson's centrality to Rich's new ethics and poetics. The title of the poem is taken from one of Dickinson's letters to Higginson, who apparently suggested that she regularize—or eliminate entirely—her rhyme and meter. Dickinson replied: "You think my gait 'spasmodic'—I am in danger—Sir—You think me 'uncontrolled'—I have no Tribunal" (*Letters* 2: 408). Rich's title capitalizes on the ambiguity of Dickinson's response. Her unorthodox metrics are a sign of the danger and risk of engaging her poetic powers and pushing beyond the bounds of conventional womanhood. But there is another kind of danger: both Dickinson's life and her language are endangered by the patriarchal culture in which she lives.

Imitating some of Dickinson's "half-cracked" poetic strategies, including the dash, Rich attempts to break through the mothballed legend to discover who Dickinson is:

> "Half-cracked" to Higginson, living,
> afterward famous in garbled versions,
> your hoard of dazzling scraps a battlefield,
> now your old snood

> mothballed at Harvard
> and you in your variorum monument
> equivocal to the end—
> who are you?
>
> (*Necessities of Life* 33)

In the course of the poem, Rich undertakes to answer this question, and, in so doing, she works her way back beyond the "garbled versions" of the masculine critical tradition to discover Dickinson as a model of artistic resourcefulness. Unlike her earlier allusion to "My Life had stood—a Loaded Gun—," here Rich sees Dickinson's life and art as an emblem of the creative rather than the destructive dimensions of female power:

> Gardening the day-lily,
> wiping the wine-glass stems,
> your thought pulsed on behind
> a forehead battered paper-thin,
>
> you, woman, masculine
> in single-mindedness,
> for whom the word was more
> than a symptom—
>
> a condition of being.
>
> (33)

Behind the publicly acceptable mask of domesticity, Rich sees pulsating the mental energy of the poet: whatever seemed battered in her demeanor was the product not of weakness, but of inward power thrusting itself against a hostile world, in single-minded devotion to her own artistic creation.

In describing the word as "a condition of being" for Dickinson, Rich suggests that it was in and through language that Dickinson realized herself and her creative power. Reversing the traditional view of Dickinson as a victim forced into seclusion and renunciation by a failed love affair, Rich presents Dickinson's lifestyle as the self-conscious choice of a woman artist who, in saying yes to her creative power, had to say no to the "spoiled language" of patriarchy:

> the air buzzing with spoiled language
> sang in your ears
> of Perjury
>
> and in your half-cracked way you chose
> silence for entertainment,
> chose to have it out at last
> on your own premises.
>
> (33)

The perjury that sang in Dickinson's ears is the false witness of female lives embedded in patriarchal language and culture. Rather than perjure herself, Rich suggests, Dickinson chose withdrawal and silence as a means of surviving as a woman poet in nineteenth-century America. The repetition of "half-cracked" at the end of the poem stresses the disjunction between the "cracked" image of Dickinson and the absolute sanity of her choice: her life and her poems only appear "cracked" in the spoiled and perjured context of the phallogocentric tradition. The repetition of "chose" at the end of one line and at the beginning of another further underscores Dickinson's powerful will to survive. No longer dwelling on the image of Dickinson pinned between the boil and scum of jellies in her Amherst pantry, Rich underlines the connection between her decision to stay at home, her determination to have her own will, and her power to create herself and recreate the world, by yoking the three ideas in the final image of the poem: "on your own premises." Unlike the house of *Snapshots of a Daughter-in-Law,* here the house has become the site not of destructive female energies, but of potency and necessary economies.

As a figure of female survival and linguistic power, Dickinson was the first of a number of women Rich would invoke in her ongoing struggle to repossess her matrilineal heritage. However, if Rich begins in *Necessities of Life* to explore the sources of female power, in this volume and in the 1969 *Leaflets,* she continues to project her poetic power as a masculine daemon or male lover who comes from outside to take possession of her. Here, again, she parallels Dickinson. In fact, in "I Am in Danger—Sir—," Rich figured Dickinson's powerful will as male: she described her as a "woman, masculine / in single-mindedness." Rich, too, projects her imaginative power as a masculine figure, her "fierce half-brother" Orion, in the opening poem of *Leaflets:*

> you were my genius, you
> my cast-iron Viking, my helmed
> lion-heart king in prison.
>
> Years later now you're young
>
> My fierce half-brother, staring
> down from the simplified west.
>   (11)

It was not until the late sixties and early seventies, in the increasingly experimental and politically engaged poems of *The Will to Change* (1971), that Rich would begin to locate the sources of her creative power within herself and other women. In "Planetarium," for example, Rich associates her power to transform human consciousness with the astronomical work of Caroline Herschel (1750–1848), whose discoveries as an astromer were eclipsed by those of her brother, William:

> I am an instrument in the shape
> of a woman trying to translate pulsations
> into images   for the relief of the body
> and the reconstruction of the mind.
>
> *(The Will to Change* 14)

Unlike "Snapshots of a Daughter-in-Law" in which Rich still speaks of the experience of women in the third rather than the first person, in "Planetarium" Rich speaks for the first time as a woman poet and an "I," who identifies with the historical power and experience of other women. But while Rich names herself as a woman poet, she does not speak as what Simone de Beauvoir called a "natural species" or a "completed reality" *(The Second Sex* 30). As "an instrument in the shape / of a woman" she is the subject of a "battery of signals" and impulses rather than a fixed and biologically determined female being.

During the years of personal and social upheaval in the sixties and seventies, Rich came to see the breakup in her private life as woman, wife, and mother and the breakup in the political sphere, occasioned by black, feminist, anti-war, and other forms of social protest, as signs of the larger failure of patriarchal values. In a 1973 article in *The American Poetry Review,* she drew a direct correlation between the bombings in Vietnam and sexual violence at home:

> The bombings, for example, if they have anything to teach us, must be understood in the light of something closer to home, both more private and painful, and more general and endemic, than the institutions, class, racial oppression, the hubris of the Pentagon or the ruthlessness of a right-wing administration: the bombings are so wholly sadistic, gratuitous and demonic that they can finally be seen, if we care to see them, for what they are: acts of concrete sexual violence, an expression of the congruence of violence and sex in the masculine psyche.
>
> ("Caryatid: A Column" 10)

Although Rich did not completely discount a Marxist or class analysis of the sources of human oppression, she became increasingly uneasy with the seeming invisibility of women in the male-centered ideologies and political practices of the radical left. Like Kate Millett, Shulamith Firestone, and other early radical feminists, she came to see the sexual as opposed to the economic class system as the primary oppression, and a transformation in traditional relations between the sexes and traditional conceptions of male and female identity as the key to personal and political renewal.

It was this transformation in sexual identity and the traditional relationships of men and women that Rich emphasized in her important essay "When We Dead Awaken: Writing as Re-Vision," which was initially delivered at a

Modern Language Association session on "The Woman Writer in the Twentieth Century" sponsored by the Commission on the Status of Women in the Profession.[6] "A change in the concept of sexual identity," Rich said, "is essential if we are not going to see the old political order re-assert itself in every new revolution" (*Adrienne Rich's Poetry* 90). She emphasized the need to reread the literature of the past from a feminist perspective not to retrieve a tradition, male or female, but rather to change it: "We need to know the writing of the past, and know it differently than we have ever known it; *not to pass on a tradition but to break its hold over us*" (91; emphasis added). She also emphasized the need to break with traditional notions of male and female spheres. Reflecting on her own sense of self-division as a woman writer, wife, and mother in the fifties and sixties, she said: "The choice still seemed to be between 'love'—womanly, maternal love, altruistic love—a love defined and ruled by the weight of an entire culture; and egotism—a force directed by men into creation, achievement, ambition, and often at the expense of others, but justifiably so. For weren't they men, and wasn't that their destiny as womanly love was ours. *I know now that the alternatives are false ones*" (97; emphasis added).

Whatever else feminism would come to mean in succeeding years, for Rich as for many other feminist writers and critics, feminism was in this first stage a politically motivated movement against traditional constructions of male and female and the traditional equation of womanhood with love, nurturance, and the maternal. Exhorting both men and women to an awakening of consciousness and a change of world in the concluding passage of "When We Dead Awaken," Rich wrote: "We can go on trying to talk to each other, we can sometimes help each other, poetry and fiction can show us what the other is going through; but *women can no longer be primarily mothers and muses for men:* we have our own work cut out for us" (98; emphasis added).[7] In her work of the sixties and the seventies, Rich, like other radical feminists, mounted a provocative critique of the family, love, marriage, motherhood, and the sexual-class system. The irony, of course, is that by the mid-seventies in response to attacks by the right, the left, and feminists themselves, Rich and other radical feminists would end by reconstituting the very sexual polarities and gender ideologies that in the initial phase of the feminist movement they set out to dismantle and disown.

Rich's initial struggle against the polarization of male and female, self and other, mind and body, subject and object, nature and culture is at the psychic and linguistic center of the poems in *Diving into the Wreck*. In "The Stranger," the speaker seeks to get beyond the phallogocentric dualisms at the base of patriarchal oppression to name the being who is at once male and female, both and neither:

> if they ask me my identity
> what can I say but
> I am the androgyne
> I am the living mind you fail to describe
> in your dead language
> the lost noun, the verb surviving
> only in the infinitive
> the letters of my name are written under the lids
> of the newborn child
>
> (*Diving into the Wreck* 19)

This same sexually unidentified "Stranger" to the "dead language" of men plunges into the sources of self and world to discover the buried treasure of "I am she: I am he" in the title poem "Diving into the Wreck":

> We are, I am, you are
> by cowardice or courage
> the one who find our way
> back to this scene
> carrying a knife, a camera
> a book of myths
> in which
> our names do not appear.
>
> (24)

Even language, grammar, and the traditional distinctions between subjective and objective case begin to break down and become fractured as the speaker seeks to name this multiple being who is at once singular and plural—I and You and We—whose "names" do not appear in the patriarchal "book of myths."

Along with "When We Dead Awaken," *Diving into the Wreck*, which received a National Book Award in 1973, placed Rich and feminist poetry at the very center of the feminist movement in the United States. For Rich, at least, the early seventies also represented a high point of intraracial solidarity among women. When Rich received the National Book Award, she read a collective statement, accepting the award for herself, as well as for Alice Walker and Audre Lorde, whose *Revolutionary Petunias* and *From a Land Where Other People Live* had also been nominated. In the same year that *Diving into the Wreck* appeared, no less than three anthologies of women's poetry were published: *No More Masks!: An Anthology of Poems by Women; Rising Tides: 20th Century American Women Poets;* and *Psyche: The Feminine Poetic Consciousness—An Anthology of Modern American Women Poets.* The following year another anthology appeared: *The World Split Open: Four Centuries of Women Poets in England and America, 1552–1950.*[8] What these anthologies indicate is a growing market for women's poetry. For the first time many women poets began to speak and write for a specifically female audience. And increasingly, women poets, particularly Adrienne Rich, but also Audre Lorde, June Jordan, Marge Piercy, Judy Grahn, and Alta, among others, began to play a more visible role in seeking to call forth and name what the future direction of the American feminist movement would be.

Lesbian Feminist Politics and Poetics

In *Sexual Politics* Kate Millett observed: "Perhaps patriarchy's greatest psychological weapon is simply its universality and longevity. A referent scarcely exists with which it might be contrasted or by which it might be refuted. While the same might be said of class, patriarchy has a still more tenacious or powerful hold through its successful habit of passing itself off as nature" (58). As Rich began to assume a more powerful role as poet, spokesperson, and theorist of American feminism, her work became increasingly split between, on the one hand, her desire *not* to name a biologically specific and determined female nature and, on the other, her desire for a specific female "referent" and "nature" in which to ground her opposition to patriarchal history and patriarchal power. Like Hélène Cixous, Luce Irigaray, Julia Kristeva, and other French feminist theorists, who sought to respond to the phallic emphasis of Freudian and Lacanian constructions of human nature by positing a two-lipped and essentially female body out of which women speak, write, and name themselves, Rich began to move in the seventies toward an increasingly essentialist, maternal, and transhistorical construction of women, women writers, and women's history.

This move is already evident in her 1972 essay "The Anti-Feminist Woman," a reflection on motherhood in patriarchy that anticipates her 1976 volume, *Of Woman Born: Motherhood as Experience and Institution*, one of the landmark texts of cultural feminism. Drawing on Erich Neumann's *The Great Mother* (1952) and Elizabeth Gould Davis's *The First Sex* (1971), as well as J. J. Bachofen's *Mutterrecht* (1861) and Robert Briffault's *The Mothers* (1927), Rich explores the evidence for a matriarchal social order that preceded patriarchy and calls for a reintroduction of the "female principle" as a means of reversing the damages and dangers of patriarchal history. "I am a feminist because I feel endangered, psychically and physically, by this society," Rich says. "We can no longer afford to keep the female principle—the mother in all women and the woman in many men—straitened within the tight little postindustrial family, or within any male-induced notion of where the female principle is valid and where it is not" (*Adrienne Rich's Poetry* 105). The essay hovers between a representation of the "feminine" as a social construct—and thus a quality that can be possessed by men—and a representation of the "feminine" as a capacity for love, mutuality, and nurturance linked with biological motherhood. "It is hardly surprising," Rich concedes, "that feminist thinking has had to begin by rejecting physiology as a basis for consideration of ability and by exploring whatever else woman is and might be besides a body with uterus and breasts." But, she continues, "I believe that a radical reinterpretation of the concept of motherhood is required which would tell us, among many other things, more about the physical capacity for gestation and nourishment of infants and how it relates to psychological gestation and nurture as an intellectual and creative force" (*On Lies, Secrets, and Silence* 77). Here, as in her future work, Rich begins to articulate the main lines of what would come to be known as "cultural feminism"—a feminism grounded in the concept of gynocracy, matriarchy, and motherhood as the site and source of female intelligence, female creative power, and a higher and better order. Whereas in her earlier work, Rich sought to question traditional constructions of male and female as meaningful categories of analysis, in her new work, she, like other cultural feminists, turned toward a reclamation of the "female principle" as a means of transformation.[9]

In "Three Conversations" that she had with Barbara and Albert Gelpi in 1974, Rich's insistence on biological motherhood as the basis of personal, political, and feminist transformation is even more pronounced. *"Women's gift for relationship is fundamental,"* she says; "for women there isn't that radical split between self and others, because what was in us comes out of us and we still love it and care for it and we still relate to it. It's still part of us in some way. *I'm not antibiological by a long shot in my thinking. . . .* I'm perfectly willing to say there is something about the fact that women have borne life that is important" (*Adrienne Rich's Poetry* 118; emphasis added). Not only does Rich identify the specifically female with the maternal, but she also assumes that all women will give birth to "others" and thus gain access to the fundamentally female capacity for relationship, protectiveness, and care that will bring about a feminist and feminine transformation of the world.

"I like to think that if women were in charge of cities they would be much more habitable places," Rich says (118). Although she continues to imagine the "good society" as one in which traditional divisions between male and female—"Yourself-other, head-body, psyche-politics, them-us"—would be "broken down" and there would be "much more flow back and forth," she ends by reinscribing the very dichotomies she sets out to break down (119). Inverting rather than transforming patriarchal hierarchies, female is substituted for male, body for head, as the superior and transforming terms, and men—and presumably women who do not bear children—are demonized and outcast as "other" in the new matriarchal order. In her multiple roles as poet, theorist, political activist, and spokesperson for American feminism, Rich— along with Alice Walker, Mary Daly, and the French feminists whose work began to appear in the United States in the mid-seventies—played an impor- tant role not simply in describing but in calling forth and prescribing the renewed interest among feminist writers and critics in matriarchy, moth- erhood, and the mother/daughter bond that would characterize feminist pol- itics, women's writing, and feminist scholarship in the seventies and eighties.[10]

"There are words I cannot choose again: / *humanism androgyny*," Rich wrote in "Natural Resources": "Such words have no shame in them, no diffidence / before the raging stoic grandmothers" (*The Dream of a Common Language* 66).[11] By the mid-seventies Rich had turned completely away from the sexually undefined "Stranger" and androgynous vision of *Diving into the Wreck* to the lesbian-feminist position she articulated in her speech to the Modern Language Association in 1976: "It is the lesbian in us who is creative," Rich asserted, "for the dutiful daughter of the fathers in us is only a hack" (*On Lies, Secrets, and Silence* 201). This speech, along with her controversial essay "Compulsory Heterosexuality and Lesbian Ex- istence" (1980), represented a move toward an increasingly polarized, ex- clusive, and hierarchized definition of female and male sexual identity in Rich's work.

Although Rich intended her speech and her essay to name the "lesbian existence" and erotic bonds among women that had been part of the historical experience of women, in her tendency to equate female friendship with les- bianism, masculinity with violence, and heterosexuality with rape, she provoked both antifeminists and feminists alike, including many lesbians who wanted to preserve the sense of risk and danger and the specifically sexual "commitment of skin, blood, breast, and bone" that also defined lesbian existence (Stimpson, "Zero Degree Deviancy" 364). Moreover, in arguing provocatively that it is the lesbian in women who is creative, Rich not only assumes and romanticizes a primal lesbian identity that is shared by all wom- en across race, class, and historical bounds; she also denies heterosexual women the ability to act, choose, and create as anything other than the hacks of patriarchy. As the Marxist feminists Ann Snitow, Christine Stansell, and Sharon Thompson note in a polite but critical response to Rich's essay: "You only allow for female historical agency insofar as women exist on the lesbian continuum while we would argue that women's history, like men's history, is created out of a dialectic of necessity and choice" (Rich, *Blood, Bread, and Poetry* 69).

As Rich embraced lesbian-feminism as personal lifestyle, poetic strategy, and political vision, her effort to reclaim Dickinson as a poetic mother became part of her broader effort to reclaim motherhood—the physical capacity for conception, gestation, transformation, and nurture—as an intellectual and creative force. *Of Woman Born: Motherhood as Experience and Institution,* which is dedicated to Rich's grandmothers and which draws on the life of her mother as a "continuing example of transformation and rebirth," appeared in 1976; in the same year, Rich published her major essay on Dickinson, "Vesuvius at Home: The Power of Emily Dickinson." In this essay on Dickinson, as in her study of motherhood, Rich engages in a quest to recover the mother as a source of regeneration and power. Like the rites of Eleusis, Rich's quest begins in spring, with a return to the house of her poetic mother: "I am traveling at the speed of time, along the Massachusetts Turnpike. For months, for years, for most of my life, I have been hovering like an insect against the screens of an existence which inhabited Amherst, Massachusetts, between 1830 and 1886" (*On Lies, Secrets, and Silence* 158).

Rich's return to Dickinson's house becomes the occasion for an extended meditation in which she seeks to reclaim Dickinson's life and work for herself and other women writers. "I have been surprised," says Rich, "at how narrowly her work, still, is known by women who are writing poetry, how much her legend has gotten in the way of her being repossessed, as a source and a foremother" (167). By reading Dickinson's life and work in the context of women's culture, Rich, in the course of the essay, seeks to overturn the popular legend: she lived not in hermetic seclusion, but in relation to a self-selected and primarily female network of personal and literary relationships; she was not the quaint and sentimental girl-child popularized by *The Belle of Amherst,* but a proud, unorthodox woman of powerful will; her poems were not sublimations of failed love but signs of her self-created and self-creating power; the male demons of her poems were not reflections of male lovers but projections of her own poetic genius. Idealizing and in some sense (re)mythologizing Dickinson in the process of seeking to repossess her as a source and foremother for contemporary women writers, Rich's reading of Dickinson would have a major impact on the direction and focus of Dickinson criticism over the next decade.[12]

In her attempt to get beyond the "garbled versions" of the masculine critical tradition, Rich emphasizes Dickinson's power, particularly her linguistic power, as her prime legacy to her poetic daughters. Says Rich:

> I am thinking of a confined space in which the genius of the nineteenth-century female mind in America moved, inventing a language more varied, more compressed, more dense with implications, more complex of syntax, than any American poetic language to date; in the trail of that genius my mind has been moving, and with its language and images my mind still has to reckon, as the mind of a woman poet in America today.
>
> (163)

Moving in the trail of Dickinson's genius, Rich finds a source of power and knowledge and a self-validating and enabling figure who says to her poetic daughters: "Someone has been here before" (182).

As a figure of female power, Dickinson became part of the dream of a common language—the drive to connect word and thing, mind and body, personal and political, poet and history, woman and woman—that Rich pursues in *The Dream of a Common Language*. Just as Rich began in the mid-seventies to mythologize her bond with Dickinson as a bond of mutuality and power, so Rich's new work is centered not on an Emersonian concept of individual power, but on a lesbian-feminist ethics and poetics of female bonding, grounded in the primal mother/daughter bond, inscribed in the rites of Eleusis, and summed up in the following lines from "Transcendental Etude":

> two women, eye to eye
> measuring each other's spirit, each other's
> limitless desire,
>> a whole new poetry beginning here.
>> (*The Dream of a Common Language* 76)

Retrieving the voice of the early poet who imitated Dickinson and Millay in her private journals, and who defined herself as a woman writing in a tradition of women poets, Rich draws on female energies and female community as sources of personal, poetic, and social transformation.

At the structural center of *The Dream of a Common Language* is "Twenty-One Love Poems," a sonnet sequence in which Rich names her personal love relationship with another woman as the source of new creation and the base of political action and power in the world. In these poems, as throughout the volume, lesbian love is mythologized and, in effect, universalized as a return to a primal bond between mothers and daughters and a primal identity shared by all women. "The daughters never were / true brides of the father," Rich writes in "Sibling Mysteries":

> the daughters were to begin with
> brides of the mother
>
> then brides of each other
> under a different law
>
>> (52)

Poetically enacting the cultural feminist vision she articulated in "The Anti-Feminist Woman" and later in *Of Woman Born*, Rich divides the world into "two worlds / the daughters and the mothers / in the kingdom of the sons" (*The Dream of a Common Language* 49). Men are demonized as the bearers of evil, violence, and war, and women are idealized as superior moral creatures, who are urged "to take and use" their love:

> hose it on a city, on a world,
> to wield and guide its spray, destroying
> poisons, parasites, rats, viruses—
> like the terrible mothers we long and dread to be.
>
> (13)

In an extension of nineteenth-century Anglo-American gender ideologies, Rich seeks to relocate the traditionally domestic and maternal values of love, nurturance, and communality at the center rather than at the margins of culture. But the total effect of "The drive / to connect. The dream of a common language" is to subsume the particular histories of women into a single white female-centered narrative of return to the mother and female unity across race and class, cultural and national bounds. While this dream suggests some of the boundless optimism of American feminism in the late seventies, it was a dream sustained by suppressing difference and colonizing other women and other cultures under the sign of global sisterhood and feminist solidarity.

This essentializing and totalizing gesture of seventies feminism is perhaps most emphatic in the final poem "Transcendental Etude," in which Rich seeks to "transcend" the masculine and specifically New England orders of time and history to get back to the "rockshelf" of female creation that "persists" at the very sources of both nature and culture. Writing against an eternalized and male-identified concept of art as appropriation, mastery, and transcendence, Rich envisions a specifically female-centered art of relation, process, and commonality embedded in nature, the body, and the rituals of ordinary women's lives:

> Such a composition has nothing to do with eternity,
> the striving for greatness, brilliance—
> only with the musing of a mind
> one with her body, experienced fingers quietly pushing
> dark against bright, silk against roughness,
> pulling the tenets of a life together
> with no mere will to mastery,
> only care for the many-lived, unending
> forms in which she finds herself,
> becoming now the sherd of broken glass
> slicing light in a corner, dangerous
> to flesh, now the plentiful, soft leaf
> that wrapped round the throbbing finger, soothes the wound;
> and now the stone foundation, rockshelf further
> forming underneath everything that grows.
>
> (*The Dream of a Common Language* 77)

For all Rich's seeming "care for the many-lived, unending / forms in which she finds herself," she ends by reducing the particularity and difference of women's lives to the same transcendental script written across time and history. She also (re)locates women, women's intellect, women's creativity, and women's history in the bedrock of the body, nature, maternity, and immanence from which early feminists, including Simone de Beauvoir, Kate Millett, and Rich herself, and more recent feminists, including Monique Wittig, Teresa De Lauretis, and Gayatri Spivak, have struggled and are still struggling to wrest her.

The real political consequences and dangers of Rich's emphasis on love, nurturance, and mothering as women's essential qualities and on women as the representatives of a higher moral order would become evident in the eighties, as the work of cultural feminists began to merge with the call for a return to home, family, and the traditional female values advocated by conservative feminists, such as Betty Friedan and Jean Bethke Elshtain. Feminism—or at least the kind of feminism represented by the antipornography crusade—began to merge with the moral and maternal, profamily and prolife agenda of Ronald Reagan and the New Right.[13]

Dickinson as Other

In her next volume of poems, *A Wild Patience Has Taken Me This Far,* Rich returned to Dickinson for what she called her "third and final address." Like her final address to Dickinson, Rich's new poems represent at once a continuation and a break with the mythologizing and cultural feminist vision of *The Dream of a Common Language.* On the one hand, Rich continues her drive to (re)connect with her body, with women, with the landscape, and with the past as she interweaves reflections on the present with bits and pieces of women's lives culled from novels, diaries, letters, and histories. Her overriding concern is integrity, which she projects in the poem "Integrity" as the spider's genius,

> to spin and weave in the same action
> from her own body, anywhere—
> even from a broken web.
> 				(*A Wild Patience* 9)

On the other hand, this "broken web"—the experience of separation and limits—becomes an increasingly insistent figure in Rich's new poems, making "the drive to connect" and the achievement of any true union among and between women difficult, if not impossible. No longer dreaming of a common language, the poet is troubled by her sense of difference, distance, and separation from her sister in "Transit," from her mother-in-law in "Mother-in-Law," from her grandmothers in "Grandmothers," from her women friends and lovers in "For Memory" and "Rift," and, perhaps most significantly, from women of color in "Frame" and "Turning the Wheel."

"There are gashes in our understandings / of this world," Rich writes in "For Memory":

> We came together in a common
> fury of direction
> barely mentioning difference
> (what drew our finest hairs
> to fire
> the deep, difficult troughs
> unvoiced)
>
> (*A Wild Patience* 21)

Increasingly uneasy with her previous "drive" to absorb all women into her own lesbian-feminist reading of women and history, in "For Ethel Rosenberg," Rich writes:

> I must allow her to be at last
>
> political in her ways not in mine
> her urgencies perhaps impervious to mine
> defining revolution as she defines it
>
> (30)

Less driven by the urge to romanticize and mythologize the relations between women and sisters, mothers and daughters, Rich forces herself to imagine "the pain inflicted on" Rosenberg "by women / *her mother testifies against her / her sister-in-law testifies against her*" (30). And in "Heroines," Rich seems newly cognizant of the "class privilege" and "partial vision" of the "*Exceptional / even deviant*" nineteenth-century women whom she had formerly heroized as powerful foremothers. "How can I give you / all your due," Rich asks:

> take courage from your courage
>
> honor your exact
>   legacy as it is
>   recognizing
>   as well
>   that it is not enough?
>
> (36)

These same questions and Rich's increased sense of limitation, difference, and the *otherness* of other women enter into her final poetic reflection on Dickinson in "The Spirit of Place."

Beginning with the lines "Strangers are an endangered species," the section on Dickinson is part of Rich's more general meditation on her relationship to the "spirit of the masters" as it is represented in the shadowy landscape and history of New England. Returning once again to the danger theme of "I Am in Danger—Sir—," Rich presents Dickinson's life and legend as another instance of the ways "instantaneous violence ambush male / dominion" endanger not only women's lives but women's past and history; like the laurel in the preceding section of the poem, Dickinson is an endangered species.

In this final return to Dickinson's house, Rich finds neither frustrated energies nor female potency, but a legacy of violation, in which Rich, too, is implicated. It is not Dickinson who inhabits her house, but the scholars and legends that have continually revamped her in accordance with the fashions and "patterns" of the times:

> In Emily Dickinson's house in Amherst
> cocktails are served the scholars
> gather in celebration
> their pious or clinical legends
> festoon the wall like imitations
> of period patterns
>   (. . . *and, as I feared, my "life" was made a "victim"*)
>   (42)

Under the description of the festivities of the cultists, there appears a parenthetical fragment from one of Dickinson's letters to Susan Gilbert, in which she complains of feeling victimized by the Church leaders at an Amherst meeting: the parenthetical and italicized fragment underscores the fact that Dickinson's life is in danger of being extinguished by the imitations that festoon the wall.

Even in her death, Dickinson has been made a victim of cultish or clinical academics who paw her relics:

> The remnants pawed the relics
> the cult assembled in the bedroom
> and you whose teeth were set on edge by churches
> resist your shrine
>   escape
>   are found
>   nowhere
>   unless in words (your own)
>   (42)

In her death, as in her life, Dickinson's only avenue of escape from the restrictive patterns of the time is through the power of language—a language that, like Rich's words on the page, disrupts and transforms traditional orders in the process of seeking to escape them.

It is in Dickinson's own words that Rich finds the figure of the stranger/ woman poet—the woman poet as *other*—who eludes the scholars as she eluded her Amherst contemporaries. Rich incorporates in the poem the following passage from a letter Dickinson wrote to her girlfriend Kate Anthon in 1859:

> *All we are strangers—dear—The world is not*
> *acquainted with us, because we are not acquainted*
> *with her. And Pilgrims!—Do you hesitate? and*
> *Soldiers oft—some of us victors, but those I do*
> *not see tonight owing to the smoke.—We are hungry,*
> *and thirsty, sometimes—We are barefoot—and cold—*
> (*A Wild Patience* 43)

Recognizing Dickinson's essential "strangeness," and thus her difference from herself, Rich resolves to cease her own effort to construct Dickinson's life and work in terms of her own lesbian-feminist needs:

> This place is large enough for both of us
> the river-fog will do for privacy
> this is my third and last address to you
> (43)

After years of attempting to enter into Dickinson's mind through her poems and letters, Rich comes to an almost humbled recognition of Dickinson as stranger and other, which enables her to resist any further "intrusion" into her life.

Making explicit the mother/daughter relationship that was implicit in her earlier addresses to Dickinson, Rich enacts the process of freeing Dickinson to be herself through a series of familial images in which she addresses Dickinson first as daughter, then as sister, and finally as mother:

> with the hands of a daughter I would cover you
> from all intrusion even my own
> saying rest to your ghost

> with the hands of a sister I would leave your hands
> open or closed as they prefer to lie
> and ask no more of who or why or wherefore

> with the hands of a mother I would close the door
> on the rooms you've left behind
> and silently pick up my fallen work
> (43)

Each of Rich's actions, linked by the recurring figure of tenderly protective hands, suggests a different dimension of her relationship with Dickinson. As the daughter whose growth as a poet had been nurtured by Dickinson as mother, Rich acknowledges Dickinson's separateness and difference; she resolves to protect her from future intrusions, including her own effort to erect her as a feminist shrine. As the sister who had discovered in Dickinson's life and work a relation to her own condition as a woman poet in America, Rich resolves to accept Dickinson's strange integrity and otherness. No longer asking "who or why or wherefore," Rich turns away from the question, "who are you," which she had asked in "I Am in Danger—Sir—." Recognizing that in probing for the answer to these questions, she too, had endangered Dickinson, Rich wants to leave her to have it out at last on her *own* premises. Finally, as the mother who had given birth to new conceptions of Dickinson's life and work, Rich resolves to free Dickinson to be herself at the same time that, in taking up her "fallen work," she lays claim to her own subjectivity and power. What Rich now emphasizes in her relationship with Dickinson is not so much her power and universality, but her and their particularity and difference in a world that is, as Rich says, "large enough for both of us."

Rich's final address to Dickinson in "The Spirit of Place" is part of a more general move in her new work against the ethnocentric ahistoricism of seventies feminism. In the poems of *A Wild Patience Has Taken Me This Far,* Rich turns away from abstract, romantic, and eternalized representations of the feminine and the female toward a new emphasis on what she calls historical "particularity" in her readings of women's writing and women's history. "Forget the archetypes," she says in her reflection on native American women's culture in the final poem, "Turning the Wheel":

> do not pursue
> the ready-made abstraction, do not peer for symbols.
> So long as you want her faceless, without smell
> or voice, so long as she does not squat
> to urinate, or scratch herself, so long
> as she does not snore beneath her blanket
>   . . .
> so long as you try to simplify her meaning
> so long as she merely symbolizes power
> she is kept helpless and conventional
>
>   (56)

As in "For Ethel Rosenberg" and "The Spirit of Place," Rich is also newly cognizant of the complicity of women, particularly white women, with the "spirit of the masters." Thus in her poetic reflection on the architectural work of Mary Jane Colter (1869–1958), whose buildings were often modeled on

Native American art and design, Rich acknowledges her "remarkable accomplishment for a woman architect" at the same time that she notes that for all her lifelong love of Native American culture, her work was "inextricable from the violation and expropriation of Native culture by white entrepreneurs" (61).

In the final section of "Turning the Wheel" and the concluding passage of *A Wild Patience Has Taken Me This Far*, Rich emphatically turns "the wheel" on the "road to the great canyon," in a literal and symbolic gesture that refuses the drive "to the female core" and the "world beyond time" that had marked both her own work and the work of other feminists in the seventies. Thinking of her actual love relationship with Michelle Cliff as she travels "alone on the open plateau / of piñon jupiter," she resolves, for the moment at least, to live in a world of particular women and particular relationships, "knowing knowing knowing," as she says in "The Spirit of Place," the "world as it is if not as it might be / then as it is" (42).

"What Chou Mean *WE*, White Girl?"

The new sense of historical complexity and complicity, particularity and difference, that enters into Rich's representation of women in *A Wild Patience Has Taken Me This Far* is symptomatic of a larger divisiveness in feminism itself as the movement split in the late seventies into the competing and often contradictory agendas of liberal, radical, cultural, Marxist, lesbian, and separatist feminists, and as women of color became increasingly vocal in their protest against all brands of feminism for practicing and fostering an essentially white female–centered politics of exclusion.[14] As Bell Hooks notes in *Feminist Theory from Margin to Center:* "The vision of Sisterhood evoked by women's liberationists was based on the idea of common oppression. . . . The idea of 'common oppression' was a false and corrupt platform disguising and mystifying the true nature of women's varied and complex social reality. Women are divided by sexist attitudes, racism, class privilege, and a host of other prejudices" (44).

In what Lorraine Bethel calls "The Cullid Lesbian Feminist Declaration of Independence (Dedicated to the Proposition that all women are not equal, i.e., identical/ly oppressed)," she reflects on the experience of watching a white woman in Bonwit Teller's buying "trinkets" that would support the elderly black woman elevator operator for the rest of her life: "It is moments/infinities of conscious pain like these that make me want to cry/kill/roll my eyes suck my teeth hand on my hip scream at so-called radical white lesbian/feminist(s) 'WHAT CHOU MEAN *WE*, WHITE GIRL?' " (86)

Rich has occasionally been singled out by black women as one of the few white feminists to insist on the need for white women to educate themselves about the experiences of black women and the historical differences between black and white women. By the early eighties, however, Rich herself became increasingly conscious of her own presumption, racism, and privilege as a white daughter of patriarchy under the influence of such works by women of color as Toni Morrison's *Sula* (1973), Alice Walker's "In Search of Our Mothers' Gardens" and *Meridian,* Audre Lorde's *The Black Unicorn* (1978) and *Zami,* Ntozake Shange's *For Colored Girls Who Have Considered Suicide . . . ?,* Barbara Smith's "Toward a Black Feminist Criticism," Gloria Anzaldúa's "Speaking in Tongues: A Letter to Third World Women Writers," and "The Combahee River Collective: A Black Feminist Statement."[15]

Critical of "a form of feminism so focused on male evil and female victimization that it . . . allows for no differences among women, men, places, times, cultures, classes, conditions, movements," the essays in Rich's *Blood, Bread, and Poetry: Selected Prose 1979–1985* and the poems in *Your Native Land, Your Life* and *Time's Power* are marked by a sense of the limits of the radical feminist emphasis on patriarchy as the primary oppression and the failure of radical feminism to speak for all women, particularly women of color (*Blood, Bread, and Poetry* 221). "The radical-feminist claim to identify with all women, to wish deeply and sincerely to do so, was," Rich wrote in the foreword to *Blood, Bread, and Poetry,* "not enough. (I still hear the voice of a Black feminist saying with passionate factuality: *But you don't know us!*)" (x).

As Rich became increasingly cognizant of what Barbara Smith called the "simultaneity of oppression" and the divisions among women and within feminism itself, she became increasingly aware of her own contradictory and self-divided location as a Southern Jewish lesbian.[16] "Sometimes," she wrote in a 1982 essay on Jewish identity, "I feel I have seen too long from too many disconnected angles: white, Jewish, anti-Semite, racist, anti-racist, once-married, lesbian, middle-class, feminist, exmatriate southerner, *split at the root*— that I will never bring them whole" (*Blood, Bread, and Poetry* 122). Rich's experience of being "split at the root" as a multiply positioned social subject leads her in the poem "Sources" to a more complex understanding of her father's own particular oppression as a Jew who married a Christian Southern woman and tried to "pass" as a non-Jewish professor at Johns Hopkins University by separating himself especially from poorer Eastern European Jews. Reflecting on her own alienated status in a New England of "Protestant separatists, Jew-baiters, nightriders," Rich experiences a new sense of identification with the father she had formerly constructed and demonized as the very embodiment of "the kingdom of the fathers": "I saw the power and arrogance of the male as your true watermark; I did not see beneath it the suffering of the Jew, the alien stamp you bore" (*Your Native Land* 5, 9).

Although Rich does not say so explicitly, her new sense of herself as a displaced Southern Jew in protestant New England further distanced her from the values and world of Emily Dickinson. In "Toward a More Feminist Criticism" (1981), Rich comments on the changes that will come when the white feminist critic stops reading and speaking as the universal center: "When she deliberately tries to work from a point of view that is *not* white solipsistic, she will feel her analysis changing; she is going to see differently and further, not just about the writings of women of color but also about the writings of white women" (*Blood, Bread, and Poetry* 96). Rich's new emphasis on the importance of ethnic, race, and class differences both in herself and other women made her increasingly impatient not only with the limits of her past work but also with the limits of the heroic, rebellious, and essentially white female literary tradition she herself had helped to construct in such essays as "The Tensions of Anne Bradstreet" (1966), "When We Dead Awaken" (1971), "Jane Eyre: The Temptations of a Motherless Woman" (1973), and "Vesuvius at Home: The Power of Emily Dickinson" (1975); and in poems such as "Snapshots of a Daughter-in-Law," " 'I am in Danger—Sir—,' " "Culture and Anarchy," and "For Julia in Nebraska."

Whereas Rich had earlier celebrated white female creative power, in one of her new poems, "Education of a Novelist," she registers outright hostility to Ellen Glasgow for representing the very kind of white female privilege and racism she finds in herself (*Your Native Land* 37–40). And in a further display of discontent with the direction of feminist work in the United States, in 1984 Rich wrote a testy response to Susan Friedman's critical discussion of Rich's relationship with H. D. in " 'I go where I love': An Intertextual Study of H. D. and Adrienne Rich." Attacking Friedman for practicing the very kind of white woman-centered feminist criticism she herself had produced and promoted in her own earlier work, Rich in effect accuses Friedman of "bias," "ignorance," "privilege," and homophobia (Comment on Friedman 737). At the very least, what Rich's exchanges with Glasgow and Friedman indicate is the erosion of feminist sisterhood and the collapse of Rich's former "dream of a common language" under the pressure of race, class, sexual, and other cultural and historical differences among women.

In "North American Time," Rich reflects on the complex issues of language and accountability, and the difficulties of speaking and writing as a public and politically engaged feminist poet whose work is imbricated in the contradictory and competing agendas, ideologies, and social practices of eighties North America:

> When my dreams showed signs
> of becoming
> politically correct
> no unruly images

escaping beyond borders
when walking in the street I found my
themes cut out for me
knew what I would not report
for fear of enemies' usage
then I began to wonder
(*Your Native Land* 33)

As a poet who had from the first placed herself at the very center of feminist movement in the United States and who set out "with a mission, not to win prizes / but to change the laws of history," Rich expresses a new consciousness of the problem of her own political and poetic "accountability" and the power of her words—both past and present—to destroy as well as create, to do evil as well as good, to underwrite as well as change the existing system (23).

"We move," says Rich, "but our words stand / become responsible / for more than we intended / and this is verbal privilege" (33). The irony is that while Rich has continued to change, interrogate, and move against the premises of her own earlier feminist theory and practice, the white female–centered model of feminist "re-vision" that Rich herself did so much to define and call into being has been institutionalized and continues to shape many of the feminist works produced in the academy. As Hortense Spillers notes in a comment on the absence of black women from many of the "premier texts" of American feminism over the last decade, and the works of Dorothy Dinnerstein, Mary Daly, and Nancy Chodorow in particular: "that we read these texts—and might include along with them an impressive number of gynocritical works in women's literature—as though their emblems, their figures of thought, the purposes and motivations that precede and accompany their execution, the living conditions out of which their search comes and the shape it takes speak monolithically across the empire of women—reminds me of the period of symbolic oppression we believe we're leaving" ("Interstices" 81).

6

Race, Black Women Writing, and Gwendolyn Brooks

> meriting the gold, I
> Have sewn my guns inside my burning lips.
> —Gwendolyn Brooks, "Riders to the Blood-red Wrath"

> ESSENTIAL black literature is the distillation of black life.
> Black life is different from white life. Different in nuance,
> different in "nitty gritty." Different *from* birth. Different
> *at* death.
> —Gwendolyn Brooks, *A Capsule Course in Black Poetry Writing*

"Most of what passes for culture and thought on the North American continent" has enforced the nonexistence of black women, write Gloria Hull and Barbara Smith in the introduction to their important anthology *All the Women Are White, All the Blacks are Men, But Some of Us Are Brave* (xvii). For black women writers, the marketplace economics of last hired, first fired has translated into a literary economics of exclusion and absence. From such early works of feminist literary criticism as Patricia Meyer Spacks's *The Female Imagination* and Ellen Moers's *Literary Women: The Great Writers* in the mid-seventies to recent works such as Sandra Gilbert and Susan Gubar's *No Man's Land: The Place of the Woman Writer in the Twentieth Century,* the writings of women of color have been given little or no place in white feminist revivals, revisions, and re-readings of women's literary history. Women of color are subsumed within the category "Woman," and the writings of predominantly white middle-class women are generalized and universalized into *the* female imagination, *the* literary woman, and *the* female literary tradition.

In response to the invisibility of black women in white male and female literary criticism as well as in black male criticism, black feminist critics have called for a black feminist critical perspective that would be fully cognizant of the interlocking systems of race, class, and gender in the lives and writings of black women. Outlining the task of the black feminist critic in "Towards a Black Feminist Criticism," Barbara Smith says:

> Beginning with a primary commitment to exploring how both sexual and racial politics and Black and female identity are inextricable elements in Black women's writing, she would also work from the assumption that Black women writers constitute an identifiable literary tradition. . . . Thematically, stylistically, aesthetically, and conceptually Black women writers manifest common approaches to the act of creating literature as a direct result of the specific political, social, and economic experience they have been obliged to share.
> (163–64)

But while Smith is cognizant of the ways the specific sociohistorical experiences of black women can make their writing different from "white/male literary structures," in her desire to "find innumerable commonalities in works by black women," she fails to note the ways the specific cultural experiences of black women writers can also make them different from each other.

This problem of difference and discontinuity among black women writers is particularly evident in the work of Gwendolyn Brooks, who had no "identifiable" black female literary tradition on which to draw. Like the language, strategies, and structures of her work, Brooks's sources are multiple, complex, and not easily categorizable. This complexity in Brooks's literary work and in her relation to literary tradition is, I would argue, embedded in the heterogeneity, contradiction, and difference of her personal and historical location as a black woman writing in the United States. In *Technologies of Gender,* Teresa De Lauretis comments on "woman as a social subject and a site of differences; differences which are not purely sexual or merely racial, economic, or (sub)cultural, but all of these together and often enough in conflict with one another" (139). Although one might make Brooks fit into any one of a number of categories—modernist poet, vernacular poet, woman poet, African-American poet, Black Arts poet, black nationalist poet—in this chapter I would like to focus on the multiple and conflicting positions that Brooks occupies as an African-American woman poet and her differences not only from black and white, female and male literary traditions but also *from* and *within* herself.

Making Herself a Tradition

In an unpublished handwritten and handbound collection of early poems entitled *Songs After Sunset* (1935–36), Gwendolyn Brooks begins and ends with an inscription to a cryptic figure named "Ima Twin."[1] This figure may allude to a second volume of poems, as Erlene Stetson has suggested in an article on Brooks's unpublished poetry (*"Songs After Sunset"* 126). Or the figure may be self-referential, alluding to that sense of "twoness" or "double-consciousness" that W. E. B. DuBois described in 1903 as the governing trope of black American experience in *The Souls of Black Folk:* "One ever feels his twoness,—an American, a Negro, two souls, two thoughts, two unreconciled strivings; two warring ideals in one dark body, whose dogged strength alone keeps it from being torn asunder" (215). Whatever its precise reference, the literary twin of Brooks's early poems serves as a fitting introduction to a black woman poet whose life and work might be read as a dynamic and continually self-transforming struggle to negotiate the conflicting demands of race, gender, and class, of aesthetics and politics, craft and commitment, modernism and populism, art and activism, black Americanism and black Africanism as she moved simultaneously toward an engagement with language as a form of social action—of guns and ammunition—in the making of an African-American poetics, and an assertion of the power of "The Womanhood"—and "the mother"—in the making of an African-American community.

As the inaugural and closing inscription of Brooks's early poems, "Ima Twin" also suggests the black woman poet's problematic relation not only to a white male but to a black male and white female literary tradition that has excluded her. At the time Brooks began to write, black creativity was in flower, but the black awakening that has come to be known as the "Harlem Renaissance" was a white-sponsored and black male–centered production, associated with the work of Langston Hughes, Countee Cullen, Claude McKay, and other male writers and artists. Although black women poets were writing and supporting each other in female literary networks during the "Renaissance" years, only the work of Georgia Douglas Johnson was published in book form.[2]

It is in the context of black female absence from the literary tradition that the cryptic "Ima Twin" of Brooks's early poems begins to assume a culturally specific meaning. With no black female poetic tradition on which to draw, Brooks, in effect, invents a literary sister—black and female like herself—as the audience and muse for her earliest poems. This specifically black female inscription of *Songs After Sunset* is complemented visually by an ink drawing of a female singer with an open songbook who appears on the title page bearing the signature "Gwendolyn." The picture suggests the black female oral and folk culture from which Brooks drew in making herself the inaugural figure—the founder and inventor—of a black female poetic tradition in which she might muse and sing.

"You," Brooks's mother had early announced, "are going to be the *lady*

Paul Laurence Dunbar" (*Report from Part One* 56). The literary title conferred by her mother fostered Brooks's sense of commonality with the popular
poet of the black people, at the same time that it marked the difference of the
specifically female voice Brooks would bring to her representations of black
life in America. "I believed every word she said and just kept on writing,"
Brooks remembers. "Sometimes I turned out two or three poems or a couple
of stories in one day, all very, very, very bad" (169).

In *Naked and Fiery Forms,* the feminist critic Suzanne Juhasz comments on
the "triple bind" of "the black woman poet": "Being doubly oppressed,
because of race and sex, she experiences conflict between being poet and
woman, poet and black, black and woman" (145). What is in fact striking
about Brooks's life and work, however, is her relative lack of conflict between
woman and poet compared with her white literary sisters; nor is there a
particular conflict between Brooks's identity as black and poet. The actual site
of Brooks's oppression is her existence—or lack of existence—as a black
woman who is doubly invisible, effaced by both her race and her sex.

During Brooks's childhood and adolescence, the overwhelming fact of her
existence was her race. As a child, Brooks remembers admiring her brown
skin: "*I* had always considered it beautiful. I would stick out my arm, examine it, and smile. Charming! And convenient, for mud on my leg was not as
annunciatory as was mud on the leg of light Rose Hurd." But Brooks's early
delight in her color was not shared by her world, where racial codes of
difference and inferiority were both inter- and intraracial. "One of the first
'world'-truths revealed to me when I at last became a member of SCHOOL,"
said Brooks, "was that, to be socially successful, a little girl must be Bright
(of skin). It was better if your hair was curly, too—or at least Good Grade"
(*Report from Part One* 37). Forced to construct and measure herself within
systems of value alien to herself—one male, the other white—Brooks felt
alone, strange, "inferior to everybody." Her sense of inferiority as a dark girl
was reinforced by her inhibitions as a "reserved, quiet child": "I was timid to
the point of terror, silent, primly dressed. AND DARK. The boys did not
mind telling me that *this* was the failing of failings." In the eyes of both light
and dark men, she was either invisible or insignificant: "the little Bright ones
looked through me if I happened to inconvenience their vision, and those of
my own hue rechristened me Ol' Black Gal" (38).

Later, in her poems, Brooks would become one of the first black women
writers to record the emotional pain and complex psychic wounding of intraracial discrimination. The representation of black boys and later black men as
instruments of intraracial oppression became a recurrent motif of Brooks's
writing from "The Ballad of Chocolate Mabbie" and "Ballad of Pearl May
Lee" in *A Street in Bronzeville* to "The Anniad" in *Annie Allen* and the

rejection suffered by Maud as an "Ol' Black Gal" in Brooks's semi-auto-
biographical novel *Maud Martha*.

Whereas the "sweet and chocolate" girls of "The Ballad of Chocolate
Mabbie," "The Anniad," and *Maud Martha* suffer in silence—"taming all
that anger down"—in "Ballad of Pearl May Lee," Brooks gives full voice to
her own sense of personal rage in a fantasy of violence against the black man.
The poem tells the story of a black man seduced by a white girl and then
accused of rape and lynched by the white community. Told from the point of
view of the black woman he betrayed, the poem expresses the paradoxical
love/hate relationship between the black woman and the black man. Although
Pearl May Lee loves Sammy, she is also enraged by the fact that in his eyes
she is only "dark meat":

> Yellow was for to look at,
> Black for the famished to eat.
>
> You grew up with bright skins on the brain,
> And me in your black folks bed.
> Often and often you cut me cold,
> And often I wished you dead.
> Often and often you cut me cold.
> Often I wished you dead.
>
> (*A Street in Bronzeville* 43)

The irony and tragedy of the poem is that Pearl May Lee's vindictive wish
comes true, putting her paradoxically on the side of the black man's white
killers. The poem registers the black woman's emotional turmoil and near-
insane breakdown, as her personal sense of love and loss are intercepted by
violent feelings of rage and betrayal.

> You paid for your dinner, Sammy boy,
> And you didn't pay with money.
> You paid with your hide and my heart, Sammy boy,
> For your taste of pink and white honey,
>> Honey,
>> Honey,
> For your taste of pink and white honey.
>
> Oh, dig me out of my don't-despair.
> Oh, pull me out of my poor-me.
> Oh, get me a garment of red to wear.
> You had it coming surely.
>> Surely.
>> Surely.
> You had it coming surely.

(45)

As the story of a white girl's perfidy, "Ballad of Pearl May Lee" might be read as a parable of the black man's betrayal at the hands of the white community. But by locating the emotional effects of that betrayal in the damaged psyche of Pearl May Lee, the poem suggests the ricocheting effects of white violence and white hegemony in the black community as the black woman becomes both the agent and the victim of a killing urge directed simultaneously against white society, against the black man, and ultimately against herself.

Although Brooks speaks through the mask of Pearl May Lee, the poem articulates feelings of rage and betrayal that are clearly her own. "I don't know whether you want to include woman rage in this discussion or not," she told Claudia Tate in a 1983 interview. "But I hope you sense some real rage in 'The Ballad of Pearl May Lee.' The speaker is a very enraged person. I know because I consulted myself on how I felt. For instance, why in the world has it been that our men have preferred either white or that pigmentation which is as close to white as possible? That's *all* political" (*Black Women Writers at Work* 44).

Lacking the bright skin and good grade hair to succeed with lighter skinned blacks and lacking the "sass and brass" to achieve reverence among what were known as the "Lesser Blacks," Brooks as a young girl sought self-affirmation in dreams of a fairy-tale prince who would love only her. "I'd go to bed and dream of embracing and marrying Him, of becoming the mother of His one child, of being desperately loved by Him. The adored Gwendolyn." But most of all Brooks sought self-actualization through her art. "Other girls *Had Boy Friends. I 'Wrote,' *" Brooks said. "I spent most of my free time in my room, writing, reading, reflecting" (*Report from Part One* 57). Writing became a necessity, a means of proclaiming her being—her *I amness*—in a world that failed to recognize the existence of either her sex or her race. "*Of course,*" she said, "I would be a poet! *Was* a poet! Didn't I write a poem every day? Sometimes *two* poems" (56). What she lacked as a black girl she would make up through word power. Like Emily Dickinson, who hid hundreds of manuscript poems in her room, Brooks dreamed of burying her poetic manuscripts as a means of proclaiming her "Mind" and her value to future generations: "Once," she told interviewer Paul Angle, "I considered *burying* my precious manuscripts in the back yard so that in the future—at some time in the hundreds of years to come—they would be discovered and loved" (*Report from Part One* 132).

According to Brooks's mother, Keziah, Brooks began "putting rhymes together" when she was seven. Her earliest poetic notebooks, which she kept in imitation of the "writing girl" of L. M. Montgomery's Emily books, date from age eleven. At this time some of her first poems were published in local newspapers; at age thirteen one of her poems, "Eventide," appeared in the popular children's magazine *American Childhood*. As in Phillis Wheatley's "On Imagination," in which the poet soars on the wings of "roving Fancy," seeking "new worlds" for "th' unbounded soul," Brooks seeks in her early poems to transcend an oppressive social order, escaping into what she called "the gold worlds I saw in the sky." Her subjects were "nature, love, death, the sky," subjects that appeared to offer a natural and racially unbounded universe in which to compose her songs.

But while Brooks was writing endless poems of nature and love, as an adolescent she was already divided between the idea of art as transcendence and colorlessness and art as race consciousness. This split was accentuated by what she learned at home and at school. Whereas at school she read the canonical works of English and American literature—Shakespeare, Wordsworth, Shelley, Keats, Byron, Emerson, and Bryant—at home she was reading Paul Laurence Dunbar, Robert Kerlin's *Negro Poets and Their Poems,* and the writings of the Harlem Renaissance poets in Countee Cullen's anthology *Caroling Dusk* (1927). She was particularly drawn to the work of Langston Hughes, whom she later met and who dedicated his book of short stories *Something in Common* (1963) to her. Commenting on her excitement upon reading Hughes's *Weary Blues* (1926), she said: "I realized that writing about the ordinary aspects of black life was important" (*Report from Part One* 70).

More than any other writer, Hughes was the catalyzing figure of Brooks's literary career. Remembering the early encouragement he gave to her and others, she described him in parturient images as a giver of black literary life, who planted and cultivated the seeds of a new generation of black writers: "Langston held high and kept warm the weapons until the youngsters could cut the caul, could wipe away the webs of birth and get to work. Indeed, he preceded them with a couple of chores, a couple of bleedings. . . . The plantings of others he not only welcomed but busily enriched" (70–71). Brooks admired Hughes's race pride, the race rhythms of his work, and his commitment to the black community before the beauty of blackness became "the thing." He was a model of literary creation who cultivated art not as a highbred aesthetic flower removed from the world, but as action, weapon, and power amid the "holocaust" of black life in America.

"Langston Hughes," she wrote in her poetic tribute to him in *Selected Poems:*

> Holds horticulture
> In the eye of the vulture
> Infirm profession.
> In the Compression—
> In mud and blood and sudden death—

In the breath
Of the holocaust he
Is helmsman, hatchet, headlight.
(123)

For Gwendolyn Brooks, seeking to enter a literary tradition in which all the blacks were men, there was no black male equivalent of what Gilbert and Gubar call "Milton's Bogey" (*The Madwoman in the Attic* 187–212). Like her relationship with her biological father, Brooks's relationship with Hughes as a kind of literary father seems relatively untroubled. While her gender might have placed her in a potentially oppositional relation to Hughes, her race consciousness and her sense of a shared historical and cultural heritage gave her a feeling of solidarity with her literary precursor.

If Hughes turned Brooks toward blues form and the black street, the poet James Weldon Johnson, whom she also met, turned her toward Western form and literary modernism. When she sent him some of her poems in 1933, he responded: "Dear Miss Brooks—You have an unquestionable talent and feeling for poetry. Continue to write—at the same time, study carefully the work of the best modern poets—not to imitate them, but to help cultivate the highest possible standard of self-criticism" (*Report from Part One* 202). Encouraged by Johnson, who carefully annotated several of her poems, Brooks began reading the work of several modern poets, including T. S. Eliot, Ezra Pound, and e.e. cummings.

Brooks's apprenticeship in literary modernism was further encouraged by Inez Cunningham Stark, the socialite rebel, poet, and reader for *Poetry* magazine who came to South Side Chicago to teach a poetry writing workshop for blacks in 1941. As a member of this workshop Brooks was exercised in Western literary forms and the modernist rules of literary economy, ambiguity, and precision. She also had her first experience of being part of a black literary community. "How serious we were, how enchanted with each other and with ourselves!" Brooks recalled. "How diligently we learned from and taught each other. I remember long literary-inquisition walks about Woodlawn, for example, with Margaret (Danner) Cunningham" (*Report from Part One* 67).

Black Blueswomen

What is striking about Brooks's years of literary apprenticeship is her relative lack of anxiety about setting up as a black female singer in comparison with the turmoil and self-division that has characterized white women poets from Anne Bradstreet to Adrienne Rich. This relative lack of conflict is all the more striking because Brooks had no visible black female poetic precursors. Here again, however, Brooks's emergence as a poet must be understood within the context of her personal and cultural experience as an African-American woman. Brooks was raised in a family of music and song. "My father recited fascinating poetry, and sang to us jolly or haunting songs," she said in a 1984 self-interview. "My mother sang, too, and played the piano almost every day. She loved music. Classical, popular, spiritual, *all* music. She wrote music; she had gone to a class to study harmony" ("Interview" 405).

From the chants and hollers of the work field, to the gospels and spirituals of the church, to the blues and jazz performances of tent shows and cabarets, music and song had also been at the very center of African-American oral and folk culture. And within this oral tradition, black women had always sung. In fact, Nikki Giovanni argues that black music originated in women calling to each other in an African field: "The hum, the holler, the leader-call are women things. The men didn't do them. Black men were out hunting in Africa, but in America they were in the fields with the women. They learned the women things from women. So what you're hearing in our music is nothing but the sound of a woman calling another woman" (Claudia Tate, *Black Women Writers at Work* 78). In " . . . And the Old Women Gathered (The Gospel Singers)," Mari Evans suggests the overwhelming power and presence of black women's songs in a black woman's life:

> It
> was fierce and
> not melodic and
> although we ran
> the sound of it
> stayed in our ears. . .
> (Stetson, *Black Sister* 146)

Although Brooks had no black female poetic tradition on which to draw, her work, like the work of black women writers from Zora Neale Hurston to Mari Evans and Sonia Sanchez, was embedded in and in some sense authorized by a rich female oral culture of chants and hollers, gospels and spirituals.

As a black woman poet who came of age during the twenties and thirties, Brooks also had an immediate tradition of female song in the lyrics of such black blueswomen as Ma Rainey and Bessie Smith, who were translating the songs of field and church into a specifically female-centered blues tradition. Although women poets were beginning to enter the African-American literary tradition during the Harlem Renaissance, as critic Barbara Christian notes in "Afro-American Women Poets": "It might be said that the genuine poetry of the black woman appeared not in literature but in the lyrics of blues singers like Bessie Smith" (122). Unlike the women poets of the Harlem Renaissance, Georgia Douglas Johnson, Angelina Weld Grimke, and Alice Dunbar .

Nelson, who composed polite and ladylike lyrics in reaction against the popular image of the black woman as sapphire, mammy, or exotic primitive, the blueswomen, who wrote and sang for primarily black audiences, were able to speak out of their personal experiences as black women in a manner that came closer to articulating the historical experience of the race.

But for black women singing the blues was more than a communal survival ritual, a means of coming to terms with, by publicly naming and sharing, the oppressive facts of black existence. Although the songs of blueswomen like Ma Rainey, Bessie Smith, and Ida Cox were often lovesick songs of suffering, victimization, and world-weariness, as Hazel Carby argues in "It Jus Be's Dat Way Sometime," the sexual struggle between male and female was at the very heart of their songs (16). For black blueswomen, singing the blues could also become a means of self-creation and self-affirmation, offering at times empowering images of an autonomous and mobile black womanhood.

In "Young Woman's Blues" (1927), Bessie Smith declares her independence from white—and black—color codes and social rituals that fail to acknowledge the presence and desires of her own "yella brown" body:

> Some people call me a hobo, some call me a bum
> Nobody knows my name, nobody knows what I've done
> I'm as good as any woman in your town
> I ain't high yeller, I'm a deep yella brown
> I ain't gonna marry, ain't gonna settle down
> I'm gonna drink good moonshine and run these browns down
> (Bernikow, *The World Split Open* 278)

Ida Cox's "Wild Women Blues" celebrates a similarly "different system" in opposition to the black woman as "angel child":

> You never get nothing
> By being an angel child,
> You better change your ways
> And get real wild.
> I want to tell you no lie,
> Wild women are the only kind
> That really get by,
> 'Cause wild women don't worry,
> Wild women don't have the blues.
> (Bernikow, *The World Split Open* 278–79)

It is out of the songs of these black blueswomen rather than out of the traditionally feminine and socially restrained lyrics of the Harlem Renaissance women poets that Brooks's poems emerge.

In only one poem, "Queen of the Blues," does Brooks make specific use of a female blues singer and a classic blues form. But female blues figures like Sadie, who "scrapes life with a fine-tooth comb," are a recurrent source of wildness, wickedness, and social subversion in Brooks's early work:

> Sadie bore two babies
> Under her maidenname.
> Maud and Ma and Papa
> Nearly died of shame.
> Every one but Sadie
> Nearly died of shame.
>   (*A Street in Bronzeville* 14)

Brooks was fascinated by what she called the "back yard" of black female experience: "A girl gets sick of a rose," she says in "a song in the front yard," declaring her desire to live where "it's rough and untended and hungry weed grows." Rebelling against the good girl mentality of the adult world, she asserts:

> And I'd like to be a bad woman, too,
> And wear the brave stockings of night-black lace
> And strut down the streets with paint on my face.
>   (*A Street in Bronzeville* 10)

In "the rites for Cousin Vit," a poem that anticipates Jayne Cortez's later evocation of the dancer Josephine Baker shimmying and snake-hipping through Africa, Europe, and the United States in "So Many Feathers," Brooks celebrates the "too vital and too squeaking" life of a woman whose burial casket "can't hold her":

> Even now she does the snake-hips with a hiss,
> Slops the bad wine across her shantung, talks
> Of pregnancy, guitars and bridgework, walks
> In parks or alleys, comes haply on the verge
> Of happiness, haply hysterics. Is.
>   (*Annie Allen* 45)

Despite or perhaps because of her own respectable upbringing, Brooks was continually drawn to blues figures like Sadie and Cousin Vit, who wickedly defy the social and gender rituals of polite and white middle-class society.

Poetry and Black Motherhood

In *The First Wave: Women Poets in America 1915–1945*, William Drake comments on the fact that the (white middle-class) women he discusses were often forced to choose between motherhood and literary creation: "The majority of women poets who rose to prominence between the World Wars did not . . . have children" (121). This notion that motherhood and poetry are fundamentally at odds has become a critical given in discussions of twentieth-century women poets. In *A World of Difference,* for example, Barbara Johnson notes the rivalry between poems and children in the work of women poets, including Gwendolyn Brooks: "It is as though male writing were by nature procreative, while female writing is by nature infanticidal" (198). In fact, however, the life and work of Gwendolyn Brooks challenge traditional and feminist constructions of the woman writer and the differences between male and female writing.

Brooks's first volume of poems, *A Street in Bronzeville,* was published by Harper and Row in 1945, six years after her marriage to Henry Blakely in 1939 and five years after the birth of their first child, Henry Blakely Jr., in 1940. Although Brooks admits that "there was about a year—after the birth of my first child—when I scarcely put pen to paper," she resolutely refuses to posit any conflict between her roles as mother and poet (*Report from Part One* 178). Asked if she agreed with Sylvia Plath's representation of motherhood and writing in *The Bell Jar* as "an either-or proposition," Brooks said: "No, I certainly disagree. I feel that writing is part of life. I often say that poetry is 'life distilled,' and I believe that's true of any other aspect of writing. Being a wife and mother and having other interests in life did not do anything except enrich my work—nourish it" (Martha Brown 48). Brooks's response might be compared with Rich's description of the difficulties she had reconciling poetry and motherhood in "When We Dead Awaken: Writing as Re-Vision": "About the time my third child was born, I felt that I had either to consider myself a failed woman and a failed poet, or to try to find some synthesis by which to understand what was happening to me. . . . I was writing very little, partly from fatigue, that female fatigue of suppressed anger and loss of contact with my own being; partly from the discontinuity of female life with its attention to small chores, errands, work that others constantly undo, small children's constant needs." "To be maternally with small children all day in the old way," Rich concludes, "*is* in direct conflict with the subversive function of the imagination" (*Lies, Secrets, and Silence* 42–43).

The differences between Brooks and Rich may, of course, be a matter of individual temperament. But I believe something larger is at stake here, suggesting more general differences between the historical experience of black and middle-class white women in America that have not been taken into account in white male or female representations of literary history. Within the black community historically, black women have never had the leisure to conceive of motherhood as a privatized activity that takes place apart from labor. Black women have long combined "work and family without seeing a conflict between the two," writes Patricia Hill Collins in *Black Feminist Thought* (49). For some black women, motherhood has been an oppressive institution. But for others, Collins argues, motherhood has provided "a base for self-actualization, status in the Black community, and a catalyst for social activism" (118).[3]

As in *Maud Martha,* in which motherhood becomes a form of self-realization registering a movement from silence to voice, Brooks's role as mother appears to seed and catalyze her work as a poet. In fact, Brooks's development from her early years to her more recent work might be read as a progressive unmasking and expansion of the voice and figure of the mother, as Brooks articulates a larger and larger role both for the mother in the black community and for herself as a kind of cultural mother to the political project of black literary and social creation.

In the African folktale "The Black Cloth," a young girl, Aiwa, is restored to her family, social status, and a place in history by singing to her mother who died in childbirth (Dadie 12–16). The story might be read as an allegory of black female restoration, suggesting the historical presence and legitimacy that Brooks and other black women writers have sought to achieve through their own songs to the black mother. Although Brooks's career reveals no literary equivalent to Alice Walker seeking to place a tombstone on the unmarked grave of Zora Neale Hurston as a means of saving the life and work of her literary mother, much of Brooks's poetic work might be read as an attempt to articulate and mark the hitherto unvoiced and invisible place of the black woman—and particularly the black mother—in a world that has failed to acknowledge her existence. Years before such white women writers as Adrienne Rich, Alicia Ostriker, and Sharon Olds began to return to motherhood as a subject and a source of creative power, Brooks sought to retrieve the voice and place of black motherhood as the foundation of what Zora Neale Hurston, in *Their Eyes Were Watching God,* had called "ancient power that no longer mattered" (26).

In a comment on the subject matter of the black writer, Gwendolyn Brooks said: "He has the American experience and he also has the black experience; so he's very rich" (*Report from Part One* 166). Like all of Brooks's early work, *A Street in Bronzeville* is two-toned, drawing on African-American and American, female and male, oral and written, black folk and white Western literary culture to produce a volume of poems that is not only "differently 'black' " but differently black and female.[4] The poems are rooted in Brooks's experiences as a black woman living in a section of South Side Chicago popularly known as "Bronzeville." "I lived on 63rd Street—at 623 East 63d Street," she said, "and there was a good deal of life in the raw all about me. . . . I wrote about what I saw and heard in the street. I lived in a small second-floor apartment at the corner, and I could look first on one side and then on the other. There was my material" (*Report from Part One* 134).

In the poems of *A Street in Bronzeville* these "raw" facts of black life are mediated by a multiplicity of black and white forms, ranging from spirituals, blues, folktales, and ballads to more traditional Western aesthetic forms such as rhymed quatrains, iambic pentameter verse, and Shakespearean and Petrarchan sonnets. The relation between Brooks's black content and her use of white literary forms is never simple or static. The irony of T. S. Eliot merges with the tragicomedy of Langston Hughes's laughter amid tears; the allusive and elliptical mode of modernist verse merges with the oblique and cryptic utterance of black folk forms; and the traditional sonnet is transformed into a vehicle of contemporary black protest and irresolution, as the social consciousness of the Harlem Renaissance and the technical experimentation of literary modernism are joined in a dynamic interaction.

The voice and vision of *A Street in Bronzeville* is communal, moving from the vignettes of black life in "the old marrieds" and "kitchenette building," to the close-ups of particular black characters in "The Sundays of Satin-Legs Smith" and "Ballad of Pearl May Lee," to the disillusionment and protest of black soldiers returning from World War II in the concluding sonnet sequence "Gay Chaps at the Bar." Rather than speak in her own voice, Brooks adopts a variety of masks and speaks in a multiplicity of voices that range from the subjective monologue of "the mother," to the "dialect" poems of "Hattie Scott," to the blues idiom of "Queen of the Blues," to the omniscient narration of "of De Witt Williams on his way to Lincoln Cemetery." These voices and masks, along with Brooks's technical strategies and her irony, become a means of formal and emotional control, enabling Brooks to handle the potentially volatile social content of her poems.

The poems explore the complex psychology of black men and women, boys and girls, and mothers and lovers, as they seek to negotiate and survive the brutal and cramped conditions of their lives. From the "Grayed in, and gray" physical environment of "kitchenette building," where "onion fumes" and "yesterday's garbage ripening in the hall" keep dreams from rising, to the broader social enclosures of racist America, with "a box for dark men and a box for Other," *A Street in Bronzeville* is about the fact of entrapment— physical, social, and psychological—and the multilayered oppression of black people in the United States.

Perhaps the most controversial poem in the volume is "the mother," a poem that revises both the black mammy figure of white literary tradition and the idealized figure of the black mother that had become a staple of the black male literary tradition. Long before the confessional verse of Sylvia Plath and Anne Sexton had made controversial "female" topics the subject of poetry, Brooks focuses on the subject of abortion. Her treatment of the subject in "the mother" is, in fact, so disturbing, that even Richard Wright, who evaluated the manuscript for Harper's, recommended that the poem be dropped.

The mother's dramatic monologue begins as an address to a generalized reader and then turns in the second half into an address to her "dim killed children." Her emotions are kept under tight control by an insistent rhyme scheme that prevents the poem's free verse lines from spilling over into a chaos of raw feeling. The power of the poem rests on the fact that Brooks refuses to simplify or sentimentalize the complexity of the mother's emotions. She loves her dead children, and she has killed them:

> I have contracted. I have eased
> My dim dears at the breasts they could never suck.
> I have said, Sweets, if I sinned, if I seized
> Your luck
> And your lives from your unfinished reach,
> If I stole your births and your names,
> Your straight baby tears and your games,
> Your stilted or lovely loves, your tumults, your marriages, aches, and your
>   deaths,
> If I poisoned the beginnings of your breaths,
> Believe that even in my deliberateness I was not deliberate.
>
> (*A Street in Bronzeville* 3)

In this poem, as in black women's writing from Sojourner Truth's "Ain't I a Woman" and Frances Harper's "The Slave Mother" to Toni Morrison's *Beloved,* the black woman, and particularly the black mother, becomes the site of social rupture, the place where the contradictions of American culture are located and exposed.

Knowing firsthand the oppressions of race and poverty, the mother chooses to kill her unborn children as a means of saving them from the violations of the social order:

> Believe me, I loved you all.
> Believe me, I knew you, though faintly, and I loved, I loved you
> All.
>
> (4)

As a sign of the black mother's powerlessness in an oppressive social system, abortion becomes at once a perverse form of mother love, and, paradoxically, a manifestation of maternal power. "Hardly your crowned and praised and 'customary' Mother," Brooks said of the poem; "but a Mother not unfamiliar, who decides that *she,* rather than her World, will kill her children" (*Report from Part One* 184).[5]

For all Brooks's desire to name the historical experience of black women, however, there is a kind of sexual division of labor in *A Street in Bronzeville.* Whereas the Bronzeville poems are woman-centered and draw on the folk idiom of the blues, the ballad, the spiritual, and the sermon, "The Sundays of Satin-Legs Smith" and "Gay Chaps at the Bar," which were specifically written for publication by Harper's, are male-centered and rendered in the ironic, allusive, imagistic, and elliptical mode of literary modernism. What this suggests is the role that the literary marketplace of the forties, and publishing companies in particular, played in producing a black literature that was Western, male, and white-inspired. Brook's tone of social protest is also more muted in her poems about women. It is through the soldier figure of "Negro Hero" that Brooks gives full voice to her rage against America's "white-gowned democracy," "with her knife lying cold, straight, in the softness of her sweet-flowing sleeve" (*A Street in Bronzeville* 31).

This note of disillusionment and protest intensifies in "Gay Chaps at the Bar," a title that, as D. H. Melhem suggests, "evokes the color bar, justice, and the 'bar' between life and death" (42). In this concluding sequence of twelve off-rhyme sonnets, the patriotism and democratic idealism that had led black soldiers to fight in World War II continually collides with the unchanging bar/law of American racial injustice. In an address that conflates America and God, the black soldier demands:

> If Thou be more than hate or atmosphere
> Step forth in splendor, mortify our wolves.
> Or we assume a sovereignty ourselves.
>   (*A Street In Bronzeville* 54)

As the integrationist faith in God and Country collapses under the pressure of war, Brooks's black soldier has already begun to move toward an assertion of black identity and black solidarity that anticipates the emergence of "Black Power" two decades later.

By 1945, Brooks, like her "gay chaps at the bar," appears to have lost her faith in traditional religious structures. The God of the whites cannot be trusted, and the God of the blacks seems powerless against the "hooded gaze" of white hegemony. Her faith in the saving grace of "white-gowned democracy" seems similarly shattered. She appears to be looking for an alternative system of values to sustain black people against what she calls, in the concluding sonnet of *A Street in Bronzeville,* "A fear, a deepening hollow through the cold." Brooks finds this alternative system in black motherhood—a system she begins to construct in *Annie Allen.*

In 1950 *Annie Allen* was awarded the Pulitzer Prize for poetry, making Brooks the first black person to be so honored. The award was in some sense a sign of her mastery of Euro-American poetic forms and her successful appeal to white audiences. But Brooks's success has also led Black Arts poet and critic Don L. Lee (Haki Madhubuti) to criticize the Brooks of *A Street in Bronzeville* and *Annie Allen* as a "conditioned" poet who failed to define herself in relation to African and African-American historical and cultural traditions. The focus of *Annie Allen*, he says, "was not on history or tradition, but poetic style. *Annie Allen* (1949), important? Yes. Read by blacks? No. *Annie Allen* more so than *A Street in Bronzeville* seems to have been written for whites" (*Report from Part One* 17).

Brooks herself acknowledged that the "Anniad" section of *Annie Allen* was "labored, a poem very interested in the mysteries and magic of technique" (*Report from Part One* 158). And in a comment on the experimental nature of *Annie Allen*, she admitted: "In writing that book I didn't always have the best motives. I wanted to *prove* that I could *write* well" (Hull and Gallagher, "Update on *Part One*" 32). In Brooks's work, as in the work of Melvin Tolson and Robert Hayden, mastering Euro-American poetic forms to *prove* black artistic worth and to gain entrance into the mainstream of American literature was a kind of literary equivalent of the integrationist politics of the forties and the fifties. The Negro writer was not "to be content with offering raw materials," Brooks said in a 1950 article entitled "Poets Who Are Negroes": "The Negro poet's most urgent duty, at present, is to polish his technique, his way of presenting his truths and beauties, that those may be more insinuating, and therefore, more overwhelming" (312).

It was this mastery of technique for white audiences that Lee objected to in Brooks's early work, and the fact that his critical essay introduces Brooks's 1972 autobiography, *Report from Part One*, suggests that she agreed with him. The problem, however, is that the simple opposition between early Euro-American and politically incorrect Brooks and later African-American and politically correct Brooks breaks down in any careful reading of her work. In fact, Brooks herself later challenged the idea that her early work was lacking in political, and specifically race, consciousness. "Many of the poems, in my new and old books, are 'politically aware,' " she asserted in a 1983 interview with Claudia Tate; "I suggest you reread them. . . . But I'm fighting for myself a little bit here because I believe it takes a little patience to sit down and find out that in 1945 I was saying what many of the young folks said in the sixties" (42). While she agrees with the "black aesthetic" idea of blacks writing as blacks, about blacks, and to blacks, in her view this represents nothing new. "An announcement that we are going to deal with 'the black aesthetic' seems to me to be a waste of time. I've been talking about blackness and black people all along" (46).

To argue, as Don L. Lee and others have, that Brooks's early work lacks a sense of African-American historical and cultural traditions is simply wrong. In fact, the critical emphasis on the conditioned, crafted, and integrationist nature of Brooks's early work has obscured the extent to which her poems are embedded in her historical experience as a black woman. In search of a male-defined racial politics, both black and white male critics have failed to note the female-defined racial and sexual politics that are at the very center of *Annie Allen*.

As its title suggests, *Annie Allen*'s center of consciousness is female. The book is, in effect, an epic of black womanhood that tells the story of a black woman's quest for identity and power beyond her double subjugation as "daughter of dusk" under the laws of both black and white fathers. As the first black and, arguably, the first female epic, the book traces Annie's growth from rebelliousness and pride in "Notes from the Childhood and the Girlhood," to her romantic entrapment in love and marriage in "The Anniad," to her movement toward self-definition and new social consciousness in "The Womanhood."

In the opening poem, "the birth in a narrow room," Annie gives voice to the black girl's lack of place and space in the social order:

> "How pinchy is my room! how can I breathe!
> I am not anything and I have got
> Not anything, or anything to do!"
>
> *(Annie Allen* 3)

Throughout the childhood and girlhood sequence, Annie's sense that "There was somewhat of something other" struggles against her mother's lesson of resignation and acceptance, domesticity and marriage. Annie's "inner scream" for "something other" is finally silenced in smiles and dreams of a magical prince.

In "The Anniad" Brooks tells Annie's story in mock heroic form, seeking through a combination of irony, humor, and pathos to exorcise the black girl's romantic enthrallment to the myth of the prince. The poem begins:

> Think of sweet and chocolate,
> Left to folly or to fate,
> Whom the higher gods forgot,
> Whom the lower gods berate;
> Physical and underfed
> Fancying on the featherbed
> What was never and is not.
>
> (19)

The lines underscore the intersection of racial and sexual caste systems in Annie's life: as a chocolate brown girl she is subjugated by the color and gender codes of black men ("the lower gods") who berate her and white men ("the higher gods") to whom she is invisible.

She is also shaped and subjugated by white romantic myths of the prince: "Watching for the paladin / Which no woman ever had," Annie seeks to remake herself in the image of the fair-skinned maiden:

> Think of thaumaturgic lass
> Looking in her looking-glass
> At the unembroidered brown;
> Printing bastard roses there;
> Then emotionally aware
> Of the black and boisterous hair,
> Taming all that anger down.
>
> (20)

Although Annie's thaumaturgy is treated comically, her attempt to print "bastard roses" on her "unembroidered brown" skin reveals the underlying pathos and tragedy of the black woman's situation as the subject of white romantic mythologies that scorn and exclude her. Color and hair grade emerge over and over as sites of contest and pain for the black heroines of Brooks's verse. Here, as in "Ballad of Pearl May Lee," Annie's tamed down anger registers Brooks's own rage against an impossible ideal of white female beauty that is enforced by black and white men alike.

When the "paladin" arrives in the form of a "man of tan," he comes bearing male "dominion" and subjection to an intraracial color code that devalues Annie's "sweet and chocolate" womanhood. In the course of the poem, Annie's dreams of love and marriage continually clash with the reality of her bereavement, as her husband goes off to war, returns wanting his "power back again," abandons her for "a maple banshee," and finally returns to Annie to die of his "overseas disease." The entire story is told in a densely metaphoric and elliptical style that marks Brooks's attempt to reconcile her experience as a black woman with her desire to "prove" herself as a poet. Although Brooks later dismissed the poem as "just an exercise, just an exercise," the modernist language and form that appear to entrap Brooks's own representation in "The Anniad" function as the perfect stylistic cognates for the debilitating sexual, racial, and romantic mythologies that entrap and silence the poem's black heroine (Hull and Gallagher, "Update on *Part One*" 32).[6]

"Oh mother, mother, where is happiness?" Annie asks in an "Appendix to the Anniad." The poem serves as a transition between the teachings of the old mother in the first two parts of *Annie Allen* and the teachings of the new and more militant black mother who emerges in "The Womanhood." The poem also represents a move away from the third-person, mock-heroic voice of "The Anniad" to the first-person female and racial voice of "The Womanhood." It is only after the death of her husband and the failure of the promise of the old mother that Annie speaks for the first time in her own voice. As in *Maud Martha*, it is not finally in love and marriage but in motherhood and children that the heroine finds both her voice and a source of self-actualizing power and social vision.

In the opening sonnet sequence of "The Womanhood," entitled "the children of the poor," Brooks/Annie speaks from the point of view of the black mother as she begins to articulate a new personal and communal ethos rooted in the moral and emotional complexity of the mother/child bond. "People who have no children can be hard," she says, representing motherhood—and particularly black motherhood—as an experience that tests any easy moral positions in a "bitten and bewarred" world. The "lifting helplessness" and "whimper-whine" of children, she says, speaking in the collective voice of the mother,

> makes a trap for us.
> And makes a curse. And makes a sugar of
> the malocclusions, the inconditions of love.
>
> (*Annie Allen* 35)

As the very figure of "the inconditions of love," a phrase that suggests both the unconditional nature of mother love and the oppressive historical conditions in which mothering has occurred, motherhood is represented as a morally complex base of social action.

"What shall I give my children? who are poor, / Who are adjudged the leastwise of the land," Annie asks in the opening lines of sonnet no. 2. The question underscores the intersecting oppressions of race, class, and gender in the black mother's life. Brooks's mother revises the easy and dehumanizing myth of the black mammy prevalent in the culture. She is "less than angelic, admirable or sure," and she lacks the means to provide for her children:

> My hand is stuffed with mode, design, device.
> But I lack access to my proper stone.
> And plenitude of plan shall not suffice.
>
> (36)

Although Brooks stresses the mother's frustration, pain, and lack of political or social means, she also emphasizes her presence, her power, and the actual historical role she has played in compensating for the failures of both the social system and God. In sonnet no. 3, "And shall I prime my children, pray, to pray?," the love of the mother replaces the love of God as the ultimate source of social salvation. Behind and beyond traditional religious structures, the mother waits "At forehead and at fingers rather wise, / Holding the bandage ready for your eyes" (37).

But while the mother/child bond is at the center of the values of love, nurturance, and social community that Brooks stresses in "The Womanhood," the mother of these poems is also a militant figure who insists on the need for hate, violence, and war in the battle for social justice. In "First Fight, Then Fiddle," Annie exhorts her children to give up fiddling—a term that suggests both artistic creation and playing around—for militant social action:

> But first to arms, to armor. Carry hate
> In front of you and harmony behind.
> Be deaf to music and to beauty blind.
> Win war. Rise bloody, maybe not too late
> For having first to civilize a space
> Wherein to play your violin with grace.
>
> (38)

In urging her children to fight for the immediate needs of black survival in order to "civilize a space" for the leisurely pursuit of art and beauty, Annie anticipates the more militant posture of Brooks's later poems. Unlike "First Fight, Then Fiddle," however, which presents art and action as antithetical social practices, in her later poems Brooks will reconceive art as a form of political action.

Focusing on the historical experience of black motherhood, Brooks begins to speak in *Annie Allen* as a kind of racial mother who speaks from and of and to the collective needs and desires of the black community. The final poem of the sequence "Men of careful turns, haters of forks in the road" is at once a protest against the white/male social order and a call to black social action. Whereas in "The Sundays of Satin-Legs Smith" and "The Anniad," comic irony functioned as a gently mocking weapon against the potentially debilitating illusions of black people's lives, in "Men of careful turns," this weapon is turned against the white community itself, exposing the "uncaring mouth," the "traditional blow," and cool "indifference" of the white man as "drunken mate."

The poem is split between the old integrationist faith in blacks and whites sharing what Brooks calls "our mutual estate" at the outset of the poem, and the sermonic appeal of the final lines, in which the speaker renounces the gradualist promises of white society and calls for new faith in black solidarity and black self-determination:

> The toys are all grotesque
> And not for lovely hands; are dangerous,
> Serrate in open and artful places. Rise.
> Let us combine. There are no magics or elves
> Or timely godmothers to guide us. We are lost, must
> Wizard a track through our own screaming weed.
>
> (60)

Like the personal and social transformation she imagines for her black heroine in *Annie Allen,* the transformation Brooks imagines for the black community will come not from outside—from the old magics and myths of white hegemony—but from within black people themselves as they "wizard" their own black track through the "screaming weed" of the present and future. Thus, the book that began enmeshed in what Brooks called the "mysteries and magic of technique" ends as a call to black action that anticipates the more direct and hortatory voice of the female preacher and orator in her later verse. The cryptic, riddled, and highly phonic style of *Annie Allen* appears to have worked as a kind of conjure—a black "rap"—that exorcises not only Annie's but some of Brooks's own white demons.

Words as Weapons

Toward the close of *Maud Martha,* Brooks registers her most violent expression of rage against the white male order. When the Santa Claus in a local department store looks right through Maud and her daughter, failing to hear the black girl-child's gift list, Maud challenges his cool indifference: " 'Mister,' said Maud Martha, 'my little girl is talking to you.' " Maud's rage leads her to imagine gouging out the eyes that have made both black mother and daughter invisible in the white man's world: she yearns "to jerk trimming scissors from purse and jab jab jab that evading eye." Unable either to allay or to dismiss her anger, Maud realizes, "There were these scraps of baffled hate in her, hate with no eyes, no smile and—this she especially regretted, called her hungriest lack—not much voice" (*Maud Martha* 176).

The black mother's wicked desire to gouge out the eyes of Santa Claus in *Maud Martha* signals the new direction of Brooks's work in *The Bean Eaters.* In the poems of this 1960 volume, Brooks's own "scraps of baffled hate" are redirected outward against the white community in a protest that is at once more vocal, more violent, and more rooted in the historic moment. The volume responds to the politically transforming energies of the civil rights movement, which was spurred by the 1954 Supreme Court decision (*Brown* vs. *Board of Education*) that banned racial segregation in public schools. The movement was officially inaugurated when in 1955 Rosa Parks sat in the white section of a bus in Montgomery, Alabama, and when the young Martin Luther King, Jr., arrived to lead the Montgomery Bus Boycotts of 1955–56. Southern opposition to school integration climaxed in Little Rock, Arkansas, in 1957 when Governor Orval Faubus tried to prevent nine black students from entering Central High School, and President Dwight D. Eisenhower had to send federal troops to ensure their safe admission. The agitation for integration of schools, buses, and eating places throughout the South gave rise to the black and white Freedom Riders of 1961, and what Brooks called "their fellows the sit-ins, the wade-ins, read-ins, pray-ins, vote-ins, and all related strugglers for what is reliably right" (*Report from Part One* 187).

In *The Bean Eaters,* Brooks's political subjects—race, gender, segregation, poverty, protest, and war—are once again mediated by a multiplicity of voices, masks, and narrative forms, ranging from the "Too saddled" and "addled" voice of the male speaker in "Strong Men, Riding Horses," who protests against the ubiquitous myth of the West, "I am not brave at all"; to the objective, almost flattened narration of "The Bean Eaters" ("They eat beans mostly, this old yellow pair"); to the suicidal monologue of the middle-aged woman in "A Sunset of the City" ("I am a woman, and dusty, standing among new affairs / I am a woman who hurries through her prayers"). But while Brooks's political protest and her personal voice are mediated—and in some sense muted—in a complex web of narrative and dramatic strategies, in these poems she also begins to move toward a looser, more direct, free verse style. This new style is particularly evident in "We Real Cool," one of the few early poems that Brooks would later feel comfortable reading to black people in streets, taverns, and prisons. The haunted and haunting voice of the seven pool players at the Golden Shovel is grounded in black speech and the musical phrasing of a jazz tune:

> We real cool. We
> Left school. We
>
> Lurk late. We
> Strike straight. We
>
> Sing sin. We
> Thin gin. We
>
> Jazz June. We
> Die soon.
> (*The Bean Eaters* 17)

The "We" that enjambs each of the lines except the last death-bearing line underscores the self-defensive posturing of the boys who are defined and entrapped by the nihilistic and ultimately deadly mythology of the black gang.

The overarching theme of *The Bean Eaters* is the erosion of dreams—of life, of love, of America itself—under the pressure of experience and the blood facts of history. This theme receives its fullest articulation in "Bronzeville Mother Loiters in Mississippi. Meanwhile Mississippi Mother Burns Bacon," the longest poem in the volume and the poem that Brooks wanted to place first. Perhaps because of the poem's insistence on the red blood of American racial and sexual violence, the editors at Harper's convinced her to begin with the more socially disembodied male voice of "The Explorer," a poem that symbolically suggests social turmoil—"There were no bourns / There were no quiet rooms"—without insisting on the specificity of either race or gender violation.

Like "The *Chicago Defender* Sends a Man to Little Rock," which responds to the "hurling spittle, rock, / Garbage and fruit" of racial conflict in Little Rock in 1957, "A Bronzeville Mother Loiters in Mississippi" represents a new turn in Brooks's work toward the historic event—a turn that anticipates the verse journalism of "In Montgomery" (1971) and the more direct political inscription of *Riot* (1969), *Family Pictures* (1970), and *Beckonings* (1975). "A Bronzeville Mother" responds to the circumstances surrounding the 1955 murder of Emmett Till, a fourteen-year-old boy from Chicago who was tortured and then killed while visiting relatives in Mississippi after he allegedly made passes at a white woman in a local store. Brooks dramatizes these circumstances within the consciousness of the white woman who was the putative subject of his advances.

As the title suggests, the maternal feeling of both the boy's Bronzeville mother and the Mississippi mother is at the center of the poem, enabling the white mother to bond with the northern black mother against the murderous white man—her husband—who is their common oppressor:

> She did not scream.
> She stood there.
> But a hatred for him burst into glorious flower,
> And its perfume enclasped them—big,
> Bigger than all magnolias.
>   (*The Bean Eaters* 25)

Rooted in the white mother's sense of identity and commonality with the black mother as "Other Woman," this blossoming flower of hatred for the white man—"Bigger than all magnolias"—bursts through the traditional race, class, and regional bounds signified by the flower of the Old South. Like Alice Walker's "Revolutionary Petunias," Brooks's "glorious flower" of hatred suggests the revolutionary power of female anger and female bonding as a source of potentially transforming social energies.

Brooks's vision of the bond between a black mother and a white mother as a source of revolutionary power against an oppressive white/male system anticipates the work of Adrienne Rich, Audre Lorde, and Alice Walker, among others. But it is an integrationist move toward interracial sisterhood that Brooks herself did not pursue in her later work. Her new direction is suggested in *The Bean Eaters* by her biting satire of the middle-class white women's "loathe-love largesse" in "The Lovers of the Poor." It is also evident in the prophetic voice of "Leftist Orator in Washington Park Pleasant-

ly Punishes the Gropers," which foretells the fall of America; and in the
militancy of "The Ballad of Rudolph Reed," a poem that anticipates the
message of James Baldwin a few years later in *The Fire Next Time* (1963) in
telling the story of a black man who is finally forced to take up arms in
defense of his right to live peacefully with his family in a "bitter white"
neighborhood.

It is only through the male figure that Brooks projects acts of physical
violence against the white system in the poems of *The Bean Eaters*. Black
women register their protest in less public acts of social resistance. In "Mrs.
Small," Mrs. Small soils the very white shirt of a white insurance man "With
a pair of brown / Spurts (just recently boiled) / Of the 'very best coffee in
town'" as a means of asserting her "small" protest against the intersecting ·
economies of racial, sexual, and class oppression represented by the insurance
man on his "morning run." Brooks's vision of Mrs. Small "Continuing her
part / Of the world's business" within the small space of her home works
toward a conception of the female heroic that she would articulate in "Weap-
oned Woman," one of the new poems published in 1963 in *Selected Poems:*

> Well, life has been a baffled vehicle
> And baffling. But she fights, and
> Has fought, according to her lights and
> The lenience of her whirling-place.
>
> She fights with semi-folded arms,
> Her strong bag, and the stiff
> Frost of her face (that challenges "when" and "If.")
> And altogether she does Rather Well.
>
> (125)

Brooks's representation of ordinary black women fighting and challenging the
world in small but not insignificant acts of social resistance and defiance
transforms traditional (male) definitions of the heroic. But while she locates a
place for the heroic in the domestic and maternal sphere, she also tends to
limit female heroism to acts of love, nurturance, and social provision. Thus,
in "A Penitent Considers Another Coming of Mary," Mary's "Coming" is
equated with Christ's, but her heroism is limited to the merciful and maternal
role of providing another son:

> She would not shake her head and leave
> This military air,
> But ratify a modern hay,
> And put her Baby there.
>
> (*The Bean Eaters* 52)

Similarly, in "Big Bessie throws her son into the street," the mother enjoins
her son to "Go down the street" rather than going down the street herself. In

the late sixties, as the black revolution moved out of the courtroom and into the streets of the United States, Big Bessie, like Gwendolyn Brooks, would go out into the street herself.

Black Power

In 1966 riots broke out in the black sections of Chicago, the same black sections that had chased away the "scented bodies" of the white middle-class women of "Lovers of the Poor": "But it's all so bad! and entirely too much for them. / The stench; the urine, cabbage, and dead beans" (*The Bean Eaters* 36). Like the riots in Watts, California, the previous summer and the riots throughout the country from Tampa and Atlanta to Newark and Detroit in 1967, the riots in Chicago were part of a more general social upheaval in America in the sixties—a decade that began with an integrationist appeal for civil rights and ended with an increasingly violent antiwar movement on campuses across the country and a growing radicalization and militancy not only among blacks, but among women, Chicanos, Native Americans, and other oppressed groups in the United States. The rioting in American cities was a sign of the increasing disaffection among urban blacks with traditional religious, integrationist, and nonviolent solutions to the socioeconomic problems of the ghetto. The riots marked a turn away from the passive resistance and black and white "dream" of Martin Luther King toward the increased radicalism and militancy signified by Malcolm X's call for black separatism, black nationalism, and black self-defense.

The disaffection of American blacks was intensified by the fact that many of those leaders who had stood for racial equality had been assassinated. Medgar Evers, head of the National Association for the Advancement of Colored People (NAACP), was assassinated in June 1963. The March on Washington was led by Reverend King in August 1963 and was followed in November by the assassination of President John F. Kennedy. Malcolm X was assassinated at a rally in Harlem in February 1965; Martin Luther King was assassinated in 1968 in Memphis, Tennessee, which gave rise to further rioting across the country. And a few months later, Senator Robert Kennedy, who had stressed the needs of poor people and blacks in his campaign for the presidency in 1968, was assassinated after the June primary in California.

The increasing radicalism of American blacks was given a name and a rallying cry when Stokely Carmichael called for Black Power at a Student Nonviolent Coordinating Committee (SNCC) march in Jackson, Mississippi, in the spring of 1965.[7] Initially used by Carmichael and his fellow organizer Willie Ricks to describe the supporting rather than controlling role that blacks wanted whites to play in the movement, the term Black Power quickly gained cultural, political, and mythological power as a term that symbolized the multiple and conflicting aspirations of a new generation of black people.

In *Black Power: The Politics of Liberation in America,* Carmichael and Charles Hamilton defined Black Power as "a call for black people in this country to unite, to recognize their heritage, to build a sense of community. It is a call for black people to begin to define their own goals, to lead their own organizations and to support those organizations. It is a call to reject the racist institutions and values of this society" (43–44). Black Power meant black pride, black beauty, black solidarity, and black love, with a corresponding emphasis on African and African-American cultural forms, including black music, African costume, and the Afro hairdo. But Black Power also signified the separatist and nationalist aspiration of blacks to define and empower themselves from within and to overthrow their American oppressors by violence if necessary: "Nigger / Can you kill," Nikki Giovanni chanted to black audiences in 1968:

> Can you kill
> Can a nigger kill
> Can a nigger kill a honkie
> Can a nigger kill the Man
> Can you kill nigger
> Huh? nigger can you
> kill
>
> *(Black Feeling* 19)

Her words register the angry and revolutionary mood of a new generation of blacks as it was manifesting itself in the growing militancy of Carmichael's SNCC, the increasingly violent posture of the Black Panther Party of Huey Newton and Eldridge Cleaver, and the separatist nationalism of Malcolm X and the Black Muslims.

Gwendolyn Brooks's first experience of Black Power as a new physical and cultural presence came at a Writer's Conference at Fisk University in the spring of 1967. "First," she said, "I was aware of a general energy, an electricity, in look, walk, speech, *gesture* of the young blackness I saw all about me" (*Report from Part One* 84). The new heroes of the Fisk conference included the poet LeRoi Jones (Imamu Amiri Baraka), the novelist John Killens, and the editor Hoyt Fuller, all advocates of the "The Black Aesthetic," the cultural and artistic counterpart of Black Power. "*I* had never been, before, in the general presence of such insouciance, such live firmness, such confident vigor, such determination to mold or carve something DEFINITE," Brooks wrote (*Report from Part One* 85). As she listened to the heady shouts

Figure 10. Photograph of Gwendolyn Brooks. "The slender, shy, and sensitive young girl / is woman now / Her words a power in the Ebon land," wrote Margaret Walker in "For Gwen—1969." (Courtesy of Gwendolyn Brooks)

of Baraka and Ron Milner—"Up against the wall, white man!"—she realized: "There is indeed a new black today. He is different from any the world has known. He's a tall-walker. Almost firm. By many of his own *brothers* he is not understood. And he is understood by *no* white" (85).

At the Fisk Writers Conference, Brooks underwent a kind of sociocultural conversion that catalyzed a transformation in her post-1967 life and work. She described the transformation in *Report from Part One:* "I—who have 'gone the gamut' from an almost angry rejection of my dark skin by some of my brainwashed brothers and sisters to a surprised queenhood in the new black sun—am qualified to enter at least the kindergarten of new consciousness now. New consciousness and trudge-toward-progress" (86). Brooks's "surprised queenhood" figures the new sense of personal power, pride, and hopefulness that were called forth by her tall-walking black brothers at Fisk University.

What this new black consciousness meant politically was that Brooks began to move toward a black separatist and black nationalist ideal for the black community, as this ideal was being articulated locally by the poet Don L. Lee and the Chicago youth organizer Walter Bradford. "I know now that I am essentially an essential African," Brooks wrote in her autobiography. "I know now that black fellow-feeling must be the black man's encyclopedic Primer. I know that the black-and-white integration concept, which in the mind of some beaming early saint was a dainty spinning dream, has wound down to farce, to unsavory and mumbling farce. . . . I know that the black emphasis must be, not *against white,* but FOR *black*" (*Report from Part One* 45). As the aesthetic counterpart of "not *against white,* but FOR *black,*" Brooks redirected her address away from the white and toward the black community, seeking to write poems not only for and about blacks but poems that she "could take into a tavern, into the street, into the halls of a housing project" (Claudia Tate, *Black Women Writers at Work* 44).

But while Brooks's post-1967 transformation led to a new sense of black power and consciousness, her commitment to a strongly male-identified Black Power movement also led to an increased sense of ambivalence about her identity and role as a black woman poet writing in America. Before 1967, Brooks's specific concerns as a black woman were at the center of her poems, sometimes, as in "A Bronzeville Mother," even crossing race and class bounds to create a bond between black and white women as mothers within and common victims of a hegemonic white male order. In her post-1967 works, as she turned toward an increased emphasis on black power and black community, she tended to mute or marginalize the particularity of her interests as a black woman writer and to silence or displace the anger she had formerly expressed against black men who enforced white hegemony and female subordination by favoring and indeed idolizing the "lemon-hued lynx" over the "Ol' Black Gal."

Brooks's self-division, self-contradiction, and self-difference are evident in the 1968 *In the Mecca,* which begins with the title poem, "In the Mecca," and concludes with a section of more recent poems, entitled "After Mecca." The inscription on the jacket cover—"I was to be a Watchful Eye; a Tuned Ear; a

Super-Reporter"—embodies Brooks's new conception of the artist's role, a
role that encompasses the watchfulness of the mother, the musical respon-
siveness of the black blues artist, and the reportorial skills of the contemporary journalist. The Mecca of the long opening poem, "In the Mecca," is at
once an actual black tenement building, formerly "a splendid palace, a show-
place of Chicago," and an ironically nuanced symbol, suggesting a religious
ideal, the historic vision of America as Mecca or Promised Land, and the
Black Mecca of the Nation of Islam envisioned by Malcolm X and other black
nationalists. The gap between ideal and real—between Mecca as a religious
site and Mecca as America, between Mecca as new Black Nation and Mecca
as the dark-lit maze of a Chicago tenement building—informs the action of
the poem. "And the fair fables fall," says Brooks at the entrance of both
Mecca building and poem, in words that figure the collapse of old mythologies in preparation for a new black consciousness that is at once the
subject and the hope of the poem.

Interweaving a panorama of Mecca inhabitants in a descriptive and dialogic
narration that encompasses a multiplicity of verse forms and styles, allusions
to current black politics, and a range of moods from despair to hopefulness,
"In the Mecca" is, in effect, a black blues epic of the urban ghetto. "To touch
every note in the life of this block-long block-wide building would be to
capsulize the gist of black humanity in general," Brooks said of the poem
(*Report from Part One* 190). Her epic of black life is once again female-
centered, unified by the overarching story of Mrs. Sallie Smith, a domestic
worker and mother of a fatherless household of nine, whose quest for her lost
daughter, Pepita, culminates at the end of the poem in the discovery of
Pepita's murdered body.

Mrs. Sallie's search for her daughter, inaugurated in the poem by the black
vernacular construction " 'WHERE PEPITA BE?' " rewrites and blackens the
Demeter and Persephone myth as a black mother-centered female resurrection
myth. The lost and ultimately invisible Pepita, whose name suggests both her
speck-like existence and her potential power as a little "pip," seed, or root, is
associated in the course of the poem with the emotional and psychic deaden-
ing of the black community. "*Ain seen er I ain seen er I ain seen er* / Ain seen
er I ain seen er I ain seen er," echoes refrain-like through the corridors of the
Mecca, signifying both the black community's indifference and the black girl-
child's invisibility as Mrs. Sallie searches frantically for her missing daughter:

> Knock—knocking down the martyred halls
> at doors behind whose yelling oak or pine
> many flowers start, choke, reach up,
> want help, get it, do not get it,
> rally, bloom, or die on the wasting vine.
>
> (*In the Mecca* 15)

As in "the mother" and "The Womanhood," the violation of the mother-child bond becomes the very emblem of the ways the black community's growth is continually stunted and "choked" by the socioeconomic conditions of black life in the United States. Like the "many flowers" that "rally, bloom, or die" behind the closed doors of the Mecca, the fate of Pepita represents both the failure and loss of the black community as well as its possibility for future renewal and growth.

"The loss of the daughter to the mother, the mother to the daughter, is the essential female tragedy," Adrienne Rich wrote in *Of Woman Born: Motherhood as Experience and Institution* (237). In Brooks's poem, this loss under patriarchy is compounded by the socioeconomic oppressions of race and poverty. The loss of the black daughter in "In the Mecca" is linked with the lost and invisible lives of an entire cast of women characters who seek self-affirmation in men, God, and *Vogue* magazine; or, like the wife and mother, Marian, in fantasies of self-mutilation that will make her visible to her community. "At ire with faucet, husband, young," Marian

> Craves crime: her murder, her deep wounding, or
> a leprosy so lovely as to pop
> the slights and sleep of her community,
> her Mecca.
> A Thing. To make the people heel and stop
> And See her.
>   . . .
> Her husband never Saw her, never said
> her single silver Self aloud.
>   (*In the Mecca* 29–30)

What the poem suggests, finally, is that the violation of the black daughter and the mother's inability to save the daughter from the Plutonian forces of destruction and death that surround her are at the very sources of black oppression in the United States. It is only by seeing the black daughter and saying "her single silver Self aloud" that black men and women will be able to find their way out of the old "way of the Mecca" as the site of both physical oppression and false fables.

The mother's quest for her lost black daughter engages the separate losses, hungers, desires, and fears of the black community. Her quest takes her not only through the underworld of the black ghetto but through the dim-lit mazes of the American past and current world history. The racial memory of Great-great Gram associates Pepita's fate with the violations of slavery and the brutal conditions of the slave child's life. " 'I ain seen no Pepita. But / I remember our cabin," says Great-great Gram:

> "We six-uns curled
> in corners of the dirt, and closed our eyes,

> and went to sleep—or listened to the rain
> fall inside, felt the drops
> big on our noses, bummies and tum-tums. . . ."
>
> (15)

Through the memory of Loam Norton the loss of Pepita is also associated with the horrors of the Holocaust and the ultimate failure of God's grace:

> Although he has not seen Pepita, Loam
> Norton considers Belsen and Dachau,
> regrets all old unkindnesses and harms.
> . . . The Lord was their shepherd.
> Yet did they want.
>
> (15)

Whereas in Brooks's 1963 poem "Riders to the Blood-Red Wrath," the Freedom Rider measures the failures and promise of the white and black community against the promise of America, proclaiming "Democracy and Christianity / Recommence with me" (*Selected Poems* 118), in the world of "In the Mecca," traditional religious structures have failed. The white man's law is inadequate: "The Law arrives—and does not quickly go / to fetch a Female of the Negro Race" (*In the Mecca* 19). And the fair fable of America has itself collapsed: "so long grand, / flogging her dark one with her own hand, / watching in meek amusement while he bled" (23).

In "In the Mecca" the failures and possibility of the black community are measured not in relation to the promise of America but in relation to its own capacity to care or not to care about the plight of the black mother in search of her lost daughter. Isolated, self-interested, and self-absorbed, most of the inhabitants of the Mecca are indifferent to the life and growth and future of the black community emblematized in the mother's quest for her lost daughter. "How many care, Pepita?" asks the maternal and ever watchful narrator, as she catalogues the lack of watchfulness and care in the black community. Like Darkara, who looks at *Vogue* magazine but does not look for Pepita, and Boonsie De Broe, who "has / not seen Pepita Smith: but is / a Lady," the Mecca inhabitants pursue their separate survival strategies in isolation and solitude. " 'Pepita who?' " says Prophet Williams and "yawns," as he goes about his business of getting rich on the sale of religion, false prophecies, and miracle cures.

Brooks even faults the black literary tradition itself in the figure of the poet, Alfred, who projects some of her own early absorption with the craft of poetry:

> No, Alfred has not seen Pepita Smith.
> But he (who might have been a poet-king)
> can speak superbly of the line of Leopold.
>
> (20)

Although Alfred cares passionately about the process of literary creation and the Negritude Movement of Leopold Senghor, who "sings in art-lines / of Black Woman," he fails to notice the small and unromanticized black female lives in his own community.

The way out of the mazes of the ghetto and the false fables of the past is represented in the poem by the contemporary voice of Don L. Lee:

> Don Lee wants
> not a various America.
> Don Lee wants
> a new nation
> under nothing;
>
>   . . .
>
> wants
> new art and anthem; will
> want a new music screaming in the sun.
>
>   (21)

As the only historical character to appear in the poem, Don Lee figures Brooks's own move away from the integrationist politics and poetics of her early poems toward the separatist vision of a new black nation celebrated and indeed called forth by new black art and anthem. Lee's prophetic call is answered in the poem by the transformation of Alfred. "Something, something in Mecca / continues to call!," Alfred murmurs at the end of the poem as he turns away from the stylized romanticism and negritude of an old black literary tradition toward a new engagement with the political and artistic possibilities of his own black community:

> And steadily
> an essential sanity, black and electric,
> builds to a reportage and redemption.
> A hot estrangement.
> A material collapse
> that is Construction.
>
>   (31)

Alfred's words, which embody the new black consciousness as it was being articulated by Don Lee, Lerone Bennett, LeRoi Jones, and other spokesmen for the Black Power movement, represent Brooks's own turn toward the promise and possibility of the black community as the ultimate Mecca not only at the end of the poem but in her own life and work after her 1967 Fisk University transformation.

Like the black nationalist voice of Don Lee, however, which was interpolated into "In the Mecca" after the poem was completed, Alfred's faith in a "black and electric" redemption seems imposed from without and fundamentally at odds with the false faith and general indifference of the black community in the poem—a community that consistently fails to respond to the quest of the black mother and the fate of her black daughter. Nor does the "Construction" envisioned by Alfred fully address or encompass the dead body of Pepita, which is discovered under the cot of the madman, Jamaican Edward, in the final passage of the poem:

> Beneath his cot
> a little woman lies in dust with roaches.
> She never went to kindergarten.
> She never learned that black is not beloved.
>
> (31)

Within the context of the new black consciousness articulated in the poem by Don Lee and the poet Alfred, the evocation of Pepita's death in the final lines of the poem might be read as part of the "material collapse / that is Construction":

> She whose little stomach fought the world had
> wriggled, like a robin!
> Odd were the little wrigglings
> and the chopped chirpings oddly rising.
>
> (31)

But by associating Pepita's "little wrigglings" and her "chopped chirpings oddly rising" with the process of black construction, the lines also inadvertently figure the problematic place of the black woman in a new black consciousness and a new black nation that appears to arise out of the sacrificial silencing and death of the black daughter.

Ultimately, Pepita's "chopped chirpings" do not really work in unison with the black male voices of renewed consciousness that punctuate and in some sense rupture the black female quest myth of "In the Mecca." Like the blank space that separates Alfred's constructive vision from the dead body of Pepita in the concluding passage of the poem, the gap between the voices of new black consciousness and Pepita's "chopped chirpings" indicates Brooks's own failure to negotiate the split between the black female-centered quest myth—with which the poem begins—and the male-centered mythos of Black Power—with which the poem ends.

Begun in the fifties as a novel for juveniles, "In the Mecca" is a kind of palimpsest that inscribes Brooks's changing and conflicting designs as she moved from the female-centered vision of her earlier poems toward the increasingly male-centered vision of her work after 1967. "Kinswomen! Kinswomen!" Brooks exclaims parenthetically after she describes the death in self-defense of Prophet Williams's wife:

> His wife she was a skeleton.
> His wife she was a bone.
> Ida died in self-defense.
> (Kinswomen!
> Kinswomen!)
> Ida died alone.
>
> *(In the Mecca 6)*

The narrator's appeal to her kinswomen in the black community suggests that before Brooks underwent the conversion to new black consciousness (represented in the poem by Don Lee and the poet Alfred), she may have been moving toward a concept of female bonding as a means of collective defense and political renewal. But this call to her black sisters, like her criticism of male and female relations in the black community, appears to have been silenced by Brooks's transformation of consciousness under the impact of the Black Power movement in 1967.

If "In the Mecca" still seems split between what Lee called the "black womanness" of Brooks's early poems and the black maleness of the late sixties, in "After Mecca" Brooks's move toward the male-identified mythos of the Black Power movement becomes complete. The title signifies the act of writing after and beyond the Mecca as the site at once of physical oppression, false fables, and the fallen promise of America. In the poems of "After Mecca," Brooks seeks to evolve a black-directed, communal, open-ended, and politically engaged art form that will respond to Lee's call for "new art and anthem." The tone of the poems is celebratory rather than critical and ironic as Brooks focuses on contemporary heroes in poems on "Medgar Evers," "Malcolm X," and the Chicago street gang "The Blackstone Rangers"; and contemporary events such as the dedication of The Wall of Respect on August 27, 1967. "It is the Hour / of ringing, rouse, of ferment-festival," says Brooks in her dedicatory poem "The Wall," signifying the constructive energies of the new black consciousness in the transformation of the side wall of a Chicago slum building into "a mural communicating black dignity": "The old decapitations are revised," she says; "the dispossessions beakless. / And we sing" *(In the Mecca 43)*.

As in "The Wall," in which "Black / boy-men on roofs fist out 'Black Power!' " the heroes of the new black construction are male. Commenting on the late sixties as "a male time," Brooks said: "I remember that when Haki [Don L. Lee] was working with Baraka, they were both very firm about men being the leaders. The women assisted" (Hull and Gallagher 38). This emphasis on male leadership and the "maleness" of Black Power is particularly evident in the poem "Malcolm X," which is dedicated to Dudley Randall, the editor of the important black publishing company Broadside Press:

He had the hawk-man's eyes.
We gasped. We saw the maleness.
The maleness raking out and making guttural the air
and pushing us to walls.

                    . . .

He opened us—
who was a key,

who was a man.

                                        (*In the Mecca* 39)

Like Nikki Giovanni's "Beautiful Black Man" and Mari Evans's "Brother . . . the twilight," Brooks's celebration of black manhood is meant to counter an oppressive and emasculating white mythology and social practice. "On account of everything that had been done to smash our men down," said Brooks, "there was this tendency on the part of the women—announced too—to lift the men up, *to heroize* them" (Hull and Gallagher 36). As in "The Blackstone Rangers" poems, however, in which "The Leaders" "construct, strangely, a monstrous pearl or grace" while the "Gang Girls" settle for "aborted carnival" and the "rhymes of Leaning," the emphasis on the maleness of Black Power tended to create a potentially oppressive sexual order in which black women were expected to support rather than to construct, to love rather than to lead.

And yet, if the sexual politics of Black Power led to a diminution of the female characters in Brooks's post-1967 poems, the racial emphasis of the new black consciousness had an empowering effect on Brooks's poetic voice. Until she published *In the Mecca* in 1968, Brooks, like Rich in her poetry of the fifties and early sixties, spoke through a number of dramatic and sometimes ironic masks. Unlike Rich, however, whose personal voice was released by a return to the specifically female sources of power in herself and the world, Brooks's personal "*I*" was released by an energizing sense of relation to the racial and specifically African sources of her identity and power.

This racially empowered "I" emerges for the first time in the concluding poems of *In the Mecca,* "The Sermon on the Warpland" and "The Second Sermon on the Warpland," poems that signify in their titles both the warped land of America and the new militancy of blacks imaged in the war planned. Moving toward a more direct, public, and sermonic form of black expression, Brooks addresses the black community as a kind of female preacher, a role that would have been denied to her in the more traditional structures of the black church. In "The Sermon on the Warpland," this voice is still contained in quotation marks as Brooks speaks to her sisters and brothers in the collective voice of the black community. As in "In the Mecca," her emphasis is on the "coming of hell and health together," the new construction that will come from the collapse of the old white systems of value and power:

"Build now your Church, my brothers, sisters. Build
never with brick nor Corten nor with granite.
Build with lithe love. With love like lion-eyes.
With love like morningrise.
With love like black, our black—
luminously indiscreet;
complete; continuous."

(*In the Mecca* 49–50)

In "The Second Sermon on the Warpland," which is dedicated to Walter
Bradford, Brooks addresses the black community directly in her own sermonic voice:

This is the urgency: Live!
and have your blooming in the noise of the whirlwind.

(51)

In both sermons, the maternal voice of "The Womanhood" is politicized as
Brooks speaks in a public space and a public form, emphasizing the transforming and revolutionary power of blackness, and preaching the values of
black love, black community, and black social action. Representing herself in
the figure of Big Bessie who moves out of the house and stands "bigly" in the
"wild weed," Brooks reconceives a role for black art, for the black woman
poet, and for the maternal at the very center of the black community:

In the wild weed
she is a citizen,
and is a moment of highest quality; admirable.

(54)

Thus, while the new heroes of *In the Mecca* are male, the vision and voice of
the black woman as a kind of culture mother are still at the very center of
Brooks's poems. The problem, however, is that even as Brooks reconceived
black motherhood as an active, political, and revolutionary power, her vision
was potentially conscriptive in failing to imagine any role for black women
writers or the new black woman apart from the maternal.

"There Will Be Differences"

"My aim, in my next future," Brooks said, "is to write poems that will
somehow successfully 'call' (see Imamu Baraka's 'SOS') all black people: .
black people in taverns, black people in alleys, black people in gutters,
schools, offices, factories, prisons, the consulate; I wish to reach black people
in mines, on farms, on thrones; *not* always to 'teach'—I shall wish often to
entertain, to illumine. My newish voice will not be an imitation of the contem-

porary young black voice, which I so admire, but an extending adaptation of today's G. B. voice" (*Report from Part One* 183). In issuing her own "call" to black people, Brooks almost self-consciously avoided the violent, fist-bearing, and antifemale rhetoric of Baraka's famous call in "Black Art." "We want poems / like fists beating niggers out of Jocks," Baraka said:

> Black poems to
> smear on girdlemamma mulatto bitches
> whose brains are red jelly stuck
> between 'lizabeth taylor's toes. Stinking
> Whores! We want "poems that Kill."
> Assassin poems, Poems that shoot
> guns. Poems that wrestle cops into alleys
> (Jones and Neal, *Black Fire* 302)

Although Brooks shared Baraka's desire to "Clean out the world for virtue and love," in her own work she emphasized the process of loving and creating *within* rather than *after* the black revolution. As an extension and adaptation of her old voice to the new black consciousness, the "newish voice" of Brooks's post-1968 work is "annunciatory, curative, inspiriting," emphasizing the values of relation and creation—her belief that "blacks should care for each other, nourish each other and communicate with each other" (Brooks, *A Capsule Course* 4; Hull and Gallagher 22).

One of Brooks's first steps in redirecting her voice to her people was to break with Harper & Row after the publication of her collected early work in *The World of Gwendolyn Brooks* (1971). She published and has continued to publish all of her new work with black presses.[8] In her new work, Brooks also broke from traditional Western forms and measures as they had been practiced by black as well as white writers of the past. "I'm trying to create new forms, trying to do something different," Brooks said, as she sought to move in the direction of "Blackening English" through the invention of a free, direct, musical, pictorial, and vernacular black expression that would ideally emerge from and be given back to the black community (Claudia Tate, *Black Women Writers at Work* 41; Martha Brown 55). Published in pamphlet form, Brooks's new volumes of poetry are polemical, didactic, and embedded in the immediacy of the historic moment. Beginning with an epigraph from Martin Luther King—"A riot is the language of the unheard"—*Riot* (1969) responds to the speech of physical riot that broke forth in American cities following King's assassination on April 4, 1968. *Family Pictures* presents snapshots from the black community as an extended black family, including a sequence of portraits of the "Young Heroes"—Keoropetse Kgositsile, Don Lee, Walter Bradford, and Paul Robeson—who embody the new black ideals of black self-possession, black solidarity, and black African roots.

"After the Grim Greatnesses, / an apathy rides the blackness / in this little land," Brooks wrote in "In Montgomery" (43), registering the fall away from the ideals of the black revolution that would mark the seventies and eighties. In her work of these years, *Beckonings, Primer for Blacks,* and the "To the Diaspora" poems of *To Disembark,* Brooks assumes the role of a kind of black Jeremiah, exhorting her people to turn away from aloneness, self-interest, and the perils of white thinking toward the revolutionary ideals of black unity, black pride, and black social responsibility. "Force through the sludge," she urges in "Another Preachment to Blacks," as she seeks to lead her people back to the personal and politically transforming power of blackness at a time when "the eyeless Leaders flutter, tilt, and fail / The followers falter, peculiar, eyeless too" (*To Disembark* 61).

In her attempt to adapt her old voice to her new black consciousness, Brooks sought to write poems that would combine her ongoing aesthetic interest in "the magic of carefully-chosen *words*" with her political interest in achieving an "*expression* relevant to all manner of blacks." "I happen to think," she said, "that the valid poem I want to write . . . can be significant for the unique word and still be accessible to all manner of life" (Brooks, "Interview" 409; Claudia Tate, *Black Women Writers at Work* 44; Hull and Gallagher 21). As an attempt to reconcile the demands of art and access, *Beckonings* is a transitional volume, a work in which Brooks's aesthetic reflexes seem to war with and short circuit her political desire to reach all manner of black people. *Primer for Blacks* comes closer to achieving Brooks's ideal of access, but the poems lack the subtlety and complexity of her early work. Beginning with the poetic exhortation of "Primer for Blacks" and "To Those of My Sisters Who Kept their Naturals" and ending with the exhortatory prose of "Requiem Before Revival," *Primer for Blacks* is an extended and urgent call back to the primal and politically empowering ground of blackness, issued at a time when "Swarms of Blacks" had begun once again to "trot along to the rear of Pied Piper whites" (*Primer* 15).

This split between the potentially conflicting demands of aesthetics and politics, form and content, art and activism was accompanied by other signs of self-division in the text of Brooks's life and work after her 1967 transformation. Although her commitment to revolutionary black ideology gave her a new sense of identity and power as a black person and a new sense of mission as a Black Arts poet, in speaking as, for, and to her people, Brooks also had to deny or silence differences between herself and other blacks, and among black people themselves, in order to sustain the ideal of black nationalism and pan-Africanism.

On her trip to East Africa in 1971 Brooks seems uneasily aware of her difference from the African people. "I look about at my brothers and sisters, and I am aware of both a warm joy and an inexpressible irrepressible sadness. For these people, who resemble my 'relatives' on Chicago's Forty Seventh and King Drive, or on Thirty Sixth and Calumet or in the depths of the West Side, are neatly separate from me" (*Report from Part One* 88). Although she feels that she has returned home to "Mother Africa," she also senses that any real return to Africa is impossible: her historical experience as an American black has made her different from her African brothers and sisters—an African-American, not an African. "THE AFRICANS!," she exclaims in frustration. "They insist on calling themselves Africans and their little traveling brothers and sisters 'Afro Americans' no matter *how* much we want them to recognize our kinship" (*Report from Part One* 130).

And yet, despite Brooks's recognition of her separation and difference from "THE AFRICANS," she continued to insist on her essential African identity: "The cultural experience of being Afro-American is integrally important to my work," she said, "but I call myself an African" (Claudia Tate, *Black Women Writers at Work* 47). In her work, she continues to celebrate a pan-African community that is not a continent on a map but a continent within black people themselves. "When you set out for Afrika / you did not know you were going," Brooks writes in "To the Diaspora":

> Because
> you did not know you were Afrika.
> You did not know the Black continent
> that had to be reached
> was you.
>
>   (*To Disembark* 41)

Brooks's vision of blackness as a "going to essences and to unifyings," as she says in her poem to the African poet Keorapetse Kgositsile, tends to reinscribe an essentialist notion of race that has been historically the ideological ground of racial oppression. Moreover, her celebration of the sameness and universality of black nature across personal, historical, and national bounds also tends to efface the very multiplicities and differences among black Americans, male and female, that had always given Brooks's work its particular texture, power, and appeal.

In celebrating the ideal of black unity and solidarity, Brooks also had to silence or gloss over dimensions of her own personal and historical experience as a black woman. Declaring her fundamental allegiance to her race rather than to her sex, she looked on the feminist demand for women's liberation as a potentially divisive force in the black community. "I was asked recently how I felt about Women's Lib," she said in her autobiography: "I think Women's Lib is not for black women for the time being, because black men *need* their women beside them, supporting them in these tempestuous days" (*Report from Part One* 179). Whereas in her earlier work Brooks was openly critical of what she called the "Black Man's blondes, blues, blunders," in her later work she emphasizes the power of love and union among black men and women: "I wish you the daily forgiveness of each other," she says in "A Black Wedding Song,"

> For war comes in from the World
> and puzzles a darling duet—
> tangles tongues,
> tears hearts, mashes minds;
> there will be the need to forgive.
>
> I wish you jewels of Black love.
> Come to your Wedding Song.
> (*Beckonings* 10)

Although Brooks acknowledges that relations among black men and women are troubled, like Mari Evans, she insists that these are "family matters," not to be aired in public or poetic form. "There's a lot going on in this man-woman thing that bothers me," she said in 1983. "I'm always saying, yes, black women have got some problems with black men and vice versa, but these are family matters. They must be worked out within the family. At no time must we allow whites, males or females, to convince us that we should split. . . . The women are not going to be winners on account of leaving their black men and going to white men, to themselves, or to nobody" (Claudia Tate, *Black Women Writers at Work* 47).

But at the very time Brooks was insisting on the need for love and solidarity among black men and women, she herself was experiencing an increasing conflict between her private life as wife, mother, and family woman and the public role she imagined for herself as a black revolutionary. In December 1969 she separated from her integrationist husband and declared her un-willingness ever to marry again: "I can say that I have no intention of ever getting married again. No, not to God. One general reason for this decision is that marriage is a hard, demanding state. Especially if you're a woman, you have to set yourself aside constantly. Although I did it during my marriage, I couldn't again. After having had a year of solitude, I realize that this is what is right for me, to be able to control my life" (*Report from Part One* 179). The separation, Brooks says, enabled both of them to "proceed to arrivals, to adventures, to a peace, to personal shapings not possible before" (58).

Although Brooks was reconciled with her husband in 1973, her concluding remarks in *Report from Part One* suggest that her new black consciousness inspired an increasing dissatisfaction with both the traditional marriage bond and with traditional male-centered definitions of the black female life:

Black Woman must remember, through all the prattle about walking or not walking three or twelve steps behind or ahead of "her" male, that her person- hood precedes her femalehood; that, sweet as sex may be, she cannot endlessly brood on Black Man's blondes, blues, blunders. She is a person in the world— with wrongs to right, stupidities to outwit, *with* her man when possible, on her own when not. And she is also here to enjoy. She will be here, like any other, only once.

(204)

This passage resists the rhetoric of black solidarity and a primarily sexual or maternal definition of black womanhood as Brooks articulates an almost existential vision of a black woman's unconditional responsibility for a per- sonhood that is finally hers *alone* to create.[9]

But if Brooks's autobiography bears traces of a black woman moving toward a new sense of self-dependence, adventure, and "personal shapings not possible before," in her poems of the seventies this new black female consciousness is absorbed by the male terms of the Black Power movement. As Brooks committed herself to the politics of Black Power and the creation of a communal black art form, her work began to lose the concreteness and specificity that came from its embeddedness in her historical experience as a black woman. Although she continued to speak as a maternal source of racial uplift, her poetic exhortations are consistently dedicated to and addressed to the sons rather than the daughters of the black revolution. Not only does the presence of women decrease in her poems of the seventies, but when they do appear, as in the "Women in Love" sequence that follows the "Young He- roes" sequence in *Family Pictures,* they are presented in the role of lovers rather than actors and heroes in the black revolution. Even in her children's book, *Aloneness,* which was inspired by her daughter, Nora Blakely, Brooks features a little boy as the representative black child/reader she seeks to reach and to teach as mother/poet; and in her allegorical children's story *The Tiger Who Wore White Gloves* (1974), it is the gloves as a sign of both whiteness and the feminine that diminish the fierce black stripes of the male tiger's power.

In silencing or glossing over her historical needs, desires, voice, and expe- rience as a black woman, Brooks's later work suggests the problematic place of black women in relation to the Black Power movement. While the call to Black Power was aimed at uniting black people, within the black nationalist movement, women's issues were generally regarded as divisive and marginal to the cause of black liberation. In pledging her allegiance to black pride and black solidarity, the black woman was not only expected to subordinate her gender identity to the demands of race; she was also expected to play, at best, a supporting role, as the term "black woman" was absorbed by the generic term "black man" in the new black consciousness.

"The only position for women in SNCC is prone," Stokely Carmichael had famously declared in 1964. Although his comment was uttered partly in jest, to many women in the civil rights movement and later in the Black Power movement, Carmichael's words had the ring of truth. Having responded to the call of Malcolm X and LeRoi Jones in 1968, says Michele Wallace: "It took me three years to fully understand that Stokely was serious when he'd said my position in the movement was 'prone,' three years to understand that the countless speeches that all began 'the Black man . . .' did not include me." "The 'new Blackness,' " she concludes, "was fast becoming the new slavery for sisters" (6, 9). Kathleen Cleaver experienced a similar sense of invisibility among the leadership of the Black Panther Party: "Women are always relegated to assistance, and this is where I became interested in the liberation of women" (Hull, Scott, and Smith, *All the Women Are White* 147).

In the poem "Hard Love Rock # II," Audre Lorde protests the double oppression experienced by black women both within and without the Black Power movement:

> Black is
> not beautiful baby
>   . . .
>
> not
> being screwed twice
> at the same time
> from on top
> as well as
> from my side.

(*The New York Head Shop and Museum* 24)

Carole C. Gregory expresses a similar sense of frustration with the "new/old custom" of her black brothers in "A Freedom Song for the Black Woman." *"Why do you reject us?"* she asks:

> The brothers say this is a class for
> African Religion and Philosophy,
> not personal questions,
> Jim Crow racism is our struggle,
> not Jane Crow sexism.

(Stetson, *Black Sister* 188)

Even Nikki Giovanni, Sonia Sanchez, and Carolyn M. Rodgers, who began as strong black nationalist poets, have come to question the problematic place and space of black women in the movement. "We are lonely," says Carolyn Rodgers in "Poem for Some Black Women," as she registers the self-division and struggle of the "talented, dedicated, well read/BLACK COMMITTED" woman who must continually remake herself in the image of male desire:

"We grow tired but must al-ways be soft and not too serious . . . / not too smart not too bitchy not too sapphire" (Stetson, *Black Sister* 178).

The emphasis on black roots and new black consciousness has led in recent years to the emergence of an empowered new group of strongly black- *and* female-identified poets, including Audre Lorde, Alice Walker, June Jordan, Ntozake Shange, and Jayne Cortez, whose works are embedded in the particularities and dailiness of black women's lives. Brooks, on the other hand, has moved in the opposite direction—away from the black female–centered work of her earlier period toward the more public, collective, and male-identified voice of her post-1968 poems. Questioned about the relative lack of women in her later work in a 1977 interview with Gloria Hull, Brooks seemed genuinely surprised, and then realized that this reflected the male-directed nature of the movement: "Well what were the women doing, Gloria, aside from amening what the others did?" (Hull and Gallagher 36). But she indicates an eagerness to address this problematic absence of women in her new work. "I hadn't even thought about it but it is true. It is true. And this afternoon will have a bearing on my future. Seriously, because I too feel that it's a very bad omission—and—especially in times when women are really rousing themselves and doing some fiery things, and even more than that, thinking fiery things" (37).[10]

Compared with the amount of work she did before 1968, there was also a sharp decrease in Brooks's published writing in the seventies and eighties. This is in part a sign of the difficulty Brooks had living up to the ideals of the Black Arts movement. "I'm not as prolific as I used to be," she admitted in her interview with Hull. "Part of that is laziness and part of that is fear—not the Ellisonian fear of coming below your standards but of not being able to achieve what I want to do here—this urge of mine to write poems that will appeal to people who quotes, 'don't like poetry' " (Hull and Gallagher 24). In seeking to write as and for everybody in the black community, Brooks had to struggle not only against the complex aesthetic reflexes of her earlier poetry; she has also had to struggle against the complexity of the historical and specifically black female experience that was at the very sources of her early poetic creation. "What affects society affects a poet," Brooks said in a 1967 interview; "So I, starting out, *usually* in the grip of a high and private suffusion, may find by the time I have arrived at a last line that there is quite some public clamor in my product" (*Report from Part One* 138). Whereas Brooks's earlier works began in the "grip" of "a high and private suffusion" and ultimately registered a "public clamor," her later poetry begins with the "public clamor" and ends by repressing the private, the personal, and the specifically black female in the interests of reaching as many black people as possible.

But the relative falling off in Brooks's published work in the seventies and eighties was not only a sign of the potentially conflicting demands of art and access or of the personal and the political. It also marks a radical transformation in her view of art. After publication of *In the Mecca* in 1968, Brooks began moving away from the Western notion of art as a fixed, fetishized, and privatized aesthetic object. "The new feeling, among the *earnest* new young creators," said Brooks in *A Capsule Course in Black Poetry Writing* (1975), "was that concern for long-lastingness was western and was wrong. One created a piece of art for the enrichment, the instruction, the extension of one's people. Its usefulness may or may not be exhausted in a day, a week, a month, a year" (5). Brooks's turn toward a more functional, fluid, and non-Western notion of art as a collective cultural exchange among black people has led her increasingly to political work in the black community as an extension of the process of artistic creation and, as she says in "To the Diaspora," the work "to be done to be done to be done" (*To Disembark* 41).

Measured in terms of its power to enrich, instruct, and extend her people, Brooks's work in the black community may in fact be her most effective and revolutionary artistic creation in recent years.[11] Underlying all this work is a consistent emphasis on the political power of black writing and the black word. From her poetry writing workshop with the Blackstone Rangers to her recent visits to United States prisons, Brooks has sought to foster the process of "blooming in the noise and whip of the whirlwind" by teaching writing as a means of translating potentially destructive and criminal energies into a form of black artistic creation that is finally a force for political creation in the black community.[12]

"Who Said It Was Simple"

Brooks's presence as cultural worker and muse to the black community and the rising generation of new black writers is nowhere more evident than in the public tribute to her staged by black writers and artists from across the country at the Affro-Arts Theater in Chicago on December 28, 1969. Memorialized in the poems, short stories, and essays of *To Gwen with Love,* which were compiled and edited by Patricia Scott Brown, Don L. Lee, and Francis Ward, the performance publicly enacted the role Brooks played in calling forth the cultural creation of the black community. Invoking Brooks as "SPIRIT-LIGHT," "goddess," "priestess," "Mother of the world," and "the poet-laureate of the Black World," this gathering of what one poet called "this teeming / Tribe-of / -Gwen" pays tribute both to the poet and to the "blak people to / for / from whom Gwendolyn Brooks writes." Playing on Brooks's name, Nikki Giovanni invokes her as a brook that collects "the earth's essence" and inspires:

> pure spring fountain
> of love/knowledge
> for those who find
> and dare drink
> of it
>
>   (48)

Sonia Sanchez presents Brooks as "a fo real bad one" in "we a bad people," a poem that is, in effect, an affirmative rewriting of Brooks's "We Real Cool." To the fiction writer John Oliver Killens, Brooks is "QUEEN OF POETS, QUEEN OF WOMEN, QUEEN OF ALL OUR INSPIRATIONS AND OUR ASPIRATIONS" (105).

In paying tribute to Brooks, the black writers stress the interrelation of her life and work in the cultural creation of the black community. "The slender, shy, and sensitive young girl / is woman now / Her words a power in the Ebon land," writes Margaret Walker in "For Gwen—1969" (95). "Let there be no mistake about it," says the historian Lerone Bennett, Jr.: "Gwen Brooks is being honored here not only because of the quality of her poetry but also because of the quality of her life. And by all this we mean to say that she *is* a poem. She is a poem of commitment and dedication to her craft and her community, she is a poem which teaches us the value of vision and will and growth, she is a poem which vibrates with our inner dynamics" (3).[13]

But for all their celebration of Brooks as a kind of African *griot*, or story-teller, who unifies her race across time in an ongoing, communal, and socially empowering dynamics of black cultural exchange, it is important to keep in mind that "this teeming / Tribe-of / -Gwen" represents a particular construc-tion of Brooks as a Black Arts poet that leaves out the historical experience of difference, self-contradiction, and struggle within and against herself and the black community that had marked and would continue to mark Brooks's work. The multiple transformations in Brooks's life and work and its multiple registers of difference and self-division as she moved from an integrationist to an essentially black separatist poetics have in fact made Brooks a particularly problematic figure in critical representations of both American and African-American literature.

Troubled by the insistent political markings of Brooks's recent work, some critics, like George Kent, would argue—against Brooks herself—that her art ultimately transcends her specifically political and black revolutionary de-signs.[14] Others, like Haki Madhubuti and many of the writers who contrib-uted to *To Gwen with Love,* would dismiss Brooks's early poetic creation and would privilege only those later works that bear the markings of a revolution-ary black political consciousness. Brooks's failure to fit into any easy critical category has meant that as a Pulitzer Prize–winning black woman poet who has produced some of the most psychologically complex, technically dazzling, and socially compelling work of our time, she has not finally received the sustained critical attention she deserves from either white or black, male or female critics. As Houston Baker notes in "The Achievement of Gwendolyn Brooks," in a comment on Brooks's divided critical status in the worlds of white and black arts: "The real duality appears when we realize that Gwendolyn Brooks—though praised and awarded—does not appear on the syllabi of most American literature courses, and her name seldom appears in the annual scholarly bibliographies of the academic world" (44).[15] To white critics, it would seem, Brooks is too black; to some blacks she seems too white; to other blacks she seems too political; and to at least some black women writers and critics she seems too male-identified.

Although several black women poets, including Mari Evans, Sonia Sanchez, Lucille Clifton, Carolyn Rodgers, and Audre Lorde, have continued to write in the "English-nourishing *and* blackness-preserving" tradition of Brooks's work, Brooks has also been a potentially problematic model for black women poets seeking to clear a space for themselves as blacks *and* as women in the African-American poetic tradition. The problem posed by Brooks as muse and ancestor figure is particularly evident in her relationship with the Chicago-based poet Carolyn Rodgers, who was a member of the poetry workshop that met regularly at Brooks's house during the late sixties and early seventies. Along with Hoyt W. Fuller, Gwendolyn Brooks was, said Rodgers, the "major influence" on her creative development (Claudia Tate, *Black Women Writers at Work* 374). In the poem "to Gwen, mo luv" Rodgers pays tribute to Brooks as a muse of black artistic creation and a powerful cultural presence, an "eternal" source of inspiration, tenderness, and care in the creation of the black community:

> you are the song that Billie
>   was born into singing
> you are the picture that Black
>   people eternal go on painting
> true, you are love & lovelier & lovingest
>   all that we be and are yet to become
> you are mo luv and mo luv and mo luv and mo luv and mo luvvvvvv
>   (Brown et al., *To Gwen with Love* 85)

Unlike Brooks, however, Rodgers, even in her early work, challenged the terms of Black Power and her own relation to it as a black/woman/writer. In the poem "BREAKTHROUGH" from *Songs of a Black Bird* (1969), Rodgers expresses her uneasiness with a rhetoric of Black Power that threatens to engulf her:

I am very tired of trying
and want Blackness which is my life, want this to be
easier on me, want it not to suck me in and
out so much leavin me a balloon with no air, want it
not to puff me up so much sometimes
that I git puffed up and sucked in in to the
raunchy kind of love Black orgy I go through.
                                              (31–32)

Making use of black idioms and speech rhythms that "remind u of the people on the corner," Rodgers in some sense takes up where Brooks's *Bronzeville* poems left off in representing the local and common lives of black people from a particularly black and woman-centered perspective (*How I Got Ovah* ix).

But whereas Brooks moved toward a redefinition of herself in collective black consciousness, Rodgers moved in the opposite direction, away from the male-centered new black consciousness of the sixties toward a redefinition of her personal identity as a black woman: "and—who—am i now," she says in "I Have Been Hungry,"

but a
saved
sighing
singular thing. a woman . . .
        (*How I Got Ovah* 52)

In "Some Me of Beauty," Rodgers seeks to define a personal sense of self and vision that will include her historical experience as a woman, black, and human:

just like that i woke up one morning
and looked at my self
and what i saw was
            carolyn

not imani ma jua or soul sister poetess of
the moment
i saw more than a "sister" . . .
i saw a Woman. human.
                and black.
                            (53)

In defining herself against the rhetoric of the Black Power movement, the "carolyn" who emerges in these lines returns to take up the woman-centered work of Brooks's early verse even as she makes a move against the collective new black consciousness of her literary ancestor. Having begun as a black nationalist poet in *Paper Soul* (1968) and *Songs of a Black Bird* (1969), Rodgers has recently broken with the term "Black"—and in some sense with Brooks herself—adopting the term "Brown" as a means of defining her own particular voice and location as an African-American woman poet: "I write as a human, a woman, who is Brown," she says. "I am questioning the use of the word Black, i.e., Blacks. I now prefer the word Brown, i.e., Brown people, and with this change goes an ideology and a set of new ideas" (Claudia Tate, *Black Women Writers at Work* 375).

In her important collection of essays, *In Search of Our Mothers' Gardens*, Alice Walker presents a record of her journey into the past to retrieve her historic and literary mothers. Her essay "Looking for Zora," in which Walker describes her quest to mark the unmarked grave of Zora Neale Hurston, might indeed serve as a model of the empowering relation between black literary mothers and daughters, as Walker seeks both to retrieve for her own uses and to transmit to others the powerful black creation of her literary ancestor. Given Walker's "desperate need to know and assimilate the experiences of black women writers," however, one is struck by her relative lack of interest in reclaiming the literary heritage of Gwendolyn Brooks (*In Search of Our Mothers' Gardens* 9). Whereas Zora Neale Hurston, Flannery O'Connor, Jean Toomer, Rebecca Jackson, Buchi Emecheta, and Langston Hughes receive extended treatment and tribute in separate essays, Brooks is mentioned only in passing. In fact, Walker appears to resent the apparent status Brooks has achieved among the male "giants of black literature": "It is shocking to hear that the only black woman writer white and black academicians have heard of is Gwendolyn Brooks," Walker said at a Convocation at Sarah Lawrence in 1972 (*In Search of Our Mothers' Gardens* 84; 36). When Walker taught her own first course in black women writers at Wellesley, Gwendolyn Brooks did not appear on her reading list. In addition to Hurston, she taught "Nella Larsen, Frances Watkins Harper (poetry and novel), Dorothy West, Ann Petry, Paule Marshall, among others. Also Kate Chopin and Virginia Woolf—not because they were black, obviously, but because they were women and wrote, as the black women did, on the condition of humankind from the perspective of women" (260).

Although Walker appears to admire Brooks as a "*born* poet" (258), *In Search of Our Mothers' Gardens* might also be read as a sustained protest against the kind of Black Arts work Brooks was doing at the very time Walker was trying to define her own "duties" as a black revolutionary artist. Setting herself against a celebratory and specifically black-centered poetics, Walker observes in "The Unglamorous But Worthwhile Duties of the Black Revolutionary Artist, Or of the Black Writer Who Simply Works and Writes" (1971): "I am impressed by people who claim they can see every person and event in strict terms of black and white, but generally their work is not, in my long-contemplated and earnestly considered opinion, either black or white, but a dull, uniform gray. It is boring because it is easy and requires only that the reader be a lazy reader and a prejudiced one. Each story or poem has a formula, usually two-thirds 'hate whitey's guts' and one-third 'I am black, beautiful, strong, and almost always right.' Art is not flattery, necessarily, and the work of any artist must be more difficult than that" (137).

To say all this is not to blame Walker for her seemingly unjust exclusion of Brooks from the tradition of black women writers that she seeks to "know and assimilate" in *In Search of Our Mothers' Gardens*. Given Walker's particular black feminist politics, her former position as editor of the woman-centered and primarily white-directed *Ms.* magazine, and her notion that "to the extent that black women dissociate themselves from the women's movement, they abandon their responsibilities to women throughout the world" (379), her exclusion of Brooks from any kind of sustained analysis makes perfect sense.

But this is precisely the point. The black female literary tradition that Walker "reclaims" in *In Search of Our Mothers' Gardens* is in fact a historical construct, grounded in specific personal and political choices and a specific exercise of cultural power and authority. Like the white male literary tradition and the process of canon formation in general, and like the literary work of Brooks herself, what has come to be known as the American and the African-American female literary tradition has been historically a site of discontinuity, struggle, and difference; it has not been the site of any natural or naturally continuous and harmonious relation among black and/or white women writers across time and history. In the words of Audre Lorde's poem—"Who Said It Was Simple."

NOTES

Chapter 1: Rethinking Women's Literary History

1. "Our first task," writes Monique Wittig in "One Is Not Born Woman," "is to always thoroughly dissociate 'women' (the class within which we fight) and 'woman,' the myth. . . . 'Woman' is there to confuse us, to hide the reality 'women' " (50–51). In "Changing the Subject," Nancy K. Miller similarly wonders "what it might mean to be women beyond the always already provided identity of Woman, with which we can only struggle" (117). See also Alcoff (405–406); Butler (1–6); and De Lauretis, "Eccentric Subjects" (115).

2. See, for example, Gilbert and Gubar, *The Madwoman in the Attic;* Bernikow, *Among Women;* Washington; Faderman, *Surpassing the Love of Men;* Marcus; Abel; Alice Walker; Friedman; Donovan; Erkkila, "Emily Dickinson and Adrienne Rich"; Wendy Martin; and De Shazer.

3. Shulamith Firestone and Anne Koedt used the phrase "to dare to be bad" in their editorial statement to *Notes from the Second Year* (1970) (Echols, *Daring To Be Bad* 300). In *Daring To Be Bad: Radical Feminism in America 1967–1975,* Alice Echols argues that the cultural feminist emphasis on global sisterhood was itself a response to the growing discord in the feminist movement over the issues of lesbianism and class (11).

4. In 1981 the Modern Language Association Division on Women's Studies in Language and Literature sponsored a series of sessions under the title "Chloe Liked Olivia," a phrase taken from Virginia Woolf's *A Room of One's Own,* which was intended to emphasize the bonds among women in literature and professional life.

5. In *Inspiriting Influences,* Michael Awkward also argues that "While male texts in the Afro-American canon follow a traditionally Western male pattern of textual competition, women's novels seem to form a more harmonious system, characterized aptly by Alice Walker's almost obsessive efforts to 'save' Zora Neale Hurston's texts and personal history from obscurity" (6).

6. For a criticism of American feminism from the point of view of French theory, see also Moi; and Jacobus. For a study of the differences between American sociohistorical feminist criticism and French deconstructive and psychoanalytical theory, see Janet Todd. In *Essentially Speaking,* Diana Fuss deconstructs the essentialist/social constructionist binary that has taken hold of feminist theory.

7. For criticism of poststructural theory by women of color, see, in particular, Joyce; Christian, "The Race for Theory"; Hooks, *Talking Back* and "Essentialism and Experience"; McDowell; and Valerie Smith.

8. For a discussion of the new sexual category of the mannish lesbian, see Newton; and Smith-Rosenberg, *Disorderly Conduct* (245–96).

9. As Joan De Jean argues in *Fictions of Sappho,* it was only after Sappho had been

heterosexualized that she was accepted into the canon as *mascula Sappho*—a phrase that associates her poetry with masculine rather than feminine power (70). For a discussion of women modernists' empowering but at times ambivalent relation with Sappho, see Gubar, "Sapphistries."

10. See Butler (111–49); and De Lauretis, "Eccentric Subjects."

11. In *Talking Back*, Bell Hooks similarly emphasizes the fact that "women can and do participate in politics of domination, as perpetrator as well as victims—that we dominate, that we are dominated" (20).

Chapter 2: Emily Dickinson and the Wicked Sisters

1. See also Taylor and Lasch; Cott; and Faderman, *Surpassing the Love of Men.*

2. For a study of the ritual of gift-giving in early societies, see Mauss.

3. Dickinson returned a copy of the book to Eldridge Bowdoin about December 1849 (*Letters* 1: 77). For Dickinson's comment on *Jane Eyre*'s "electric" effect, see *Letters* 3: 775.

4. Dickinson's practice of letter writing both as an art form and as a form of female social resistance has roots in the eighteenth century. See, for example, the revolutionary correspondence of Abigail Adams and Mercy Otis Warren, in *Adams Family Correspondence;* see also Hannah Foster's *The Coquette,* in which women friends employ letters as a means of challenging traditional domestic bounds. In *The Bonds of Womanhood,* Nancy Cott says: "The diaries and letters of young women in the late eighteenth century . . . suggest a pattern of reliance on female friendships for emotional expression and security" (173).

5. In "The Cult of True Womanhood, 1820–1860," Barbara Welter describes the qualities of piety, purity, domesticity, and dependence that characterized "true womanhood" (152).

6. For a discussion of Dickinson's use of the figurativeness of language as a means of challenging traditional patriarchal structures, see Homans. In *Emily Dickinson: A Poet's Grammar,* Cristanne Miller also studies Dickinson's use of disrupted norms of grammar, syntax, and typography as a means of challenging traditional male orders.

7. This oppositional voice may have been even more emphatic than we know, for Dickinson's exchanges with Elizabeth Holland and Sue Gilbert have been carefully edited, and there is a mysterious break in Dickinson's correspondence with Holland in the crucial years between 1860 and 1865.

8. For a discussion of the difficulty that Todd had in attaining letters from them, see Sewall (626–29).

9. For a discussion of Austin's "work" and the attempt to erase the specifically lesbian dimensions of this relationship, see Martha Nell Smith.

10. In actuality, Sue's father was the owner of a tavern and livery stable in Amherst.

11. See for example, Faderman, "Emily Dickinson's Letters to Sue Gilbert"; Mudge; and Oberhaus. In " 'To Fill a Gap,' " Martha Nell Smith argues that "their relationship knew anger as well as joy, ambivalence as well as clarity in feeling," but even she suggests that theirs was a higher because a more egalitarian kind of love. Dickinson's poems to Sue, she says, "do not reflect the hierarchy and difference of

heterosexual relations, but the sameness and equality of lesbian relations" (18). Adelaide Morris makes a similar argument in " 'The Love of Thee—a Prism Be.' "

12. In *The Riddle of Emily Dickinson,* Rebecca Patterson argues that repressed homosexuality is the key to Dickinson's life. For a discussion of the homoerotic dimension of Dickinson's relationship with Susan Gilbert, see Faderman, "Emily Dickinson's Homoerotic Poetry" and "Emily Dickinson's Letters to Sue Gilbert"; see also Martha Nell Smith. In *Dickinson: The Anxiety of Gender,* Vivian Pollak stresses the more negative, guilt-ridden homosexual dimension of Dickinson's love relationships with women, especially Sue Gilbert. (133–56).

13. For a comparison of the rhetoric of Dickinson's "Master" letters and her letters and poems to Sue Gilbert, see Morris.

14. In *The Poetry of Emily Dickinson,* Ruth Miller argues that these groupings are bound by imagery, theme, and mood into long link-poems that progress from "quest" to "suffering" to "resolution."

15. In fact, Dickinson appears to echo Josiah Holland's rather conventional notion of women's role: "Her mission is to love, and it argues depravity of soul when a woman pants to enter the race and contend with man in the labor of life" (cited in Peckham 55).

16. In " 'To Fill a Gap,' " Martha Nell Smith argues: "If, in fact, she devised her own method of publication, which was to send her poems out in letters, then the manuscripts themselves, not their printed versions, should be the locus of study" (3).

17. See, for example, Diehl, *Dickinson and the Romantic Imagination;* Gilbert and Gubar, *The Madwoman in the Attic;* Gilbert, "The American Sexual Poetics of Walt Whitman and Emily Dickinson"; Wendy Martin; Mossberg; and Pollak, *Dickinson: The Anxiety of Gender.*

18. See, for example, Cody; Mossberg; and Pollak, *Dickinson: The Anxiety of Gender.*

19. For a study of the class formation of Dickinson's work see Erkkila, "Emily Dickinson and Class."

20. In *History of Amherst College,* William S. Tyler says of Samuel Fowler Dickinson: "His business which was so large as to require all his time and care, suffered from his devotion to the public. He became embarrassed and at length actually poor. And in his poverty he had the additional grief of feeling that his services were forgotten" (121).

21. On April 20, 1855, the *Hampshire and Franklin Express* noted that Edward Dickinson had regained possession of their property. "Thus has the worthy son of an honored sire the pleasure of possessing the 'Old Homestead' " (Leyda 1: 331).

22. See Zagarell. For a discussion of Dickinson's relation to the Sentimental Love Religion of Lydia Sigourney, Harriet Beecher Stowe, and Elizabeth Stuart Phelps, see also St. Armand (13–153).

23. Conrad Aiken's essay introducing *Selected Poems of Emily Dickinson* (1924) and Allen Tate's 1932 essay "Emily Dickinson" were central in establishing her critical reputation. Tate begins his essay by setting Dickinson's work against "Marxian criticism" as the latest form of "heresy" (16). See also Blake; and Lubbers.

Chapter 3: Dickinson, Women Writers, and the Marketplace

1. The two editors to whom Dickinson refers may be Samuel Bowles and Josiah Holland, the editors of *The Springfield Republican.*

2. For studies of feminine literary production in nineteenth-century America, see, in particular, Douglas; Kelley; Watts; and Dobson.

3. In *A Literature of Their Own,* Elaine Showalter notes that "the male pseudonym was much more popular in England than in the United States" (59).

4. Jack Capps lists the book in Emily Dickinson's library in *Emily Dickinson's Reading: 1836–1886.*

5. In *The Hidden Life of Emily Dickinson,* John Evangelist Walsh argues that *Jane Eyre* is echoed in about twenty Dickinson poems (114).

6. An 1858 edition of Elizabeth Gaskell's *Life of Charlotte Bronte* is inscribed by Emily Dickinson: "Sister from Sister" (Capps 174).

7. Although Thomas Johnson presents this elegy as a single poem (*Poems* #148), the manuscript indicates that it is actually two separate poems (Dickinson, *The Manuscript Notebooks of Emily Dickinson* 112).

8. Vivian Pollak, in "Dickinson, Poe, and Barrett Browning: A Clarification," was the first to point out the clear allusion to "A Vision of Poets" and to suggest that Emmons had sent Dickinson a copy of *Poems of 1844.*

9. Letter to John Kenyon in the Dedication to *Aurora Leigh* (Browning, *The Poetical Works* 254).

10. Proposing Elizabeth Barrett as a candidate for poet laureate in 1850, the *Athenaeum* noted that there "is no living poet of either sex who can proffer a higher claim than Mrs Barrett Browning" (June 1, 1850, 585).

11. In a review of *Aurora Leigh,* the *Dublin University Magazine* noted: "Indeed in the effort to stand, not on a pedestal beside man, but actually to occupy his place, we see Mrs. Browning commit grave errors. She assumes as it were the gait and the garb of man, but the stride and strut betray her" (470). For studies of the contemporary response to Barrett Browning's work, see also Kaplan; and Helen Cooper.

12. See Walsh; Patterson, "Elizabeth Browning and Emily Dickinson"; and Moers, *Literary Women* (55–62).

13. For a discussion of the conservative politics and essentialist feminine ideology of *Aurora Leigh,* see David (143–58).

14. See, in particular, Patterson, "Elizabeth Browning and Emily Dickinson"; Moers, *Literary Women* (55–62).

15. In *Dickinson: The Anxiety of Gender,* Vivian Pollak cites "Her—'last Poems'—" as an example of Dickinson's sense of jealousy and competition with other women writers. She reads the poem as a "transformation of jealousy into grief" and an expression of "Dickinson's unconscious hostility toward Barrett Browning" (242–43).

16. In *The Hidden Life of Emily Dickinson,* John Walsh suggests that this poem was intended for Barrett Browning (134–35).

17. In her article, "Life's Empty Pack: Notes Toward a Literary Daughteronomy," Sandra Gilbert mistakenly reads the poem as a response to *The Life of George Eliot* by Eliot's husband, John Cross. But Cross's biography did not appear until 1884. As

Dickinson's letter to Thomas Niles indicates, she wrote the poem in 1883 in response to Mathilde Blind's biography, *George Eliot,* which was published the same year.

18. There is a volume of Jackson's *Verses* (1870) inscribed "Sue from Vinnie" in the Houghton Library at Harvard University.

19. For other discussions of Dickinson's relationship with Helen Hunt Jackson, see Thomas Johnson, *Emily Dickinson: An Interpretive Biography* (155–80); Cheryl Walker (87–116).

20. Holland in fact rejected *Mercy Philbrick's Choice,* but it was quickly published and popularized by Thomas Niles as the first of his No Name Series in 1876.

21. When the correspondence between Dickinson and Jackson began is unclear. Among Dickinson's papers are two envelopes addressed to Helen Hunt, one in the handwriting of 1868 and the other dating from about 1872 (*Letters* 2: 544).

22. Jackson visited Dickinson twice: once in October 1876 and again in October 1878.

Chapter 4: Differences That Kill: Elizabeth Bishop and Marianne Moore

1. In "Efforts of Affection: A Memoir of Marianne Moore," Bishop remembers that Moore never referred to Emily Dickinson, and when she commented on the fact that Moore walked the same Brooklyn streets as Whitman, "She exclaimed in her mock-ferocious tone, 'Elizabeth, don't speak to me about that man!' " (Bishop, *The Collected Prose* 143).

2. For an excellent study of the transformations in Moore's poetic development, see Holley.

3. In his introduction to a special Moore issue of *Twentieth-Century Literature,* Andrew Kappel comments on the desire to manage the world that characterizes Moore's poems, as well as her meetings with people. Determined to create a formal order that would eliminate the possible dangers of unpredictability and surprise, "she plays the gentle bully to have her slightly unnatural way" (vi). See also Taffy Martin: "It quickly becomes clear that control is indeed the subject of Moore's poetry" (7).

4. In her study of the Bishop/Moore correspondence, Lynn Keller emphasizes a similar mother/daughter paradigm. Once Moore and Bishop found a proper balance between "bonding and separation," she argues, their "relationship stabilized as one between equals, based on mutual generosity and mutual need" (426). See also my discussion of the anti-Bloomian dimensions of their relationship in Erkkila, "Elizabeth Bishop and Marianne Moore: The Dynamics of Female Influence."

5. For a study of the ways Mrs. Moore's moralism and acerbity may have undermined Marianne Moore's sense of achievement, see Moran.

6. In "Efforts of Affection," Bishop remembers that Moore objected to her "Valentine" sparrows in which "dust" rhymed with "lust" (Bishop, *The Collected Prose* 145).

7. Many of the letters that Moore sent to Bishop in the late thirties, the period of her most intense involvement in Bishop's work, are missing. Although these letters could have been lost in the course of Bishop's travels, it is also possible that Bishop de-

stroyed them out of embarrassment at the clear marks of Moore's hand in her early work.

8. In responding to an earlier version of this essay, Pat Willis—the former curator of the Rosenbach Museum and Library—said that she always disliked "Invitation" because it made Moore seem like Mary Poppins.

9. See also Williamson, who censures Bishop's love poems, and "Insomnia" in particular, for "melodramatic indulgence" and failure to observe "a middle ground of normal human judgment" [!] (97, 98).

Chapter 5: Adrienne Rich, Emily Dickinson, and the Limits of Sisterhood

1. As Marilyn Farwell points out in her article on "Adrienne Rich and an Organic Feminist Criticism," Rich has had a major impact on the philosophy and practice of feminist criticism, and yet her work is frequently not cited in review essays on feminist criticism. For studies of Anglo-American women poets, see, in particular, Juhasz; Watts; Gilbert and Gubar, *The Madwoman in the Attic* and *No Man's Land;* Homans; Diehl, *Dickinson and the Romantic Imagination;* Cheryl Walker; Ostriker, *Writing Like a Woman* and *Stealing the Language;* Wendy Martin; and Bennett.

2. See, for example, Du Plessis; Goldstein; Farwell; Diehl, "Cartographies of Silence"; Gentile; Friedman; Jane Cooper; De Shazer; Keyes; Diaz-Diocaretz; Humm; and Meese. See also my own early attempt to theorize a model of female influence through a study of Rich's relationship with Emily Dickinson in Erkkila, "Emily Dickinson and Adrienne Rich: Toward a Theory of Female Poetic Influence." Jan Montefiore, in *Feminism and Poetry,* takes a more critical attitude toward Rich, as does Cora Kaplan in *Sea Changes: Essays on Culture and Feminism* (50–56). In one of the best discussions of Rich's lesbian feminist poetics to date, Catherine Stimpson, in "Adrienne Rich and Lesbian/Feminist Poetry," acknowledges the potential problems of Rich's cultural feminism, but then goes on to argue that "Rich has wonderfully escaped the nets she fears, the 'impasse' at which some critics pin her" (258).

3. Anne Bradstreet's *The Tenth Muse Lately Sprung Up in America* (1650) was introduced by her brother-in-law, John Woodbridge. *The Memoirs of the Life and Death of the Pious and Ingenious Mrs. Jane Turell* (1735) was edited posthumously by her father. Phillis Wheatley's *Poems on Various Subjects, Religious and Moral* (1773) was preceded by a notice signed by the Governor, Lieutenant Governor of Massachusetts, and other notable men in the colony. Thomas Higginson wrote the preface to the first edition of *Poems by Emily Dickinson* (1890), ed. Mabel Loomis Todd and T. W. Higginson. Robert Lowell wrote the "Foreword" to Sylvia Plath's *Ariel* (1965).

4. In "Vesuvius at Home: The Power of Emily Dickinson," Rich refers to "My Life had stood—a Loaded Gun—" as the "real 'onlie begetter' of my thoughts here about Dickinson; a poem I have mused over, repeated to myself, taken into myself over many years" (*On Lies, Secrets, and Silence* 172). She used the image of "a loaded gun" a few years later in "Face to Face" to suggest the power of unexpressed energies in early American life: "burning under the bleached scalp; behind dry lips / a loaded gun" (*Necessities of Life* 49).

5. Rich's interest in Dickinson's formal experiments is evident in her review of Ann

Stanford's *The Woman Poets in English*. She is critical of Stanford's decision to regularize Dickinson's form: "I deeply regret that Dickinson suffers in this anthology from Miss Stanford's decision to publish her in the regularized style conformed to by her early editors, rather than the style of the original manuscripts in the Thomas Johnson edition of 1959. The dashes and capitalizations of Dickinson are, as Johnson has said, 'an integral part of the structure of her poetry'; they suggest an awareness of pause and emphasis, a dynamic tension, that neoclassical formalism may be deaf to, but which is part of her genius. Especially in the formal context of her sisters' work, I deplore seeing Dickinson tamed, sheared down, in this way" (6).

6. The essay was first published in an issue of *College English* on "Women Writing and Teaching," edited by Elaine Hedges in 1972.

7. In a revised version of this essay published in *American Poets in 1976*, ed. William Heyen, Rich deleted both the concluding vision of men and women working together and her earlier refusal to define women "primarily as mothers and muses for men." The 1976 version concludes with a polarized vision of good women battling against the essentially masculine and destructive demons of patriarchy: "The creative energy of patriarchy is fast running out; what remains is its self-generating energy for destruction. As women, we have our work cut out for us" (*On Lies, Secrets, and Silence* 49).

8. Howe and Bass, eds., *No More Masks!*; Chester and Barba, eds., *Rising Tides*; Segnitz and Rainey, eds., *Psyche*; and Bernikow, ed. *The World Split Open*.

9. I follow Echols ("The New Feminism of Yin and Yang") in maintaining a distinction between early radical feminism and cultural feminism, which emerged in the mid-seventies. In addition to Rich's *Of Woman Born*, other major cultural feminist texts include Daly, *Gyn/Ecology*; Raymond; Barry; Griffin; and Morgan.

10. See for example, Daly, *Beyond God the Father* and *Gyn/Ecology*; Alice Walker; Cixous; Chodorow; Flax; Irigaray, "And the One Doesn't Stir Without the Other"; Kristeva, "Motherhood According to Giovanni Bellini," in *Desire in Language* (237–70); Davidson and Broner; Marcus; Hirsch, "Mothers and Daughters" and *The Mother/Daughter Plot*; Gilligan; Benjamin; and Ruddick. Critical of feminist celebrations of the pre-Oedipal mother, Nina Baym, in "The Madwoman and Her Languages," notes that mothers themselves are often silenced, even in Rich: "In much criticism, it is the pre-Oedipal mother who is looked for, sought not to combat patriarchy, but to defend against the real mother" (57).

11. For a discussion of the controversy over the term androgyny, see, in particular, the articles by Stimpson ("The Androgyne and the Homosexual"), Gelpi, and Secor in *Women's Studies*, a special issue on the question of androgyny.

12. In "A Poet's Feminist Prose," a review of *On Lies, Secrets, and Silence*, Ellen Moers says that Rich's essay on Dickinson is the "single best critical essay we have" (12). This essay, along with Rich's "When We Dead Awaken: Writing as Re-Vision," has had a significant impact on feminist criticism of Dickinson, including works by Juhasz; Gilbert and Gubar, *The Madwoman in the Attic*; Homans; Diehl, *Dickinson and the Romantic Imagination*; Cheryl Walker; Wendy Martin; and Bennett.

13. See Friedan; and Elshstain. In "The New Conservative Feminism," Judith Stacey observes: "The new conservatives' development of this maternal goddess

theme, a theme implicit in a good deal of contemporary feminist writing, suggests the political dangers of such formulations" (575). For a consideration of the political effects of the feminist emphasis on women's difference in the Sears Case, see Milkman; Scott. See also Echols, "The New Feminism of Yin and Yang."

14. For criticism of white feminist racism by women of color, see, in particular, Barbara Smith, "Toward a Black Feminist Criticism" and " 'Fractious, Kicking, Messy, Free' "; Lorde, "An Open Letter to Mary Daly" and "The Master's Tools Will Never Dismantle the Master's House" in *Sister Outsider* (66–71; 110–13); Moraga and Anzaldúa; Bethel and Smith, "The Black Women's Issue"; Hooks; Carby, "White Women, Listen!"; Hull, Scott, and Smith; Spillers; and Valerie Smith. For a study of the problems of exclusion in feminist thought, see Spelman.

15. In "The Master's Tools Will Never Dismantle the Master's House," Audre Lorde singles out Rich as one of the few white feminists to acknowledge and challenge the racism of the women's movement (*Sister Outsider* 113); Hortense Spillers also finds Rich, along with Catharine MacKinnon, the two exceptions to the rule of white feminist exclusion of black women (81). For Rich's comments on the racism of the women's movement and the limitations of her own early work, see, in particular, "Disloyal to Civilization: Feminism, Racism, Gynephobia" (*On Lies, Secrets, and Silence* 275–310) and "Toward a More Feminist Criticism" and "Resisting Amnesia: History and Personal Life" (*Blood, Bread, and Poetry* 85–99; 136–59).

16. Barbara Smith uses the term "simultaneity of oppression" in " 'Fractious, Kicking, Messy, Free' " (582).

Chapter 6: Race, Black Women Writing, and Gwendolyn Brooks

1. This manuscript of thirty-three poems is in the Lilly Library at Indiana University, Bloomington.

2. For studies of the Harlem Renaissance women poets, see Wall; Hull.

3. See also Davis.

4. In "Criticism in the Jungle," the term "differently black" is used by Henry Louis Gates, Jr., to distinguish between the black texts of writers like Ralph Ellison and Wole Soyinka and "Canonical Western texts" (6).

5. When Brooks was invited to the White House in 1980, she chose to read "the mother" in what was no doubt a politically nuanced gesture (Melhem 14).

6. For a discussion of the discursive function of the style of *Annie Allen*, see Claudia Tate, "Anger So Flat."

7. For a discussion of the socioeconomic significance of the term black power, see Boggs.

8. *Riot* (1969), *Family Pictures* (1970), and *Beckonings* (1975) were published by Dudley Randall's Broadside Press, the same press that published the early work of Nikki Giovanni and Sonia Sanchez; *To Disembark* (1981), which collects her post-1968 work and includes a new selection of poems entitled "To the Diaspora," was published by Madhubuti's Third World Press; *Primer for Blacks* (1980) was published by Brooks's own Black Position Press; and *Blacks* (1987)—which collects her early work, including *Maud Martha*—, *The Near-Johannesburg Boy and Other Poems*

(1986), and *Gottschalk and the Grande Tarantelle* (1987) were published by Brooks's The David Company.

9. Although Brooks was reunited with her husband, in her projected sequel to her semiautobiographical novel *Maud Martha,* she imagines killing off Maud's husband after she has her second baby. "Well, she has that child and she has another child and then her husband dies in the bus fire that happened in Chicago in the fifties," she told Gloria Hull in 1977. "So I put her husband in that fire. Wasn't that nice of me? I had taken him as far as I could. He certainly wasn't going to change. I could see that." Maud's response, said Brooks, would be "unbidden relief," as she moves toward a number of "additional adventures," including an affair at age fifty and a trip to Africa (Hull and Gallagher 26–27).

10. Brooks's conversation with Hull may have inspired a new turn toward women in some of her more recent work. In "To Those of My Sisters Who Kept Their Naturals," which appears in *Primer for Blacks,* Brooks pays tribute to her black sisters who have refused to be seduced by the hair-straightening and black-denying mythologies of whiteness. In *To Disembark,* "Boys Black," which was initially addressed to black boys in *Beckonings,* is transformed into a call to all black people, entitled "Another Preachment to Blacks"; and the "To the Diaspora" sequence in the same volume includes a specific call "To Black Women." *The Near-Johannesburg Boy and Other Poems* includes a poem on South African activist Winnie Mandela entitled "Winnie," which, in a personal conversation with me in 1989, Brooks described as one of her "most satisfying" recent poems.

11. Impressed by a preview of *Opportunity, Please Knock,* a musical show directed by Oscar Brown, Jr., and performed by members of the Blackstone Rangers gang, in 1967 Brooks started a poetry workshop for interested Blackstone Rangers, college students, and teen organizers. The group, which included Don Lee, Walter Bradford, Johari Amini Kunjunfu, Mike Cook, Jim Cunningham, and Carolyn Rodgers, continued to meet over several years, making Brooks's home a center for the intersecting energies of black artistic and political creation in the Chicago community. Named the poet laureate of Illinois in 1968, in 1970 Brooks initiated a series of Poet Laureate Awards for Illinois high school students because she said "a 'poet laureate' should do more than wear a crown—should be of service to the young" (*Report from Part One* 212). As part of her continued service to the young, Brooks also organized T.H.E.M.—Trying Hard to Express Myself—a group of eighteen teenagers on her block who met regularly at her house from 1972 to 1974 to discuss issues and to read, write, and communicate. Brooks has also been an active participant in community projects, including the 1967 dedication of the Wall of Respect, which includes a picture of Brooks painted by Edward Christmas. Like other poets in the Chicago community, including Haki Madhubuti and Carolyn Rodgers, Brooks has taken her works not only into taverns and the streets; she has also read her works and sponsored poetry writing contests in prisons in Illinois, New York, Missouri, Massachusetts, and Indiana. Like LeRoi Jones and Larry Neal, who edited *Black Fire: An Anthology of Afro-American Writing* as a means of making the "Founding Mothers and Fathers" of the new black nation available to the black community, Brooks has consistently sponsored, edited, and introduced the work of the new young writers. In 1971, she founded

an annual called *The Black Position* as a means of providing a forum for the political and cultural creation of the Chicago community. In the same year, she edited *Jump Bad: A New Chicago Anthology*, a collection of work by the young poets who had been in her workshop; and *A Broadside Treasury*, a collection of poems originally published by Broadside Press. In addition to writing the preface to Etheridge Knight's *Poems from Prison*, she introduced Keorapetse Kgositsile's *My Name is Afrika* (1971), and she helped her mother publish a collection of her writings entitled *The Voice and Other Short Stories* (1975).

12. Brooks's emphasis on the political power of the black word is also evident in the number of works she has published on the process of writing, including *Young Poet's Primer* (1980) and *Very Young Poets* (1983). *A Capsule Course in Black Poetry Writing*, a handbook (suggested by Brooks), includes advice on poetry writing by Brooks, Keorapetse Kgositsile, Haki Madhubuti, and Dudley Randall.

13. In 1987, on the occasion of Brooks's seventieth birthday, Haki Madhubuti edited a similar collection of poems, essays, and tributes entitled *Say That the River Turns: The Impact of Gwendolyn Brooks*. Describing Brooks as "a Living National Treasure" and "a Queen Mother" in his introductory essay, Madhubuti says: "Ms. Brooks is a woman who cannot live without her art, but who has never put her art above or before the people she writes about."

14. "The result of Miss Brooks's way with form and technique is usually a legitimate universalism," argues George Kent in his essay "The Poetry of Gwendolyn Brooks" (112); later, in "Aesthetic Values in the Poetry of Gwendolyn Brooks," he traces the aesthetic values that link Brooks's early and later work, concluding that "it is difficult to be more than tentative" about what he calls "the liberation poems" (93). In his uncompleted and posthumously published biography, *A Life of Gwendolyn Brooks*, Kent brings a similarly formalist and aesthetic perspective to his analysis of Brooks's work. In "Gwendolyn Brooks and a Black Aesthetic," Norris B. Clark also argues that Brooks's craft and her broadly humanistic concerns ultimately transcend the polemics and rhetoric of the black aesthetic.

15. Although Baker's comment was written in 1972, to date there are only three book-length studies of Brooks's work: a slim volume entitled *Gwendolyn Brooks* by Harry Shaw; *Gwendolyn Brooks: Poetry and the Heroic Voice*, written by Brooks's former student D. H. Melhem; and *A Life of Gwendolyn Brooks* by George Kent, which ends in 1978 with the death of Brooks's mother, Keziah Brooks. There is also a fine collection of essays entitled *A Life Distilled: Gwendolyn Brooks, Her Poetry and Fiction*, edited by Maria K. Mootry and Gary Smith.

BIBLIOGRAPHY

Abel, Elizabeth. "(E)Merging Identities: The Dynamics of Female Friendship in Contemporary Fiction by Women." *Signs* 6 (1981): 414–35.

Adams, Abigail and John. *Adams Family Correspondence.* Ed. L. H. Butterfield. 2 vols. Cambridge, Mass.: Harvard University Press, 1963.

Alcoff, Linda. "Cultural Feminism versus Post-Structuralism: The Identity Crisis in Feminist Theory." *Signs* 13 (1988): 405–36.

Althusser, Louis. "Ideology and Ideological State Apparatuses." *Lenin and Philosophy and Other Essays.* New York: Monthly Review Press, 1971. 127–86.

Anzaldúa, Gloria. "Speaking in Tongues: A Letter to Third World Women Writers." *This Bridge Called My Back: Writings by Radical Women of Color.* Ed. Cherríe Moraga and Gloria Anzaldúa. 165–74.

Ashberry, John. Review of Elizabeth Bishop's *The Complete Poems. New York Times Book Review* 1 June 1969: 8, 25.

Athenaeum (June 1, 1850): 584–85.

Austen, Jane. *Emma.* Ed. Stephen M. Parrish. New York: Norton, 1972.

Awkward, Michael. *Inspiriting Influences: Tradition, Revision, and Afro-American Women's Novels.* New York: Columbia University Press, 1989.

Baker, Houston. "The Achievement of Gwendolyn Brooks." *Singers of Daybreak: Studies in Black American Literature.* Washington, D. C.: Howard University Press, 1972. 43–53.

Banning, Evelyn I. *Helen Hunt Jackson.* New York: Vanguard, 1973.

Barry, Kathleen. *Female Sexual Slavery.* Englewood Cliffs, New Jersey: Prentice-Hall, 1979.

Baym, Nina. "The Madwoman and Her Languages: Why I Don't Do Feminist Theory." *Feminist Issues in Literary Scholarship.* Ed. Shari Benstock. Bloomington: Indiana University Press, 1987. 45–61.

Beauvoir, Simone de. *The Second Sex* (1949). Trans. H. M. Parshley. New York: Knopf, 1953.

Benjamin, Jessica. *The Bonds of Love: Psychoanalysis, Feminism, and the Problem of Domination.* New York: Pantheon, 1988.

Bennett, Paula. *My Life a Loaded Gun: Female Creativity and Feminist Poetics.* Boston: Beacon Press, 1986.

Bercovitch, Sacvan. *The American Jeremiad.* Madison: University of Wisconsin, 1978.

Bernikow, Louise. *Among Women.* New York: Harmony Books, 1980.

———, ed. *The World Split Open: Four Centuries of Women Poets in England and America, 1552–1950.* New York: Vintage, 1974.

Bethel, Lorraine. "What Chou Mean WE, White Girl?" *Conditions* 5 (1979): 86–92.

Bethel, Lorraine and Barbara Smith, eds. "The Black Women's Issue." *Conditions* 5 (1979).

Bianchi, Martha Dickinson. *The Life and Letters of Emily Dickinson*. New York: Houghton Mifflin, 1924.

Bingham, Millicent Todd. *Ancestors' Brocades: The Literary Debut of Emily Dickinson*. New York: Harper, 1945.

————. *Emily Dickinson's Home: Letters of Edward Dickinson and His Family*. New York: Harper & Brothers, 1955.

Bishop. Elizabeth. "As We Like It." *Quarterly Review of Literature* 4 (1948): 129–35.

————. *The Collected Prose*. Ed. Robert Giroux. New York: Farrar, Straus and Giroux, 1984. [*Collected Prose*]

————. *The Complete Poems, 1927–1979*. New York: Farrar, Straus and Giroux, 1983. [*Complete Poems*]

————. *Diary of "Helena Morley."* New York: Farrar, Straus and Giroux, 1957.

————. Letters to Robert Lowell. Houghton Library, Harvard University, Cambridge, Mass. [Houghton Library]

————. Letters to Marianne Moore. Rosenbach Museum and Library, Philadelphia, Pa. [*R*]

————. Letters to Anne Stevenson. Washington University Library, St. Louis, Mo. [Washington University Library]

————. The Elizabeth Bishop Papers. Vassar College Library, Poughkeepsie, N.Y. [*V*]

Blake, Caesar Robert, ed. *The Recognition of Emily Dickinson: Selected Criticism Since 1890*. Ann Arbor: University of Michigan, 1964.

Blind, Mathilde. *George Eliot* (1883). Ed. Frank Waldo and G. A. Turkington. Boston: Little, Brown, 1904.

Bloom, Harold. *The Anxiety of Influence: A Theory of Poetry*. New York: Oxford University Press, 1973.

Boggs, James. "Black Power—A Scientific Concept Whose Time Has Come." *Black Fire: An Anthology of Afro-American Writing*. Ed. LeRoi Jones and Larry Neal. 105–18.

Brontë, Charlotte. "Biographical Notice of Ellis and Acton Bell" (1850). *Agnes Grey* by Anne Brontë. Edinburgh: John Grant, 1924.

————. *Jane Eyre*. Ed. Richard J. Dunn. New York: Norton, 1971.

Brontë, Emily. *The Complete Poems of Emily Jane Brontë*. Ed. C. W. Hatfield. New York: Columbia University Press, 1941. [*Complete Poems*]

Brooks, Gwendolyn. *Aloneness*. Detroit: Broadside Press, 1971.

————. *Annie Allen*. New York: Harper & Brothers, 1949.

————. *The Bean Eaters*. New York: Harper & Brothers. 1960.

————. *Beckonings*. Detroit: Broadside Press, 1975.

————. *Blacks*. Chicago: The David Company, 1987.

————. *A Capsule Course in Black Poetry Writing*. Detroit: Broadside Press, 1975.

————. *Family Pictures*. Detroit: Broadside Press, 1970.

————. *Gottschalk and the Grande Tarantelle*. Chicago: The David Company, 1987.

————. *In the Mecca*. New York: Harper & Row, 1968.

————. "In Montgomery." *Ebony* (1971): 42–48.

————. "Interview." *Triquarterly* 60 (1984): 405–10.

————. *Maud Martha*. New York: Harper & Brothers, 1953.

————. *The Near-Johannesburg Boys and Other Poems*. Chicago: The David Company, 1986.

————. "Poets Who Are Negroes." *Phylon* 11 (1950): 312.

————. *Primer for Blacks*. Chicago: The Black Position Press, 1980.

————. *Report from Part One*. Detroit: Broadside Press, 1972.

————. *Selected Poems*. New York: Harper & Row, 1963.

————. *A Street in Bronzeville*. New York: Harper & Brothers, 1945.

————. *The Tiger Who Wore White Gloves, or What You Are You Are*. Chicago: Third World Press, 1974.

————. *To Disembark*. Chicago: Third World Press, 1981.

————. *The World of Gwendolyn Brooks*. New York: Harper & Row, 1971.

Brown, Ashley. "An Interview with Elizabeth Bishop," *Shenandoah* 17 (1966): 3–19.

Brown, Martha H. "Interview with Gwendolyn Brooks." *Great Lakes Review* 60 (1979): 48–55.

Brown, Patricia Scott, Don L. Lee, and Francis Ward, eds. *To Gwen with Love: An Anthology Dedicated to Gwendolyn Brooks*. Chicago: Johnson Publishing, 1971.

Browning, Elizabeth Barrett. *The Poetical Works of Elizabeth Barrett Browning*. Ed. Ruth M. Adams. Boston: Houghton Mifflin, 1974. [*Poetical Works*]

Butler, Judith. *Gender Trouble: Feminism and the Subversion of Identity*. New York: Routledge, 1990.

Capps, Jack. *Emily Dickinson's Reading: 1836–1886*. Cambridge, Mass.: Harvard University Press, 1966.

Carby, Hazel. "It Jus Be's Dat Way Sometime: The Sexual Politics of Women's Blues." *Radical America* 20 (1986): 9–24.

————. "White Women, Listen! Black Women and the Boundaries of Sisterhood." *The Empire Strikes Back: Race and Racism in 70s Britain*. Centre for Contemporary Cultural Studies. University of Birmingham. London: Hutchinson & Co., 1982.

Carmichael, Stokely and Charles V. Hamilton. *Black Power: The Politics of Liberation in America*. New York: Vintage, 1967.

Chester, Laura and Sharon Barba, eds. *Rising Tides: 20th Century American Women Poets*. New York: Washington Square Press, 1973.

Childers, Mary and Bell Hooks. "A Conversation About Race and Class." *Conflicts in Feminism*. Ed. Marianne Hirsch and Evelyn Fox Keller. 60–81.

Chodorow, Nancy. *The Reproduction of Mothering: Psychoanalysis and the Sociology of Gender*. Berkeley: University of California, 1978.

Christian, Barbara, "Afro-American Women Poets: A Historical Introduction" (1982). *Black Feminist Criticism: Perspectives on Black Women Writers*. New York: Pergamon, 1985. 119–25.

————. "The Race for Theory." *Feminist Studies* 14 (1988): 67–79.

Cixous, Hélène. "Le Rire de la Méduse" ("The Laugh of the Medusa"). Trans. Keith and Paula Cohen. *Signs* 1 (1976): 875–99.

Cixous, Hélène and Catherine Clément. *The Newly Born Woman* (1975). Trans. Betsy Wing. Minneapolis: University of Minnesota Press, 1986.

Clark, Norris B. "Gwendolyn Brooks and a Black Aesthetic." *A Life Distilled*. Ed. Mootry and Smith. 81–99.

Cody, John. *After Great Pain: The Inner Life of Emily Dickinson*. Cambridge, Mass.: Harvard University Press, 1971.

Collins, Patricia Hill. *Black Feminist Thought: Knowledge, Consciousness, and the Politics of Empowerment*. Boston: Unwin Hyman, 1990.

"The Combahee River Collective: A Black Feminist Statement." *All the Women Are White, All the Blacks Are Men, But Some of Us Are Brave*. Ed. Hull, Scott, and Smith. 13–22.

Cooper, Helen. *Elizabeth Barrett Browning: Woman and Artist*. Chapel Hill: University of North Carolina Press, 1988.

Cooper, Jane, ed. *Reading Adrienne Rich: Reviews and Re-Visions, 1951–81*. Ann Arbor: University of Michigan, 1984.

Costello, Bonnie. "Marianne Moore and Elizabeth Bishop: Friendship and Influence," *Twentieth-Century Literature* 30 (1984): 130–49.

————. "Vision and Mastery in Elizabeth Bishop." *Twentieth-Century Literature* 28 (1982): 351–70.

Cott, Nancy. *The Bonds of Womanhood: "Woman's Sphere" in New England, 1780–1835*. New Haven: Yale University Press, 1977.

Dadie, Bernard Binlin, ed. *The Black Cloth: A Collection of African Folktales*. Trans. Karen Hatch. Amherst: University of Massachusetts, 1987.

Daly, Mary. *Beyond God the Father: Toward a Philosophy of Women's Liberation*. Boston: Beacon Press, 1973.

————. *Gyn/Ecology: The Metaethics of Radical Feminism*. Boston: Beacon Press, 1978.

David, Deirdre. *Intellectual Women and Victorian Patriarchy*. Ithaca, N. Y.: Cornell University Press, 1987.

Davidson, Cathy M. and E. M. Broner, eds. *The Lost Tradition: Mothers and Daughters in Literature*. New York: Ungar, 1980.

Davis, Angela. *Women, Race and Class*. New York: Vintage, 1981.

De Jean, Joan. *Fictions of Sappho, 1576–1937*. Chicago: University of Chicago Press, 1989.

De Lauretis, Teresa. "Eccentric Subjects: Feminist Theory and Historical Consciousness." *Feminist Studies* 16 (1990): 115–50.

————. ed. *Feminist Studies/Critical Studies*. Bloomington: Indiana University Press, 1986.

————. *Technologies of Gender: Essays on Theory, Film, and Fiction*. Bloomington: Indiana University Press, 1987.

Derrida, Jacques. *Of Grammatology* (1967). Trans. Gayatri Chakravorty Spivak. Baltimore: The Johns Hopkins University Press, 1976.

De Shazer, Mary K. *Inspiring Women: Reimagining the Muse*. New York: Pergamon, 1986.

Diaz-Diocaretz, Myriam. *The Transforming Power of Language: The Poetry of Adrienne Rich*. Utrecht, The Netherlands: HES Publishers, 1984.

Dickinson, Emily. *The Poems of Emily Dickinson*. Ed. Thomas H. Johnson. 3 vols. Cambridge, Mass.: The Belknap Press, 1955. [*Poems*]

———. *The Letters of Emily Dickinson*. Ed. Thomas H. Johnson. 3 vols. Cambridge, Mass.: The Belknap Press, 1960. [*Letters*]

———. *The Manuscript Notebooks of Emily Dickinson*. Ed. R. W. Franklin. 2 vols. Cambridge, Mass.: The Belknap Press, 1981.

———. *Selected Poems of Emily Dickinson*. Ed. Conrad Aiken. London: Jonathan Cape, 1924.

Diehl, Joanne F. "Cartographies of Silence: Rich's *Common Language* and the Woman Poet." *Feminist Studies* 6 (1980): 530–46.

Diehl, Joanne Feit. *Dickinson and the Romantic Imagination*. Princeton, N. J.: Princeton University Press, 1981.

Dobson, Joanne. *Dickinson and the Strategies of Reticence: The Woman Writer in Nineteenth-Century America*. Bloomington: Indiana University Press, 1989.

Donovan, Josephine. "Toward a Woman's Poetics." *Tulsa Studies in Women's Literature* 3 (1984): 99–110.

Doolittle, Hilda. Letters to Marianne Moore. Rosenbach Museum and Library, Philadelphia, Pa. [*R*]

Douglas, Ann. *The Feminization of American Culture*. New York: Knopf, 1977.

Drake, William. *The First Wave: Women Poets in America, 1915–1945*. New York: Macmillan, 1987.

Dublin University Magazine 49 (1857): 460–70.

DuBois, W. E. B. *The Souls of Black Folk* (1903), in *Three Negro Classics*. New York: Avon Books, 1965.

Du Plessis, Rachel Blau. "The Critique of Consciousness and Myth in Levertov, Rich and Rukeyser." *Feminist Studies* 3 (1975): 199–221.

Echols, Alice. *Daring To Be Bad: Radical Feminism in America 1967–1975*. Minneapolis: University of Minnesota Press, 1989.

———. "The New Feminism of Yin and Yang." *Powers of Desire. The Politics of Sexuality*. Ed. Ann Snitow, Christine Stansell, and Sharon Thompson. New York: Monthly Review Press, 1983. 439–59.

Eliot, George. *Middlemarch: A Study of Provincial Life*. Ed. Gordon S. Haight. Boston: Riverside Press, 1956.

———. *Poems*. New York: Merrill and Baker, n.d.

———. "Silly Novels by Lady Novelists." *Essays of George Eliot*. Ed. Thomas Pinney. New York: Columbia University Press, 1963.

Eliot, Thomas Stearns. "Marianne Moore." *The Dial* (1923): 497–99.

Elshtain, Jean Bethke. *Public Man, Private Woman: Women in Social and Political Thought*. Princeton, N. J.: Princeton University Press, 1981.

Engels, Friedrich. *The Origin of the Family, Private Property, and the State*. New York: International Publishers, 1942.

Erkkila, Betsy. "Elizabeth Bishop and Marianne Moore: The Dynamics of Female
    Influence." *Marianne Moore: Woman and Poet.* Orono, Maine: National Po-
    etry Foundation, 1991.
————. "Emily Dickinson and Adrienne Rich: Toward a Theory of Female Poetic
    Influence." *American Literature* 4 (1984): 541–59.
————. "Emily Dickinson and Class." *American Literary History* 4 (1992): 1–27.
Faderman, Lillian. "Emily Dickinson's Homoerotic Poetry," *Higginson Journal* 18
    (1978): 19–27.
————. "Emily Dickinson's Letters to Sue Gilbert." *Massachusetts Review* 18
    (1978): 197–225.
————. *Surpassing the Love of Men: Romantic Friendship and Love Between Women
    from the Renaissance to the Present.* New York: William Morrow, 1981.
Farwell, Marilyn. "Adrienne Rich and an Organic Feminist Criticism." *College En-
    glish* 39 (1977): 191–203.
Flax, Jane. "The Conflict Between Nurturance and Autonomy in Mother/Daughter
    Relationships and Within Feminism." *Feminist Studies* 4 (1978): 171–89.
Ford, Emily Fowler. "Eheu! Emily Dickinson." *Springfield Republican* 11 Jan. 1891.
Foster, Hannah. *The Coquette* (1797). Ed. Cathy N. Davidson. New York: Oxford
    University Press, 1986.
Foucault, Michel. *Madness and Civilization: A History of Insanity in the Age of
    Reason* (1961). Trans. Richard Howard. New York: Random House, 1965.
Freedman, Estelle B., Barbara C. Gelpi, Susan L. Johnson, and Kathleen M. Weston,
    eds. *The Lesbian Issue. Essays from Signs.* Chicago: University of Chicago
    Press, 1985.
Friedan, Betty. *The Second Stage.* New York: Summit Books, 1981.
Friedman, Susan. " 'I go where I love': An Intertextual Study of H. D. and Adrienne
    Rich." *Signs* 9 (1983): 228–45.
Fuller, Margaret. *Woman in the Nineteenth Century.* Norton: New York, 1971.
Fuss, Diana. *Essentially Speaking: Feminism, Nature and Difference.* New York:
    Routledge, 1989.
Gallop, Jane, Marianne Hirsch, and Nancy K. Miller. "Criticizing Feminist Crit-
    icism." *Conflicts in Feminism.* Ed. Marianne Hirsch and Evelyn Fox Keller.
    349–69.
Gaskell, Elizabeth. *Life of Charlotte Brontë.* New York: Appleton and Company,
    1857.
Gates, Henry Louis, Jr. "Criticism in the Jungle." *Black Literature and Literary
    Theory.* Ed. Henry Louis Gates, Jr. New York: Methuen, 1984.
Gelpi, Barbara Charlesworth. "The Politics of Androgyny." *Women's Studies* 2
    (1974): 151–60.
Gentile, Mary. "Adrienne Rich and Separatism: The Language of Multiple Realities."
    Maenad 2 (1982): 136–146.
Gerin, Winifred. *Charlotte Brontë: The Evolution of Genius.* New York: Oxford
    University Press, 1967.
Gilbert, Sandra. "The American Sexual Poetics of Walt Whitman and Emily Dickin-

son." *Reconstructing American Literary History*. Ed. Sacvan Bercovitch. Cambridge, Mass.: Harvard University Press, 1986. 123–54.

———. "Life's Empty Pack: Notes Toward a Literary Daughteronomy." *Critical Inquiry* 11 (1985): 355–83.

Gilbert, Sandra and Susan Gubar. " 'Forward into the Past': The Complex Female Affiliation Complex." *Historical Studies and Literary Criticism*. Ed. Jerome J. McGann. 240–65.

———. *The Madwoman in the Attic: The Woman Writer and the Nineteenth-Century Literary Imagination*. New Haven, Conn.: Yale University Press, 1979.

———. *No Man's Land: The Place of the Woman Writer in the Twentieth Century*. 3 vols. New Haven, Conn.: Yale University Press, 1988–19 .

Gilligan, Carol. *In a Different Voice*. Cambridge, Mass.: Harvard University Press, 1982.

Giovanni, Nikki. *Black Feeling Black Talk Black Judgement*. New York: Morrow Quill Paperbacks, 1979.

Goldstein, Laurence. "The Evolution of Adrienne Rich." *Michigan Quarterly Review* 15 (1976): 360–66.

Gorham, Deborah. *The Victorian Girl and the Feminine Ideal*. Bloomington: Indiana University Press, 1982.

Griffin, Susan. *Woman and Nature: The Roaring Inside of Her*. New York: Harper & Row, 1978.

Gubar, Susan. "Sapphistries." *The Lesbian Issue: Essays from Signs*. Ed. Estelle Freedman, Barbara C. Gelpi, Susan Johnson, and Kathleen M. Weston. 91–110.

Hawthorne, Nathaniel. *The Letters, 1853–1856*. Ed. Thomas Woodson, L. Neal Smith, and Norman Holmes Pearson. Cleveland: Ohio State University Press, 1987.

H. D. (Hilda Doolittle). "Marianne Moore." *The Egoist* 3 (1916): 118–19.

Hemans, Felicia. *The Works of Mrs. Hemans*. With an Essay on Her Genius by Mrs. Sigourney. 7 vols. Philadelphia: Lea & Blanchard, 1840.

Higginson, Thomas. *Carlyle's Laugh and Other Surprises* (1909). Freeport, N. Y.: Books for Library Press, 1968.

———. "Helen Hunt Jackson." *Contemporaries*. Boston: Houghton, Mifflin, 1899. 142–67.

———. "Letter to a Young Contributor." *Atlantic Monthly* 9 (1862): 401–11.

Hirsch, Marianne. *The Mother/Daughter Plot: Narrative, Psychoanalysis, Feminism*. Bloomington: Indiana University Press, 1989.

———. "Mothers and Daughters." *Signs* 7 (1981): 200–222.

Hirsch, Marianne and Evelyn Fox Keller, eds. *Conflicts in Feminism*. New York: Routledge, 1990.

Holley, Margaret. *The Poetry of Marianne Moore: A Study in Voice and Value*. New York: Cambridge University Press, 1987.

Homans, Margaret. *Women Writers and Poetic Identity*. Princeton, N. J.: Princeton University Press, 1981.

Hooks, Bell. *Ain't I a Woman*. Boston: South End Press, 1981.

———. "Essentialism and Experience." *American Literary History* 3 (1991): 172–83.

———. *Feminist Theory from Margin to Center*. Boston: South End Press, 1984.

———. *Talking Back: Thinking Feminist, Thinking Black*. Boston: South End Press, 1989.

Howe, Florence and Ellen Bass, eds. *No More Masks!: An Anthology of Poems by Women*. Garden City, N. Y.: Anchor Press, 1973.

Hull, Gloria. *Color, Sex and Poetry: Three Women Writers of the Harlem Renaissance*. Bloomington: Indiana University Press, 1987.

Hull, Gloria and Posey Gallagher. "Update on *Part One:* An Interview with Gwendolyn Brooks." *College Language Journal* 21 (1977): 19–40.

Hull, Gloria, Patricia Bell Scott, and Barbara Smith, eds. *All the Women Are White, All the Blacks are Men, But Some of Us Are Brave*. Old Westbury, N. Y.: The Feminist Press, 1982.

Humm, Maggie. *Feminist Criticism: Women as Contemporary Critics*. New York: St. Martin's Press, 1986.

Hurston, Zora Neale. *Their Eyes Were Watching God* (1937). Urbana: University of Illinois Press, 1978.

Irigaray, Luce. "Et l'une ne bouge pas sans l'autre" ("And the One Doesn't Stir Without the Other"). Trans. Helene Vivienne Wenzel. *Signs* 7 (1981): 60–67.

———. *This Sex Which Is Not One* (1977). Trans. Catherine Porter. Ithaca, N. Y.: Cornell University Press, 1985.

Jackson, Helen Hunt. *Bits of Talk About Home Matters*. Boston: Roberts Brothers, 1873.

———. *Poems*. Boston: Little, Brown, 1910.

Jacobus, Mary. *Reading Woman: Essays in Feminist Criticism*. New York: Columbia University Press, 1986.

Jardine, Alice. *Gynesis: Configurations of Woman and Modernity*. Ithaca, N. Y.: Cornell University Press, 1985.

Jarrell, Randall. "The Poet and His Public." *Partisan Review* 13 (1946): 488–500.

Jessup, Eunice Clark. "Memoirs of Literatae and Socialists 1929–1933." *Vassar Quarterly* 55 (1979): 16–17.

Johnson, Barbara. *A World of Difference*. Baltimore: The Johns Hopkins University Press, 1987.

Johnson, Thomas. *Emily Dickinson: An Interpretive Biography*. Cambridge, Mass.: The Belknap Press, 1955.

Jones, LeRoi and Larry Neal, eds. *Black Fire: An Anthology of Afro-American Writing*. New York: William Morrow, 1968.

Joyce, Joyce A. "The Black Canon: Reconstructing Black American Literary Criticism." *New Literary History* 18 (1987): 335–44.

Juhasz, Suzanne. *Naked and Fiery Forms: Modern Poetry by Women, A New Tradition*. New York: Harper & Row, 1976.

Kalstone, David. *Becoming a Poet: Elizabeth Bishop with Marianne Moore and*

Robert Lowell. Ed. Robert Hemenway. New York: Farrar, Straus and Giroux, 1989.

———. *Five Temperaments.* New York: Oxford University Press, 1977.

Kaplan, Cora. "Introduction." *'Aurora Leigh' and Other Poems.* London: The Women's Press, 1978.

———. *Sea Changes: Essays on Culture and Feminism.* London: Verso, 1986.

Kappel, Andrew. "Introduction: The Achievement of Marianne Moore," *Twentieth-Century Literature* 30 (1984): v–xxx.

Keller, Lynn. "Words Worth a Thousand Postcards: The Bishop/Moore Correspondence." *American Literature* 55 (1983): 405–29.

Kelley, Mary. *Private Woman, Public Stage: Literary Domesticity in Nineteenth-Century America.* New York: Oxford University Press, 1984.

Kent, George. "Aesthetic Values in the Poetry of Gwendolyn Brooks." *Black American Literature and Humanism.* Ed. R. Baxter Miller. Lexington: University Press of Kentucky, 1981. 75–81.

———. *A Life of Gwendolyn Brooks.* Lexington: University Press of Kentucky, 1990.

———. "The Poetry of Gwendolyn Brooks." *Blackness and the Adventure of Western Culture.* Chicago: Third World Press, 1972. 104–39.

Keyes, Claire. *The Aesthetics of Power: The Poetry of Adrienne Rich.* Athens: University of Georgia Press, 1986.

Kizer, Carolyn. *Knock upon Silence.* Garden City, N. Y.: Doubleday, 1965.

Kolodny, Annette. "Dancing Through the Minefield: Some Observations on the Theory, Practice, and Politics of a Feminist Literary Criticism." *Feminist Studies* 6 (1980): 1–25.

Kristeva, Julia. *Desire in Language: A Semiotic Approach to Literature and Art.* Ed. Leon S. Roudiez. Trans. Alice Jardine, Thomas Gora, and Leon Roudiez. New York: Columbia University Press, 1980.

———. "Oscillation Between Power and Denial." *New French Feminisms.* Ed. Elaine Marks and Isabelle de Courtivron. 165–67.

———. *Revolution in Poetic Language* (1974). Trans. Margaret Walker. New York: Columbia University Press, 1984.

Lacan, Jacques. *Ecrits. A Selection.* Trans. Alan Sheridan. New York: Norton, 1977.

Levi-Strauss, Claude. *The Elementary Structures of Kinship.* Ed. Rodney Needham. Trans. James Harle Bell, John Richard von Sturmer, and Rodney Needham. Boston: Beacon Press, 1969.

Leyda, Jay. *The Years and Hours of Emily Dickinson.* 2 vols. New Haven, Conn.: Yale University Press, 1960.

Lorde, Audre. *The New York Head Shop and Museum.* Detroit: Broadside Press, 1974.

———. *Sister Outsider.* Trumansburg, N. Y.: The Crossing Press, 1984.

Lowell, Amy. *The Complete Poetical Works.* Cambridge, Mass.: Houghton Mifflin, 1955.

Lowell, Robert, "Thomas, Bishop, and Williams." *Sewanee Review* 55 (1947): 497–99.

Lubbers, Klaus. *Emily Dickinson: The Critical Revolution*. Ann Arbor: University of Michigan Press, 1968.

Madhubuti, Haki, ed. *Say That the River Turns: The Impact of Gwendolyn Brooks*. Third World Press, 1987.

Marcus, Jane. "Thinking Back Through Our Mothers." *New Feminist Essays on Virginia Woolf*. Ed. Jane Marcus. Lincoln: University of Nebraska Press, 1981. 1–30.

Marks, Elaine and Isabelle de Courtivon, eds. *New French Feminisms*. Amherst: University of Massachusetts Press, 1980.

Martin, Taffy. *Marianne Moore: Subversive Modernist*. Austin: University of Texas Press, 1986.

Martin, Wendy. *An American Triptych: Anne Bradstreet, Emily Dickinson, Adrienne Rich*. Chapel Hill: University of North Carolina Press, 1984.

Mather, Cotton. *Manaductio ad Ministerium* (1726). New York: AMS Press, 1978.

Mauss, Marcel. *The Gift: Forms and Functions of Exchange in Archaic Societies*. Trans. Ian Cunnison. Glencoe, Ill.: Free Press, 1954.

McDowell, Deborah. "The Place of Black Women 'In Theory'." Paper presented at the Modern Language Association meeting in Chicago, 1990.

McGann, Jerome J., ed. *Historical Studies and Literary Criticism*. Madison: University of Wisconsin Press, 1985.

Meese, Elizabeth A. *(Ex)tensions: Re-Figuring Feminist Criticism*. Chicago: University of Illinois Press, 1990.

Melhem, D. H. *Gwendolyn Brooks: Poetry and the Heroic Voice*. Lexington: University Press of Kentucky, 1987.

Milkman, Ruth. "Women's History and the Sears Case." *Feminist Studies* 12 (1986): 373–400.

Miller, Cristanne. *Emily Dickinson: A Poet's Grammar*. Cambridge, Mass.: Harvard University Press, 1987.

Miller, Nancy K. "Changing the Subject: Authorship, Writing and the Reader." *Feminist Studies/Critical Studies*. Ed. Teresa De Lauretis. 102–20.

Miller, Ruth. *The Poetry of Emily Dickinson*. Middletown, Conn.: Wesleyan University Press, 1968.

Millett, Kate. *Sexual Politics*. Garden City, N. Y.: Doubleday, 1970.

Moers, Ellen. *Literary Women: The Great Writers*. New York: Doubleday, 1976.

———. "A Poet's Feminist Prose." *The New York Times Book Review*, 22 April 1979: 12.

Moi, Toril. *Sexual/Textual Politics: Feminist Literary Theory*. New York: Methuen, 1985.

Montefiore, Jan. *Feminism and Poetry: Language, Experience, Identity in Women's Writing*. London: Pandora, 1987.

Moore, Marianne. "Archaically New." *Trial Balances*. Ed. Ann Winslow. New York: Macmillan, 1935. 78–83.

———. *The Complete Poems of Marianne Moore*. New York: Macmillan, 1967. [*Complete Poems*]

————. *The Complete Prose.* Ed. Patricia Willis. New York: Viking, 1986. [*Complete Prose*]

————. Letters to Elizabeth Bishop. Vassar College Library, Poughkeepsie, N. Y. [*V*]

————. Letters to Bryher. Rosenbach Museum and Library, Philadelphia, Pa. [*R*]

————. "A Modest Expert." *The Nation* 163 (September 28, 1946): 354.

Mootry, Maria K. and Gary Smith, eds. *A Life Distilled: Gwendolyn Brooks, Her Poetry and Fiction.* Chicago: University of Illinois Press, 1987.

Moraga, Cherríe. *Loving in the War Years.* Boston: South End Press, 1983.

Moraga, Cherríe and Gloria Anzaldúa, eds. *This Bridge Called My Back: Writings by Radical Women of Color.* Watertown, Mass.: Persephone, 1981.

Moran, Eileen G. "Portrait of the Artist: Marianne Moore's Letters to Hildegarde Watson." *Poesis* 6 (1985): 124–36.

Morgan, Robin. *Going Too Far.* New York: Random House, 1978.

Morley, Helena [Alice Dayrell Brant]. *The Diary of "Helena Morley."* Trans. Elizabeth Bishop. New York: The Ecco Press, 1951.

Morris, Adelaide. " 'The Love of Thee—a Prism Be': Men and Women in the Love Poetry of Emily Dickinson." *Feminist Critics Read Emily Dickinson.* Ed. Suzanne Juhasz. Bloomington: Indiana University Press, 1983. 98–113.

Mossberg, Barbara. *Emily Dickinson: When a Writer Is a Daughter.* Bloomington: Indiana University Press, 1982.

Mudge, Jean McClure. "Emily Dickinson and 'Sister Sue.' " *Prairie Schooner* 52 (1977): 90–108.

Newton, Esther. "The Mythic Mannish Lesbian: Radclyffe Hall and the New Woman." *The Lesbian Issue. Essays from Signs.* Ed. Estelle B. Freedman, Barbara C. Gelpi, Susan Johnson, and Kathleen M. Weston. 7–25.

Oberhaus, Dorothy Huff. "In Defense of Sue." *Dickinson Studies* 48 (1983): 1–25.

Odell, Ruth. *Helen Hunt Jackson.* New York: Appleton-Century, 1939.

Ostriker, Alicia. *Stealing the Language: The Emergence of Women's Poetry in America.* Boston: Beacon Press, 1986.

————. "What Do Women (Poets) Want? H. D. and Marianne Moore as Poetic Ancestresses." *Contemporary Literature* 27 (1986): 475–92.

————. *Writing Like a Woman.* Ann Arbor: University of Michigan Press, 1983.

Parker, Robert Dale. *The Unbeliever: The Poetry of Elizabeth Bishop.* Urbana: University of Illinois Press, 1988.

Patterson, Rebecca. "Elizabeth Browning and Emily Dickinson." *The Educational Leader* 10 (1956): 21–48.

————. *The Riddle of Emily Dickinson.* Boston: Houghton Mifflin, 1951.

Peckham, Harry H. *Josiah Holland in Relation to His Time.* Philadelphia: University of Pennsylvania Press, 1940.

Plath, Sylvia. *Letters Home.* Ed. Aurelia Schober Plath. New York: Harper, 1975.

Pollak, Vivian. *Dickinson: The Anxiety of Gender.* Ithaca, N. Y.: Cornell University Press, 1984.

————. "Dickinson, Poe, and Barrett Browning: A Clarification." *New England Quarterly* 54 (1981): 121–24.

Ransom, John Crowe. "The Poet as Woman." *The World's Body*. New York: Scribner's, 1938. 76–110.

Raymond, Janice. *The Transexual Empire*. Boston: Beacon Press, 1979.

Rich, Adrienne. *Adrienne Rich's Poetry*. Ed. Barbara Charlesworth Gelpi and Albert Gelpi. New York: Norton, 1975.

————. *Blood, Bread, and Poetry: Selected Prose 1979–1985*. New York: Norton, 1986.

————. "Caryatid: A Column." *American Poetry Review* 2 (1973): 10–11.

————. *A Change of World*. New Haven, Conn.: Yale University Press, 1951.

————. Comment on Friedman's " 'I go where I love': An Intertextual Study of H. D. and Adrienne Rich." *Signs* 9 (1984): 733–38.

————. "Compulsory Heterosexuality and Lesbian Existence." *Signs* 5 (1980): 631–60.

————. *Diving into the Wreck: Poems 1971–1972*. New York: Norton, 1973.

————. *The Dream of a Common Language: Poems 1974–1977*. New York: Norton, 1978.

————. *Leaflets: Poems 1965–1968*. New York: Norton, 1969.

————. *Necessities of Life: Poems 1962–1965*. New York: Norton, 1966.

————. *Of Woman Born: Motherhood as Experience and Institution*. New York: Norton, 1976.

————. *On Lies, Secrets, and Silence: Selected Prose 1966–1978*. New York: Norton, 1979.

————. Review of *The Women Poets in English*, ed. Ann Stanford. *New York Times Book Review*, 15 April 1973: 6.

————. *Snapshots of a Daughter-in-Law: Poems 1954–1962*. New York: Norton, 1963.

————. *Time's Power: Poems 1985–1988*. New York: Norton, 1989.

————. *A Wild Patience Has Taken Me This Far: Poems 1978–1981*. New York: Norton, 1981.

————. *The Will to Change: Poems 1968–1970*. New York: Norton, 1971.

————. *Your Native Land, Your Life: Poems*. New York: Norton, 1986.

Rodgers, Carolyn. *How I Got Ovah*. Garden City, New York: Doubleday, 1975.

————. *Songs of a Black Bird*. Chicago: Third World Press, 1969.

Rubin, Gayle. "The Traffic in Women: Notes on the 'Political Economy' of Sex." *Toward an Anthropology of Women*. Ed. Rayna R. Reiter. New York: Monthly Review Press, 1975. 157–210.

Ruddick, Sara. *Maternal Thinking: Towards a Politics of Peace*. Boston: Beacon Press, 1989.

Rukeyser, Muriel. *The Collected Poems*. New York: McGraw-Hill, 1978.

Schwartz, Lloyd and Sybil P. Estess, eds. *Elizabeth Bishop and Her Art*. Ann Arbor: University of Michigan Press, 1983.

Scott, Joan. "The Sears Case." *Gender and the Politics of History*. New York: Columbia University Press, 1988. 167–77.

Secor, Cynthia. "Androgyny: An Early Reappraisal." *Women's Studies* 2 (1974): 161–70.

Segnitz, Barbara and Carol Rainey, eds. *Psyche: The Feminine Poetic Consciousness. An Anthology of Modern American Women Poets.* New York: Dell, 1973.

Sewall, Richard. *The Life of Emily Dickinson.* New York: Farrar, Straus and Giroux, 1974.

Shaw, Henry. *Gwendolyn Brooks.* Boston: Twayne Publishers, 1980.

Showalter, Elaine. "Feminist Criticism in the Wilderness." *Critical Inquiry* 8 (1981): 179–206.

————. *A Literature of Their Own.* Princeton, N.J.: Princeton University Press, 1977.

Sigourney, Lydia. *Select Poems.* Philadelphia: E. C. & J. Biddle, 1847.

Smith, Barbara, " 'Fractious, Kicking, Messy, Free': Feminist Writers Confront the Nuclear Abyss." *New England Review and Bread and Loaf Quarterly,* 5 (1983): 581–92.

————. "Toward a Black Feminist Criticism" (1977). *All the Women Are White, All the Blacks Are Men, But Some of Us Are Brave.* Ed. Gloria Hull, Patricia Bell Scott, and Barbara Smith. 157–75.

Smith, Martha Nell. " 'To Fill a Gap.' " *San Jose Studies* 13 (1987): 3–25.

Smith, Valerie. "Black Feminist Theory and the Representation of the 'Other.' " *Changing Our Own Words: Essays as Criticism, Theory, and Writing by Black Women.* Ed. Cheryl Wall. New Brunswick, N. J.: Rutgers University Press, 1989: 38–57.

Smith-Rosenberg, Carroll. *Disorderly Conduct: Visions of Gender in Victorian America.* New York: Knopf, 1985.

————. "The Female World of Love and Ritual: Relations Between Women in Nineteenth-Century America." *Signs* 1 (1975): 1–29.

Spacks, Patricia Meyer. *The Female Imagination.* New York: Knopf, 1972.

Spelman, Elizabeth. *Inessential Woman: Problems of Exclusion in Feminist Thought.* Boston: Beacon Press, 1988.

Spillers, Hortense. "Interstices: A Small Drama of Words." *Pleasure and Danger: Exploring Female Sexuality.* Ed. Carole S. Vance. Boston: Routledge & Kegan Paul, 1984. 73–99.

Spires, Elizabeth. "Elizabeth Bishop." *Poets at Work.* Ed. George Plimpton. New York: Viking, 1989. 365–86.

Spivak, Gayatri Chakravorty. *In Other Worlds: Essays in Cultural Politics.* New York: Routledge, 1988.

Stacey, Judith. "The New Conservative Feminism." *Feminist Studies* 9 (1983): 559–83.

Starbuck, George. " 'The Work!': A Conversation with Elizabeth Bishop." *Ploughshares* 3 (1977): 11–29.

St. Armand, Barton Levi. *Emily Dickinson and Her Culture: The Soul's Society.* New York: Cambridge University Press, 1984.

Stetson, Erlene, ed. *Black Sister: Poetry by Black American Women, 1746–1980.* Bloomington: Indiana University Press, 1981.

————. "*Songs After Sunset* (1935–36): The Unpublished Poetry of Gwendolyn Brooks." *A Life Distilled.* Ed. Maria K. Mootry and Gary Smith. 119–27.

Stevenson, Anne. *Elizabeth Bishop.* New York: Twayne Publishers, 1966.

Stimpson, Catharine R. "Adrienne Rich and Lesbian/Feminist Poetry." *Parnassus* 12
    (1985): 249–68.
———. "The Androgyne and the Homosexual." *Women's Studies* 2 (1974): 237–48.
———. "Zero Degree Deviancy: The Lesbian Novel in English." *Critical Inquiry* 8
    (1981): 363–80.
Tate, Allen. "Emily Dickinson." *Emily Dickinson: A Collection of Critical Essays.*
    Ed. Richard Sewall. Englewood Cliffs, N. J.: Prentice-Hall, 1963. 16–27.
Tate, Claudia. "Anger So Flat: Gwendolyn Brooks's *Annie Allen.*" *A Life Distilled.*
    Ed. Maria K. Mootry and Gary Smith. 140–52.
———. ed. *Black Women Writers at Work.* New York: Continuum Press, 1983.
Taylor, William R. and Christopher Lasch, "Two 'Kindred Spirits': Sorority and
    Family in New England, 1839–1846." *New England Quarterly* 36 (1963): 23–
    41.
Todd, Janet. *Feminist Literary History.* New York: Routledge. 1988.
Todd, Mabel Loomis, ed. *Letters of Emily Dickinson.* New York: Harper & Brothers,
    1931.
Travisano, Thomas J. *Elizabeth Bishop: Her Artistic Development.* Charlottesville:
    University of Virginia Press, 1988.
Tyler, William S. *History of Amherst College in the First Half Century, 1821–1871.*
    Springfield, Mass.: Clark W. Bryan and Company, 1873.
Walker, Alice. *In Search of Our Mothers' Gardens.* New York: Harcourt Brace
    Jovanovich, 1983.
Walker, Cheryl. *The Nightingale's Burden: Women Poets and American Culture Be-
    fore 1900.* Bloomington: Indiana University Press, 1982.
Wall, Cheryl A. "Poets and Versifiers, Singers and Signifiers: Women of the Harlem
    Renaissance." *Women, the Arts and the 1920's in Paris and New York.* Ed.
    Kenneth W. Wheeler and Virginia Lee Lussier. New Brunswick, N. J.: Trans-
    action Books, 1982. 74–98.
Wallace, Michele. "A Black Feminist's Search for Sisterhood." *All the Women Are
    White, All the Blacks Are Men, But Some Of Us Are Brave.* Ed. Gloria Hull,
    Patricia Bell Scott, and Barbara Smith. 5–12.
Wallace, Patricia B. "The Wildness of Elizabeth Bishop." *Sewanee Review* 93 (1985):
    95–115.
Walsh, John Evangelist. *The Hidden Life of Emily Dickinson.* New York: Simon &
    Schuster, 1971.
Washington, Mary Helen. "These Self-Invented Women: A Theoretical Framework
    for a Literary History of Black Women." *Radical Teacher* 17 (1980): 3–6.
Watts, Emily Stipes. *The Poetry of American Women from 1632 to 1945.* Austin:
    University of Texas Press, 1977.
Wehr, Wesley. "Elizabeth Bishop: Conversations and Class Notes." *Antioch Review* 39
    (1981): 319–28.
Welter, Barbara. "The Cult of True Womanhood, 1820–1860." *American Quarterly*
    18 (1966): 151–74.
Whitman, Walt. *Leaves of Grass.* Ed. Sculley Bradley and Harold W. Blodgett. New
    York: Norton, 1973.

Williams, William Carlos. *Autobiography.* New York: Random House, 1951.

Williamson, Alan. "*A Cold Spring:* The Poet of Feeling." *Elizabeth Bishop and Her Art.* Ed. Lloyd Schwartz and Sybil P. Estess. 96–108.

Willis, Patricia C. *Marianne Moore: Vision into Verse.* Philadelphia: Rosenbach Museum and Library, 1987.

Wittig, Monique. "One Is Not Born Woman." *Feminist Issues* (1981): 47–54.

———. "The Straight Mind." *Feminist Issues* (1980): 103–10.

"The Works of Alexander Dumas." *North American Review* 56 (1843): 110.

Zagarell, Sandra A. "Expanding 'America': Lydia Sigourney's *Sketch of Connecticut* and Catharine Sedgwick's *Hope Leslie.*" *Tulsa Studies in Women's Literature* 6 (1987): 225–47.

INDEX